# Finding My Vocabulary

# Finding My Vocabulary

A Gay Man's Stories of Discovery,
Survival and Self-Determination

*a memoir*

## James Philip Baran

Finding My Vocabulary

James Philip Baran

Copyright © 2024 James Baran Media LLC
All rights reserved.

A shortened version of "The Epiphany" was read by the author at Outspoken Chicago on November 7, 2023.

An early version of "The Journey of Coming Out" was published in *Adventist Today*, October 7, 2021, titled, "A Gay Man's Journey through the Adventist Church." https://atoday.org/a-gay-mans-journey-through-the-adventist-church/

The poem "A Tide of Winter" was first published in *Druid's Cave* (Spring 1986), copyright ©1986 Druid's Cave Creative Writing Club, Illinois State University, Normal, Illinois.

Published in the United States by James Baran Media LLC.
Baran, James, 1961-
Finding My Vocabulary: A Gay Man's Stories of Discovery, Survival and Self-Determination / James Philip Baran—1st ed.

ISBN 979-8-9910306-0-1
1. Non-fiction. 2. Biography. 3. Memoir. 4. LGBTQ+.

Cover design by John Yates/Stealworks.com
Cover photograph and author photograph by David Robertson

First Edition

For privacy, some names have been changed or omitted.

No part of this book may be reproduced or transmitted in any form or by any means, electronic or mechanical, including photocopy, recording, or any information storage and retrieval system now known or yet to be invented, without written permission from the publisher, except by a reviewer who wishes to quote brief passages in connection with a review written for inclusion in a magazine, newspaper, broadcast, or publisher's or writer's blog.

Chicago

# Acknowledgments

Thank you to all whose encouragement, advice, and editorial suggestions have helped bring this book into coherence and whom I can't thank enough for going on this ride down memory lane with me.

My heartfelt thanks to Judith Roof, Thom Racina, David Gilmore, Bernardine Lewis, Bruce Gomez, Kathi Sanders, Barbara Byrd Keenan, Theresa Gargano-Adamski.

Special thanks to Michael Graif and Ron Duplack for their time in detailed discussion, and especially to Brian Rosenblatt for his extensive advice.

Thank you to everyone involved with Outspoken at Sidetrack Chicago, especially: Art Johnston and David Fink, founders; Archy Jamjun, curator; Jennifer Ould, assistant curator; Anna DeShawn, host; Bradley Balof, Sidetrack general manager; and Bryan Smith, Sidetrack marketing and audio-visuals.

Most importantly, thank you to my husband, David Robertson, for long-enduring patience and unconditional love.

In memory of

Dolores Mary Samp Baran and Frederick Jacob Baran

---

Fear no more the heat o' th' sun,
    Nor the furious winter's rages,
Thou thy worldly task has done,
    Home art gone and ta'en thy wages.
Golden lads and girls all must,
As chimney-sweepers, come to dust.

–*Cymbeline*, Act IV, Scene II
William Shakespeare

For David

# Contents

| | |
|---|---|
| Introduction | 1 |
| Finding My Vocabulary | 11 |
| Valley of the Guinea Pigs | 27 |
| Dead and Buried | 35 |
| My Family Tree | 53 |
| The Epiphany | 69 |
| All in the Family | 81 |
| Love for Sale | 91 |
| The Journey of Coming Out | 105 |
| Rumor Has It | 143 |
| The Graduate Student | 151 |
| What's Love Got to Do with It? | 175 |
| In Memoriam: Mater Dolorosa | 197 |
| My Father and Mr. Hyde | 215 |
| The Three-Ring Circus | 229 |
| Wanderlust | 241 |
| The Old Apple Tree | 281 |
| | |
| Appendix: Sources and Further Reading | 291 |

# Introduction

Vocabulary is a powerful tool. It's the main building block of language, which gives us the ability to explain and understand events in history; it helps us define facts; it helps us articulate and solve problems; and—among other things—a healthy vocabulary sets us apart from the lower creatures. If you listen to a good Sunday school teacher, he or she may even tell you that God gave us the gift of intelligence, the ability to think, so that we might not waste that ability but that we might use it to improve our lives, choose peace over war, unity over divisiveness, kindness over anger, and through agreements and disagreements find common ground and threads that connect us on a path moving ever-forward toward enlightenment, or at least tolerance. I hope that's not too much to hope for.

And so it alarms me, as it should everyone, to witness a willful intolerance of vocabulary and its natural connections to problem-solving and learning by individuals and communities of people who, apparently, would prefer a society impaired by disagreement, misunderstanding, and foolishness over the more productive goal of higher beings (such as we are) to communicate clearly in order to learn, advance our culture, improve our lives with honest and accurate information, and solve problems for the mutual benefit of all. The very idea that there may be people who willfully wish to block our ability to learn about the world around us strikes me as somehow undemocratic, or at the very least worryingly suspect. I'm concerned about the agenda of such people who would block access to vocabulary, and—by extension—inhibit or stunt educational success. There's an intolerance in that agenda that bothers me—an intolerance of education, facts, science, law, and even peaceful dialog that, to me, seems to be approaching epidemic proportion.

That trend toward intolerance seems to be accompanied by an authoritarianism in politics that has spread over the past decade, and for some reason it's been particularly noticeable in the South. As I watched one governor's behavior and heard his sound bites on TV, I thought that surely his state's legislature would ignore many of his ideas and set a middle-of-the-road legislative course—government is supposed to serve *all* citizens, after all. Like so many of us, I turned my attention elsewhere and let it slide, going back to my smartphone, scrolling distractedly through videos of cats that almost seem to speak Italian! And then that state legislature took up its governor's authoritarian style with fevered urgency. It was only then that I realized anger and uninformed fear were going to spread like the pestilence so often preached from pulpits of fundamentalist and evangelical churches—organizations that are Christian in label and branding but not necessarily so in what they teach and practice. The last straw for me was when that state passed a law behind a mask of "parents' rights," which disguised what I see as its darker purpose: to silence the voices of LGBTQ+ children and youths who only want to understand themselves, be seen and valued, and to legislatively forbid

## Introduction

open and free speech on selected topics. If history could talk, it would tell us—in fact, it would scream: "Look up from those cell phones and take notice: this has happened before!"

I am determined not to let what started as a war on words—what is now a new culture war against diversity, tolerance, and on all LGBTQ+ people—go on without raising my own voice against it. And so I set about writing my own history so that my experience could not be expunged or buried by misinformation. Mine is a story of growing up in the time before social media, seeking a vocabulary that represented me, becoming more and more aware of the world around me, and in the process aware of my own identity, my own differences from those around me.

I was brought up in a conservative environment, but I was never forbidden from reading books. My story tells of success in spite of roadblocks—my growth into a perfectly normal gay man. Like many children, I, too, had no one to talk to about my immutable identity. But in the 1960s my reasons for not being able to articulate my questions stemmed from a dearth of real examples of what I was looking for—people like me.

Today, in spite of having a wide variety of positive role models for children and youths, in parts of America students are denied the opportunity to ask questions, denied access to books, because politicians and religious organizations and their leaders feel threatened—threatened because the discussion of what it means to be gay or lesbian, bisexual or transgender will reveal that LGBTQ+ people are not a threat at all. When I consider the hysterical reactions to topics touching on things LGBTQ+, I think that the underlying authoritarian motivation is to prevent young people from growing up to be tolerant, accepting citizens who might see the value in every person. That idea alone—seeing value in every person—could have prevented the Civil War. But some people don't seem to want a peaceful society; they apparently enjoy perpetuating the idea that we have to see some people as threats, as enemies, as the "Other." To me, this appears to be a goal of the anti-LGBTQ+ movement—in politics and religion. I'm not a psychologist, so I can't alleviate the fears of many in that group, but I hope someone can. The facts are these: we're not interested in recruiting children to the Gay life; we just want them to be well-adjusted and able to succeed as the best citizens they can be, without fear of being fired from their jobs or murdered. Is there no pope, archbishop, rabbi, priest, no pastor or swami, no senator or governor, no mayor, no cable news pundit, or no teacher who can explain human mysteries in a way that can change hardened attitudes of intolerance into compassion and acceptance?

In these pages, you'll see a few superscript numbers. These numbers refer to sources or further reading available in the Appendix. I provide these references so that readers who might balk and say, "James, you can't possibly be serious," will be able to explore other sources and read the evidence to see that I'm not fabricating those details—that journalists, researchers, writers, and scientific organizations have noted the same facts and ideas that I call out as markers in the longer-range authoritarian agenda which, in my opinion, is to write laws based on a narrow-focused Christian nationalist ideology. My gut instinct tells me the goal may be some form of theocracy, but I'd be relieved to be proven incorrect. One example that should alarm all Americans is that a new House Speaker actually said, "The separation of church and state is a misnomer."[1] I shudder to think of his intentions.

\* \* \*

## Introduction

I knew I was gay at age four. The vocabulary and a fuller understanding would come much later, but at four I knew I was drawn to men. I was not groomed, and no one put this idea into my head. I simply awoke to it in my own time, with no influence from anyone.

In the 1960s there were no role models for a young queer child; there appeared to be no characters on television, no people who stood out in our community, and no images or characters in books in which I could see myself. As a result, I felt certain I was alone, and so it was natural to hide my immutable self, keep him under wraps. A few years later I saw people like me on television, and I was confused by their self-caricature—simultaneously hiding and yet flaunting their apparent homosexuality. Liberace horrified me. Paul Lynde was funny, I'll admit. Truman Capote was embarrassingly dramatic, and I didn't want to emulate him. The idea of being gay in the years before Stonewall was rarely discussed; in fact, it was suppressed, ridiculed, discouraged out of fear or prejudice. The slow road to respect and inclusion for gay people began after the Stonewall riots of 1969—the first response to police raids on New York's gay bars that made national news when young people stood up to police harassment. This is considered the birth of the gay rights movement out of which evolved the LGBTQ+ community. I was eight at the time and would not become aware of the movement until I attended college a decade later. But in the meanwhile, I just continued to live my child's life, aware that I was different, looking for my own vocabulary, my own context, my own belonging.

I wasn't made gay by Bugs Bunny in drag; Harvey Korman and Tim Conway in buxom disguise on the *Carol Burnett Show* didn't do it; Tony Curtis and Jack Lemmon impersonating female band members in *Some Like It Hot* didn't do it; and Flip Wilson's character,

Geraldine, certainly didn't make me gay, either. The funny thing is, my parents—straight to the core and conservative—found all those characters hysterically funny and utterly harmless. They knew camp when they saw it, even if they didn't know what camp actually was.

Eventually religion came into the picture, but it did not help matters. Indeed, the religious sect my parents and I joined in hopes of finding an oasis became, for me, a dangerous quicksand. Instead of lifting me up, religious dogma was used as a bludgeon to beat me down and keep me suppressed. Many members of this religious denomination with whom I came in contact verbally abused and ridiculed me, and diminished my sense of worth. A much shorter, early version of "The Journey of Coming Out" was published in *Adventist Today*.[2]

Throughout my childhood and adolescence, I had an interest in reading. Subconsciously, perhaps, I had hoped to find myself in one of the stories I read or in the pictures in our family library of books and magazines. Nothing, not once, flashed to me in affirmation or recognition. That fact contributed to my desire to share my story of finding myself in a time before social media, in order to share my experiences with a new generation of LGBTQ+ people who now face a different set of challenges.

Today I am alarmed to witness a twenty-first century reincarnation of Anita Bryant spreading fear and misinformation in that old faithful call-to-arms: *"Save our children!"*[3] Today's children need to be saved—that's for sure—but in my opinion it's perfectly clear who we need to protect them from: Republican governors and Republican-led state houses—what I see as a new Reich—ultra-authoritarian and seemingly determined to stamp out diversity, at least LGBTQ+ diversity. Just look at their legislative agendas, and you'll

Introduction

see what I mean. It's my opinion that the playground bullies have grown up to become conservative legislators, and their goal seems to be to erase LGBTQ+ people from society.[4-10]

Since 2021, in an attack against some of our most vulnerable citizens, nearly every Republican-led state house has passed legislation against Trans persons.[11] In many cases, those same state houses have passed legislation against teaching—even speaking—the fact that lesbians and gay men exist. With their "war" on words and their meaning—in book bans and by policing classroom discussions—those legislators and governors seem to tamp down on diversity in an attempt to mold American society into a homogenized Aryan-American Stepford landscape where there is no diversity beyond Straight and White. It's not a subtle trend; legislators in certain states are limiting what school children may read.[12] Words have become weapons, and some politicians are expert practitioners of equivocation, apparently to confuse or anger the uninformed and gullible, and generally twist accepted dialog to challenge societal norms of understanding and logic. I often hear myself talking back to the TV news anchor: "Did [insert politician's name] really just say that? But the opposite is true!" *Am I the only one who notices this?* Their political speech and sound bites are so flagrantly false—characterizing the opposition as the enemy, that it confuses anyone who tries to explain what they've done—like sleight of hand. Our language itself seems to have become an unknown territory where accepted definitions come into question—and the result is conflict and doubt. It's as if we are being gaslit.

During my formative years, my conservative parents voted mainly for Republican candidates, but more importantly they listened to facts delivered by real journalists (not pundits). They voted for the candidate with honest, common-sense goals. And it may come as a surprise, but they encouraged me to read—any book I wanted. My parents respected the local school board, and left teaching up to the teachers; they admired institutions of higher learning, scientists and doctors who told them how to live healthier lives. They also firmly believed in the separation of Church and State. In those years, when someone in Congress was caught in a crime, they were often ousted—by their own party. I'll admit that when I came home with a college degree and new ideas about politics or job goals, my parents—hands shaking at the ceiling—implored the heavens, "Send him to college and *this* is what we get?" Yet they still accepted me, respected that I was able to think for myself. And through it all I developed some critical thinking skills, something else some politicians don't like—citizens who can separate fact from fiction.

"Those were the days," a phrase my mother often said while I was growing up, had no meaning for me—until now. A year before her death, my mom—who had never even held a smartphone—told me in prophetic terms, eyes wide as she spoke, "You'd better stop with that Facebook and Twitter nonsense; it's all just wind—a waste of your time, and it's going to bring about the end of the world." I laughed because I thought she was imagining things, but based on how misinformation spreads on social platforms—crafted by people who stoke hate and division—I'm pretty sure she was right. Now I long for a day with no social media—this would be a safer, better-informed, kinder world without it. Looking back, I see my own life as if it were a film—through the rearview mirror—with nostalgia and an echo of my mom's words—*Those were the days.*

This book is my testament, a narrative of my particular suburban context for growing up, my observations, opinions, and experi-

## Introduction

ences with bullying, religious fundamentalism, my extrication from weaponized religion, and my becoming a well-adjusted, normal and happy gay man—something that too many governors and members of Congress would probably like to blot out. These memoir stories will show you, I hope, that experiences—both good and bad—build our identities, that whatever our interests are, they add knowledge and richness to our character—and no two characters are the same. With determination, we can extract negativity and the detractors who would divert us from our best selves or who would push us out of society with their fear.

In 2023, while I was searching for a literary agent, a representative from one agency contacted me to a) thank me for submitting a thorough proposal, and b) to tell me that "really, there've been too many gay memoirs lately. The market is saturated." I suppose that's one perspective, although it bothers me that it came from a literary world gatekeeper. My view, on the other hand, is that there aren't enough stories of LGBTQ+ lives on bookstore shelves.

We as members of the vast LGBTQ+ community cannot remain silent as the political-religious march toward authoritarianism tries to erase the progress democracy has made for all Americans. As I contribute my own thread to our beautiful LGBTQ+ tapestry, I encourage you as well to tell your story. Our community is rich and diverse in its history. I am glad that I took my journey—it made me who I was meant to be. I hope you'll find moments in these stories that relate to your history, your unique journey into who you are meant to be.

—April 2024, Palm Springs

# Finding My Vocabulary

"You'll never amount to anything." That's something my father told me quite a few times during my childhood, and again during adolescence, and even in early adulthood. He finally stopped using that judgment when I landed my first job out of graduate school, at age 25, whether he was relieved or defeated, I have no idea. As a child, his assessment confused and upset me; each word was innocent enough on its own—separately, but strung together in a sentence, they were hurtful. In adolescence, I just rolled my eyes and yelled in response, "You can say that as often as you want, but it won't make it true." And in adulthood, I ignored the phrase entirely, knowing my father held a worldview entirely outside of my own. Looking back, I imagine he was trying to use reverse psychology on me—tell me I'm a failure so that I'll react by doubling down on my studies to prove him wrong. Perhaps he had a vision for my life, which he saw that I was not following, so his pronouncement was a way to reject my originality, creativity, autonomy—all those things that made me different from him. I had evolved beyond him.

Over the course of childhood and adolescence, I went about growing up, following my intrigues wherever they led, avoiding situations that didn't fit my personality, moving into the lanes of influence that closely reflected or complemented my evolving interests. And one day as an adult I realized that I had built myself from all my experiences—books read, movies watched, parental examples, friendships, lessons and the teachers who taught them, the various cultural influences of our community, its prejudices and other traits, and my travels. I had built myself into this thing I am, and I became confident in my own experience—*in fact, my authority*—to explain what I learned about the world through my own channels. I came to realize that most kids probably learn about the world around them, figure out their interests, and become who they are meant to be no matter how a parent, or anyone else for that matter, might try to stop, redirect, or otherwise impose their influence. I also realized that we learn things a lot sooner than adults think we do.

\*\*\*

In the late 1960s, Brookfield, Illinois, where I grew up, was a quiet, leafy suburb of Chicago, with grid-like streets mapped out east to west, north to south, bisected by Grand Boulevard and Broadway which crossed diagonally and met at Eight Corners, seemingly the center of town, where there was a large roundabout that in the summer featured a fountain spraying water twenty feet high, and in winter displayed a Christmas tree. When dusk settled, children ran for home. I rode my bike past the elm and maple trees, then through a copse of pine, passing under the branches of the large apple tree in the center of the garden. I put my bike away in the garage and slipped inside our cape cod to occupy myself dis-

## Finding My Vocabulary

creetly, quietly in a remote corner, reading or drawing. I would hide amongst the books and magazines, looking through *National Geographic* articles about Egypt, Japan, India or other distant places. I grew into a lanky, thin boy, awkward and delicate—an easy target. Always a picky eater, I appeared to be under-weight for my age, and my mother tried many tricks to get me to eat more. I loved apples, though—they were my favorite fruit.

I didn't have many friends, just three or four boys and girls close to my own age. By first grade, the natural selection process had already begun, where the quiet, reflective types such as myself were easy targets. By third grade, some boys would ridicule my clothes and chase me home, calling me "teacher's pet" just because I followed instructions and took assignments seriously. They thought themselves the alphas, a superior clan because they traded in violence; one of their fathers was the police chief of our town. I avoided them as best as I could. Some kids at school called me "chicken," the first to run home when a fight broke out, my boy's leather dress shoes skating on the sidewalks, my bow tie loose or lost. Now that I recall it, maybe I had it coming, with the bow tie and dress shoes.

I was enrolled in kindergarten a few months before my sixth birthday at the local public school, S.E. Gross. As a kindergartener, the day was spent being reminded how to behave, when to keep quiet, listen to our teacher, follow basic instructions, learn about colors and shapes, stacking blocks and differentiating among the differing shapes of circle, triangle, and square. At the same time, we were shown pictures and drawings of trees and animals, and learned their names. In the 1960s when I was just starting school there were no school lunches, so we all walked home for lunch, spending about thirty minutes at home, and returning to school within an hour of having left. During the afternoon period we spent time learning the alphabet and how to count starting with our fingers, then adding our toes, and finally reading the numbers that represented those progressive quantities.

Our teacher taught us the alphabet by showing us each letter in order with great drama, and then giving us words to repeat that began with that letter. So, she presented "a" and told us to repeat words that started with "a" such as apple and ant. We progressed through the alphabet slowly, and without realizing it, gained knowledge that helped us understand the world. For a creative and imaginative child such as myself the words were a way to create games and play. And on it went, weeks and weeks through kindergarten and first grade. Apple, ant, bat, boy, cake, cat, dog, duck, fly, frog, girl, gnat, rat, sat, snake, squirrel, wolf, zebra—our lessons took us through fruits, desserts, insects, indeed to the zoo, where in fact we had our first school field trip to learn all about the animals of the world. And on we went as anyone might imagine, gradually expanding our circle of knowledge and experience. Teachers and parents all seemed to revel in our newfound learning capacities and encouraged us to do more, go farther, advance.

On a fall weekend, my parents decided to take a drive to Lake Zurich to see the changing leaves. It wasn't all that far from our home, but nevertheless it was an adventure. I was proud to share my knowledge about trees, animals, even the cars we passed along the way. At the time, I seemed to be developing into an idiot savant of cars and airplanes. At Bell's Apple Orchard, my father lifted me high into the branches of an apple tree so I could pick the crisp, juicy fruit. I was captivated by the sunlight filtered through the

## Finding My Vocabulary

gnarled branches and thick leaves of the tree. The light danced and flickered as I grabbed for apples. We filled a bushel to take home, and bought apple cider donuts from the bake shop. Family road trips like that were exciting and created vivid memories. Upon my return to school, I eagerly shared my stories with classmates about the places we visited and things we did. That old orchard is paved over now, with a strip mall and brick and wood-sided houses filling the landscape. The short journey that once was a breezy weekend drive is now a competitive sport—navigating bumper-to-bumper traffic and finding a parking place.

About the time of that first orchard visit, new neighbors moved into a house not far down our block. A mother, father, and one child. Mike was the boy's name, and he and I wound up in the same class and became friends. We would play in each other's back yards in the summer, explore the shrubbery of the neighboring yards as if on safari looking for zebra or ibex and pretending our family dog, Duchess, was a horse. Our games often reflected the vocabulary lessons we had had in school. Mike was a bit of a wild kid, and I quickly learned to follow his lead and act similarly in bold ways. As we spent more and more time together, it seemed that every day had a vocabulary lesson, and we were learning more complex words. This is possibly why we felt more grown up than the other children—we had the power of words.

One sunny Saturday, having run out of ideas for our play time, Mike brought out one of his father's magazines, *PLAYBOY* spelled out in large block letters, and since we were boys and playing, we thought it was most appropriate and meant for us. Mike said the magazine was from his father's "collection," a hidden trove of magazines, and that he'd never miss this one copy. My parents had magazines in our house, but I was sure none were like this one. My mother's magazines were *Life, Ladies' Home Journal, National Geographic*—magazines that showcased the president's family, or stories that depicted various meal options and the proper running of a middle-class house, or exciting articles about parts of the world newly discovered, about people who wore loincloths and lived with cattle, herding, hunting and gathering. But Mike's dad was a modern man of the world, and the eye-popping images we saw that day expanded my vocabulary in a new direction. Mike told me the words his father said when he looked at the pictures, words that sounded forbidden, wicked. The words seemed so harmless, simple, somehow funny—tits, ass, these were the main words, and naked, naked ladies, that's what we were looking at.

At dinner that evening, both my father and mother were at the table, me at one end across from my father, and my mother to one side. My mother always had encouraged me to speak my mind, to tell her what I was learning in school and what I did on play dates, so I was eager to share my new knowledge. Joining in the conversation, I told my parents that Mike had come over and had showed me one of his father's magazines. When my mother asked what it was, I enthusiastically spoke about the tits and ass we saw in the magazine. When I uttered those words, my parents' reactions surprised me. My father's mouth popped open with a look of shock tinged with a smile, his gold incisor glinting in the light—*That's my boy!* But my mother's entire countenance was transformed. One moment she was calmly eating her potatoes and roast beef, and the next she had dropped her fork, swallowed hard and told me *never,* NEVER to use such words again, that these were bad words. I think it was tit that did it, really, but it could have been ass. She

## Finding My Vocabulary

told me that these were not words a little boy such as myself—*indeed, a young gentleman!*—should be using, and that she was going to have a talk with little Mike's mother. She was bringing me up properly, as she firmly pointed out.

After school the next day, Mike and I were hiding out in his parents' basement, and we found yet another magazine. We were curious boys after all. The pictures in this magazine were shocking. A man and a woman were doing something to each other—they were somehow interconnected. By now, I was developing into a little hellion and was pretty cocky with my expanding vocabulary, and—clearly not having learned a lesson the evening before—I shared this new word at dinner with my parents. The resulting punishment was something right out of a Russian novel, being imprisoned, of being "grounded"—yet another new word I learned that evening from my mother. I was grounded, which meant I was not allowed outside of the house for a whole week, except to go to school. No desserts, either. *And no playing with that degenerate, Mike! Those obscene words!*

The following week, while calmly sitting in the back seat of my parents' 1967 silver-blue Chevrolet Biscayne as my father drove us home from a church service, I rolled down the window and yelled with glee some of the new words I had learned—just to see if people on the sidewalks would react the same way my parents had. As we passed a small group of women, I yelled in my loudest voice—*BIG TITS*—from the back seat of the car which instantly accelerated and sped off, with my father calmly telling my mother, "Just ignore him; if you ignore the behavior, it will stop."

Later in the year, on a cold winter day, I had my friends over for a play date. I was playing teacher, and they were to play the students, and our game was "Vocabulary Lessons." I had my chalk, and as I pointed to the letters of the alphabet on the chalkboard, I began the day's lesson with authority and pride. I was the leader of this small classroom, and I was going to teach my class about words. "A is for apple," I began, and I wrote the word on the chalkboard. Continuing, I added, "But A is also for ass—a donkey or a mule." We busily continued an entertaining and informative hour, including examples for nearly every letter of the alphabet—going well beyond what our teacher at school had taught us, finding joy in the printed characters unfolding before us to expand our vocabulary. "B is for bitch, which is a female dog." The range of words continued with, "C is for cabin, which is a small house in the woods." Then "D stands for daft, which means foolish." The process of learning—even as a game—seemed to propel us forward, and I became bolder in my word choices. As you can predict, my mother walked in just as I got to "W, which stands for whore." She was not pleased with me at all with what she saw written so carefully in English, and in a very foul mood after she answered several phone calls from my friends' mothers later that day. My chalk was taken away, and the chalkboard was locked in a closet.

By now my mother had reached her limit, and she decided to try a new approach in my learning process. When I was in my formative years, we had actual children's books—designed to help us learn the alphabet and expand our vocabulary. Nowadays, I see too many children using iPads or other devices, and I wonder if their learning patterns are different now that they are visually stimulated with moving pictures on a screen. Not long after the "Big Tits" fiasco and the classroom game, my mother presented me with my first real book. Titled *My Little Golden Book of Manners*, by Peggy Parish, it

## Finding My Vocabulary

was part of a whole library of children's books that covered a wide range of topics designed both to entertain and to educate, a series that some members of today's Congress obviously never read. My mother was bringing up a gentleman, as she herself had pointed out more than once, and was going to supervise my development into the distinguished man she felt I was destined to be. I enjoyed my book on manners so much that my mother bought many more from the series. Among my favorites were *Gordon's Jet Flight,* by Naomi J. Glasson, and *Top Cat,* by Carl Memling. Other books in the series were about words, numbers, boats, dinosaurs, airplanes, dogs, church hymns, and how to tell time—something I never quite figured out until mom found a clock face with movable hands. But the most important lesson of all? I learned when to keep my mouth shut and to differentiate between public words and words spoken in private among friends.

By the first or second grade I had developed a real love of reading. A couple of my favorite books of the time were *Peter and the Big Balloon,* by Hazel W. Corson, and the most entertaining, *Teddy the Terrier,* by Virginia Hunter. Teddy was captivating because the story was illustrated with actual hand-tinted photos of a Wire Fox Terrier photographed wearing all sorts of costumes—a tuxedo while seated at the piano, shirt and overalls while working on a red wagon, yellow-rimmed glasses and a red robe while leafing through a magazine—just like a lounging Hugh Hefner.

First and second grade passed effortlessly it seemed, and my reading skills were superior to many of my classmates. In fact, I was often called on to read aloud. By the third grade I was reading more challenging material, my favorite topics being discovery- and travel-related stories or ghost stories such as *The Ghost of Dibble Hollow,* by May Nickerson Wallace.

## James Philip Baran

About this time, and under threat of being cut off from more magazines, my older sister snuck to me a cast-off copy of *Mad* magazine, which was mainly a series of black and white illustrations of strange, comic, and/or ugly characters engaged in various acts of trickery, scenes of comic hilarity involving double entendre, or funny character profiles. One comic captured my imagination, and gave me a new word which I tried to use that day, and, as a result I created a new game for myself: A word a day.

"Luxury" was my new word for the day. I surveyed the house, saying things like, "Look at the luxury chair there in the corner," or, "Here we have a luxury pork chop and mashed potatoes," when dinner was served, my mother's eyes rolling heavenward as she sliced into the tender meat. Needless to say, I should be credited by the best British grocery stores for their excessive use of the word luxury. Go into Waitrose and you'll find any number of luxury items—items you would normally not even think of as luxurious. Luxury yogurt, for instance. What could possibly make this item luxurious, the price? I get it with Luxury Christmas Pudding. And then the Luxury Toilet Tissue—now there's a plush item! But my favorite is Luxury Strawberry Conserves. Of course, conserves by their nature are the very definition of luxury. In order of lowest-cost to the highest-priced in the jellies and jams aisle, jelly is the least luxurious, followed by jam, preserves, and then the top-of-the-line conserves by Wilkin & Sons. Each step up to a higher tier means there is more real fruit in the jar, and thus more luxury. But more important, as I pondered these things, if there is so much luxury available, why is there no set of boldly marketed "economy" items? Every housing development boldly claims "luxury townhomes," "exclusive opportunity," or my favorite: "private residences"—as if there were public

## Finding My Vocabulary

ones. Seriously. What does this mean, anyway? The point is, it's just marketing gibberish that sounds nice, sounds catchy. To be perfectly honest, it sounds upper-income, and, well, who doesn't want to be associated with that? It's magnetic. And I suppose this is the point—these words make these ideas, and these houses, attractive—desirable. And because of those words and the impressions they suggest, those houses are expensive. So, then, just where do people of limited means actually live? Does anyone build homes for those with lower incomes? I haven't been able to find any.

Now let's turn to the word combination "First Class" as another example. This has come to mean exclusive, with a feeling that only a few are allowed in, and the majority—the hoi polloi—are barred from entry. Really, though, in travel, first class is the new coach, just with a red carpet or a separate check-in counter—the only real perk is that you're the first to leave the plane. Economy, or Premium Economy as they like to offer, has become so low on the totem pole that no one admits they bought these seats. And then we all try to get upgrades. If we can't, we are miserable.

As I get older, I find myself still dwelling on certain words, or finding that some old familiar words have new meaning. Take "freedom." Freedom used to be a perfectly normal word, basically a state of being free, images of blond hair blowing in a sea breeze come to mind, as well as the concept of being able to make your own decisions in any matter involving choice. See where I'm going? When I hear the word freedom being thrown around today, it is often coming from the lips of some member of Congress who felt his freedom was compromised when the Federal Aviation Authority mandated that masks be worn on airplanes during a pandemic. Or the senator who once claimed—fist pounding on a podium—that forcing Americans to buy health insurance violated our freedom of choice. It's an interesting fact, though, that if all people actually had health insurance, we would be healthier collectively as a nation and, therefore, able to be freer. But I'm sometimes overly concerned with semantics and context (there's another dangerous word). The fact is, though, that words can become double-edged swords and are used as social weapons.

And since I mentioned that words can be weapons, let's turn to the word "Christian." Oh, come on, let's just take a quick look. Christian, in its original meaning, is "one who professes belief in the teachings of Jesus Christ"[1]—I looked it up in a dictionary, so I know this is correct. And just what are the teachings of Jesus Christ, one might ask? Well, here we go. Let's start with the central concept in Christianity—love. Love guides all elements in Jesus' teachings. In fact, what can be called Jesus' only rules to live by are these two: First, love God with all your heart, mind, and soul. And second, love your neighbor as yourself (I even looked it up at Matthew, chapter 22). Based on these ideas, smart followers of Jesus can glean that we must also *act* in certain ways, do specific things, all based on concepts of love. A brief summary might include these ideas: Forgive others who have wronged us. Love, or respect—or just tolerate—the people we may not think of as friends. Don't be a hypocrite. Don't bear false witness or judge others. Considering those ideas, then, *in my view*, if we approach our life by using these guiding principles, then we'll be living a good life, whether we label ourselves Christian or not. I can feel an objection coming over my reference to the idea of love; the love so often indicated for enemies or for neighbors is not romantic, not associated with Eros, but philia, or brotherly love. It is the idea that when our actions are based

## Finding My Vocabulary

in this love, then we treat others as equals, with respect, kindness, welcome—*the way we'd treat ourselves*. But I'm not a social worker; if people don't grasp it at this point, there's no use trying to explain further. Suffice it to say that when I hear the word Christian being thrown around today, my ears perk up—especially if it's a politician saying, "America is a Christian nation." What are they really saying, anyway? What is the subtext, the agenda? So, I listen and anticipate what I might learn about the speaker of the word.

Not that long ago, there was another instance that made me reflect on vocabulary. I saw on TV a rather angry-looking man—unhinged even—on the news raising his voice in rage while saying that wokeness was a problem in his state. My interest was piqued. I'm an open-minded individual, and I can admit when I've missed something. So, thinking I had misunderstood the word's meaning, I went back to my favorite information source, *Merriam-Webster's Dictionary*, to see what "woke" meant. I was surprised to find that it really isn't a bad thing, after all, and that, *No, in fact, I hadn't misunderstood the word*. It just means "aware of and actively attentive to important facts and issues (especially issues of racial and social justice)."[2] Well, there's nothing wrong with that once you know what it means. I don't see what that governor was making such a fuss about. Maybe someone should send dictionaries to those governors who are made uneasy by words. A dictionary might help them grasp that words are not our enemy.

Over the past few years, since the Covid-19 outbreak, I often hear people—Republican politicians mainly—throwing around words like "culture" and "values," common words in our vocabulary. Always interested in learning something new, I thought I'd better investigate because I may have missed something. I'll admit I *thought* I knew what these words meant, but maybe there's a new definition. So, I picked up my old trusted information source, *Merriam-Webster's Dictionary*, to see what's what.

"Values," apparently, refers to "something (such as a principle or quality) intrinsically valuable or desirable."[3] Values can include ideas such as: to respect our citizens' rights and freedoms; that elected officials face consequences for misconduct; all citizens have equal opportunity; political debate is respectful; people agree on basic facts. Hmm, seems to me that those politicians shouting about someone or some group "trying to change our values," are, *in fact*, the ones trying to confuse the public by casting doubt on what this actually means. These highly emotional sound bites seem to always focus on voting rights, immigration, women's healthcare, and anything related to the LGBTQ+ community—all hot-button topics sure to raise the ire of conservative voters. To me, it's a mind game of "Twist the Facts" used by some politicians in an attempt to fool those without critical thinking abilities into believing that liberals, democrats, women, and the LGBTQ+ community are somehow threats to America. I know for a fact that I, for one, am not trying to change our nation's values—I'm trying to defend them.

It's a similar situation with the word "culture," which means "customary beliefs, social forms ... characteristic features of everyday existence."[4] To me, it seems our culture is made up of a large variety of components: we have language (in practical use: the ability to communicate, and, included in that, an agreement on the definition of words); our customs (we work Monday through Friday usually, we use banks, we use money for trade, that sort of thing); our beliefs (freedom of speech, acceptance of facts, belief in

## Finding My Vocabulary

equality); our institutions (the courts, schools, medical establishment, financial markets, banks); we enjoy works of art and literature (we appreciate paintings, sculpture, and we read books—all things that make us think); we live with music and other performing arts (we enjoy various kinds of music and live performance including concerts, dance, theatre—even drag shows); we have moral standards or a moral compass (a core belief that we respect others, we are honest in the way we conduct ourselves, we do unto others as we'd have them do unto us, we do not kill, and we police our own lives—generally); we have laws (follow established laws, respect law enforcement including police or FBI, and even the Justice Department!); we rely on rituals (marriage, baptism, graduations, funerals, retirement parties); we have holidays (Independence Day, Memorial Day, Thanksgiving)—all accepted facets of our society that are built upon a shared national or historic experience. These things, taken together, form our culture. Again, when politicians loudly and with venom decry that someone is trying to change our values or our culture, those people are playing mind games with the public—trying to convince some citizens that others are their enemy when, in fact, it is these politicians who are undermining democracy by spreading distrust in the bedrock ideas we take for granted. I suppose when couched in angry, venomous, and misleading rhetoric by a politician on a cable news channel of questionable integrity, words like "culture" and "values" take on a nuanced biblical, sky-is-falling, doomsday scenario. But it's just smoke and mirrors, a sleight of hand—*it's not real*. Many Republican politicians make words *sound* righteous, adding an emotional hue for the audience, riling them up just by the sound. To me, this is just part of an effort to turn words into weapons.

## James Philip Baran

And while I'm at it, why not look at the word "gay?" Sure, in the 1940s this perfectly normal word meant happy, carefree. And really, it still does, although today its primary definition is "sexual or romantic attraction to people of one's same sex."[5] Do some people actually think that speaking a word somehow makes people within earshot absorb and become that word? I hear the word straight at least five times a week, and just hearing it hasn't turned me. Or is there some fear that if asked a clarifying question they'd have to utter the word themselves, or admit that it's real, a valid option, and nothing to be feared? In fact, if they accepted scientific evidence, they might have to admit they were wrong in their assumptions. *Aha! Maybe now I'm getting to the core issue.* Perhaps this is why illogically fearful governors and legislators want to ban the word gay from use in our culture. Regardless, whatever may be the cause, their obsession with this word is unhealthy. I'm not a social worker, so I can't help these people. I can't help alleviate their fear, but I do wish someone would find a way to explain things to them.

The list of fascinating words goes on and on; in fact, it almost seems that one could spend a lifetime learning about words. Having an expansive vocabulary does not mean you've been indoctrinated, or that you have become elite. It just makes you better prepared to be a productive citizen, to communicate and understand the world around you.

# Valley of the Guinea Pigs

My childhood in the 1960s was physically constrained by the geography of the anonymous suburban block on which our house stood, in a perfect row of brick and frame bungalows and cape cods, each with their own particular paint scheme and landscape. The neighborhood was adorned by large, stately elm trees, maples that turned rich shades of burnt umber, burgundy, yellow and burnished gold in the fall, a few ash and oak, as well as a variety of cedar and pine trees in the side- or back yards, like a vast parkland with houses thrown in. In fact, our town was labeled "Tree City USA." I enjoyed the outdoors where I was entertained by the play of light coming through the high branches, the birds flitting hither and yon, squirrels and rabbits about their busy work, and my boyish tree-climbing. But my indoor life proved interesting as well. As an imaginative child, I chomped at the bit to expand my dominion from the predictable back yard to the seemingly limitless world farther afield from our front door. When the weather turned bad and didn't offer the usual entertainment and inspiration, I turned to the indoors and to books, magazines, and television. *National Geographic* picture books and magazines seemed to be everywhere in our house—in the living room bookcase, in the study area of my parents' upstairs bedroom, in the built-in bookcase along the stairs, and even in the basement. These books, along with the Sony Trinitron situated at one end of the living room, fueled my imagination and took me to new places.

My favorite books were about dogs, foreign countries, and art. I even had a little magazine that came by mail every month called *Boy's Life*, and as I recall it was a rather staid publication designed to channel boys and their ideas into straight and narrow paths (and I mean that the way it sounds), paths strictly outlined as appropriate for masculine hobbies, such as camping, being helpful at home, learning about first aid, and acting the gentleman around adults. But nothing captured my attention quite as well as the television. On it, I found vast options for entertainment and knowledge, some of which my parents were not happy about though they mostly let me watch what I chose. My favorite shows were, of course, Saturday morning Looney Tunes and Merrie Melodies, the cartoons *Bugs Bunny* and *Roadrunner*, but more interesting were such programs as *Batman*, *The Munsters*, *The Addams Family*, *Green Acres*, *The Beverly Hillbillies*, *The Monkees*, and the oh-so-mod *The Avengers*—the original, with Diana Rigg and Patrick MacNee. Now *that* was a show! It had everything going for it: the English countryside, creaky old houses with secret rooms hiding ultra-modern telecommunications and radar equipment, fast sports cars, and Emma Peel in skin-tight outfits while John Steed wore a traditional black suit accessorized with an umbrella. My closest friend of the time, Linda, and I would reenact scenes from the show, she in a pair of Go-Go boots and me holding one of my father's umbrellas, running down the street, hiding behind bushes and trees, then suddenly rushing at some invisible criminal, Linda with a karate chop and me in a standard fencing pose, umbrella extended from my arm, sword-like with a shout of *"en guarde!"* We were the talk of the block if not the town. Neighborhood wives would often phone my mother or Linda's to check up on what "those crazy kids" were doing. Too bad we didn't have social media back then—surely, we would have been influencers with a large following.

From 1970 to 1976 a Saturday night television show called "Creature Features" was broadcast on Chicago's WGN channel 9.[1] The programming encompassed the range of classic black and white horror films mainly from the 1930s and 40s. I was only nine at the time I discovered this program, so it was unusual *laissez faire* for my parents to let me stay up late and watch such films. Typically, the movies involved tales of haunted houses, werewolves, vampires, ghosts, monsters made up of spare body parts, manlike reptiles walking out of lagoons, or highly strung, angry beasts destroying the cities of Japan. One of my favorite actors was Vincent Price, who starred in *The Pit and the Pendulum*, *The Raven*, and later on, *The Abominable Dr. Phibes*—billed as comedy-horror, I found it fascinatingly creepy, if unrealistic, with an acid bath for one unsuspecting character and the highly unlikely self-embalming performed by Dr. Phibes in the concluding scene (I may have been a child, but even I knew that was *not* how it was done).[2] I laughed through *Godzilla* and found *Mothra* to be just too much—while entertaining, they were utterly preposterous, and I knew it. By the time I was ten, I had developed a high appreciation for film, and even in adulthood I have always admired the care taken in cinematography, costume, and set design to make films realistic.

## James Philip Baran

By far the most inspiring tales were the ones that transported me to a different time and place. *The Mummy's Hand* from 1940[3] and *The Mummy's Tomb* from 1942[4] captured my imagination, and I would watch, completely absorbed, taking in every detail about the Tana leaves needed for mummification, the style of Egyptian architecture and furniture, the sarcophagus, and the realistic, desolate desert. I knew the tomb scenes were shot on a stage set, but at least the films' makers took the time and made the effort to create a reasonably realistic, if fictional, tomb interior. I watched *The Mummy* in a trance, channeling Zita Johann as Ankh-su-namun, staring trancelike across the Nile and across the centuries, repeating one name—"Imhotep, Imhotep."[5] I was a born actor, I felt it in me.

I don't recall quite where or how I had first heard of Egypt, possibly in school, but certainly I had seen it in the books and magazines father left casually strewn about the house. My father's theory on education was, to quote my mother, "If books are left about, then the children will eventually open them and read." At any rate, whether I learned of Egypt in school or in the books I stumbled upon at home, by this time I had already decided I was going to become an archeologist—the fancy kind of grave-robber, traveling to far-away places and sailing down the Nile, sun on my face and a fragrant breeze in my hair. Either that, or a funeral director, one or the other. I had been set on a job in the death business because we had relatives who owned a funeral home, and since my father took me there often, I naturally felt a connection. I recall enjoying the cool, hushed interior, the shaded windows, a muffled phone ringing quietly behind a closed door, and the ever-present fragrance of chrysanthemum that seemed to mask some other, more clinical odor. I felt certain that the Tana leaves, rare spices and bandages were kept in a secret chamber at the back of the building, behind the drapery-concealed, locked double doors. This added a feeling of mystery to my visits, a puzzle to be worked out. My childish fantasy future was driven by my wish to live the life I saw on film, to explore and discover tombs of the ancients, and to bring their vast wealth back to the Field Museum which I had visited on a supervised class trip. As I saw it, the family business was my best way to start out.

While I was envisioning my future as an archaeologist/funeral director, my older sister was busy in her first year of college where she was studying math and computer science—in my father's words, she was "making something of herself!" I admired her independence, that she ventured downtown every day to go to school. She brought home so many interesting people—a girl with wild hair and a great sense of humor from a Jewish family, and a Black girl who talked about politics—and who wore men's clothes because, as she pointed out, "they're more comfortable for me." Aside from my sister's studies and her fascinating friends, her hobby was in raising a small brood of guinea pigs, each with catchy names such as Whitey or Podge. The glamorous one with silky black hair was named Elizabeth Taylor, naturally. They enjoyed a seemingly charmed life of lettuce and carrots, supplemented by some strange-smelling nuggets, all washed down with pure tap water stored in a clear inverted bottle. A friend of my sister's built a large three-story cage with ramps so that the guinea pigs had places to eat and play, and to nap on the penthouse level where the afternoon sun shone best through west-facing windows.

All was happiness and reeping calls—"reep reep reep" were the high-pitched squeals every time the kitchen faucet was turned on to wash their lettuce. When dinner was delivered they went into a joyful tizzy, reep-reep-reeping and scampering in circles, until the lettuce leaves were placed gently in front of them. What sweet creatures, these pets. And what appetites they had! What joy they brought us all, even mother, who had reservations about them because of the need for weekly cage-cleaning.

Life was normal, it seemed, until one afternoon Whitey did not wake from his nap.

My sister was at school that fateful day. We waited until she came home, and on soft-padded feet slowly followed her to her room to confirm the loss. Heartbroken, she wondered aloud about what to do. Needless to say, I was one step ahead of her and offered my services for the funeral. I was, after all, the child-prodigy funeral director, fully trained; I had recorded expansive knowledge of mummification and burial rites from Hollywood's best mummy films. And my funeral home visits taught me that lavish expense and ritual is required to honor a loved one and send them into the afterlife.

Mom's best shoebox was easily acquired, along with appropriate tissue papers usually reserved for gift wrapping. But the challenge was in getting the rare spices. I had to wait until after dinner when mother was out of the kitchen for these important supplies, the use of which she would most likely prohibit and probably even admonish me, "Oh, no you don't. You can just put that back where you found it." I had learned from my films and from my Egyptian history books that herbs and spices such as salt and cinnamon, along with sacred Tana leaves, were needed to complete the embalming process. I could not find the Tana leaves anywhere in the spice cabinet, but there was a large jar of bay leaves, so, improvising, I thought they'd do just fine. I made sure I got all the cinnamon and nutmeg because the brown aromatic spices were perfect for this

## Valley of the Guinea Pigs

job. Thankfully mother stocked up on Morton's salt—it took two full cartons to complete the mummification process.

The funeral was held the next day, and Whitey was laid to rest in an elaborate ceremony outdone only by the pharaohs of Egypt, or for that matter by any American funeral. Since we had no Hill of the Seven Jackals,[6] I chose a plot near the rear of our cape cod, under a copse of pine trees, close to mother's herbaceous border—my own Valley of the Guinea Pigs. After the grave was closed, I solemnly presented my sister with a typewritten invoice for my services. On a visit to the Baran Funeral Home I had overheard one of our relatives—on the phone with some customer—say something about timely payment being a very important matter. This, however, was to haunt me when, a week later, mother decided to bake a cinnamon-spice cake and couldn't find all the ingredients. I was reading or playing a game when I heard my mother in the kitchen, becoming increasingly agitated, "Where *is* the cinnamon? And *where* did all the salt go?" When I admitted what had become of those spices, I was promptly escorted to the A&P and forced to spend my hard-earned money restocking the spice cabinet. The injustice!

It's now fifty years since little Whitey was laid to rest in that tranquil garden in Brookfield. Next to him are other guinea pigs from our family, Podge and Liz. I am sure if it has not happened already, some budding archaeologist of that house, on an expedition in that back yard some summer day, will unwittingly exhume the mummified remains of a very loved and honored guinea pig. With any luck, that curious kid will find his or her own connection to ancient Egypt and will be inspired to travel and to learn about many different cultures of the world.

# Dead and Buried

The day my grandpa died was the happiest day of my life. The bastard had it coming. John Baran had been an angry, mean-spirited, troublemaking sort. With the onset of dementia in his last years, his worst personality traits—once under some control—became dominant. And on Tuesday, October 26, 1971, he finally gave up the ghost. My reaction to the news—whispered by my mother while gently shaking me awake—took her by surprise to say the least, and with a touch of alarm most likely. I was giddy, elated like Chief Inspector Dreyfus in *The Pink Panther Strikes Again*, who laughed when hearing of Clouseau's purported death.[1] I have had many truly happy days since then, but when I was ten, the day gramps died, I was thrilled. An added benefit was that I got to stay home from school—what a great excuse. I can still recall the look of concern on my teacher's face the following morning when I presented the explanatory note from my mother. But as the undertaker's crew from the Palucek Funeral Home was occupied in grandpa's bedroom, I crept downstairs to watch as they zipped him up and wheeled him through our front door in a heavy black bag, reclining slightly on a stretcher, neighbors in the street watching, arms crossed and hands clasped over their mouths.

That morning when I learned that grandpa had died, I was glad because I thought that *now* my father would have more time for me; I was pleased because I thought I could move into the vacated room—once it was thoroughly aired and cleaned of course. I did not accompany my father to the funeral home as he made the arrangements, chose a coffin (steel with an airbrushed brown and copper finish), burial vault (the simple concrete cemetery box would do), decided on a religious service (definitely not), picked a date for the visitation and funeral (as soon as possible), and drove out to Woodlawn Cemetery to select a grave. My father was gone most of the day. And there was a strange emptiness to the house, a quiet stillness that felt newly somber—a life came to a full stop as the soul departed. Whether he was good or bad, it mattered not—he was now gone. It turned out to be a warm, sunny fall day, the mood outdoors an uplifting and cheerful contrast to the events of the morning.

Even my mother was quiet and reflective all day. Finally, that madman was dead. She phoned all her sisters to deliver the news, quietly, seriously. For five years our lives were living hell with the old demon in our midst. I knew what an awful man he had been, and I was sure my mother was glad as well. I was only a child of ten, but I had seen the way he had behaved, the things he had done. Indeed, he had it coming. His cigar smoking, finally finished. My mother kept his bedroom windows open all day to clear the infected air. She even stripped the bed and remade it with fresh linens. Several years prior, Grandpa John had set his bedroom on fire; at one time he climbed out a window and walked down the street in nothing more than his long underwear, his usual attire at home;

## Dead and Buried

he burned our dog's nose with his cigar to test a theory that it had no physical sense; he smoked every day in our house and blew the smoke luxuriously in my mother's face, exhaling acrid clouds in the kitchen, in the living room, everywhere. But the darkest thing he did was accuse my mother of attempting to poison him. And what's worse, my father believed him. Perhaps even more vile, grandpa had tempted my father with the idea of, quite truly, getting rid of us. I overheard the two of them talking one night—I had crept downstairs because I heard voices, and I could hear Grandpa John saying to my father, "Get rid of the woman and the crazy kid. They are useless." Grandpa spoke in a broken English tinged with a heavy old-world Polish accent. When he said my father's name, Fred, it was uttered as "Fratt" (with a rolled r). "Fratt, what do you say, huh? Be rid of them." In fact, in 1967, after grandpa's encouragement, my father filed for divorce from my mother—that's how serious grandpa's meddling in family affairs had become. He had it coming. His was a fitting end: asphyxia caused by emphysema.

Grandpa John wasn't always bad, though. I've been told that after I was born, when I was brought home from Columbus Hospital, there was a small gathering to show off the new baby, at which Grandpa John, in a cloud of cigar smoke, had placed a one-hundred-dollar bill on my stomach as I squirmed in the crib. I've also been told that upon smelling the cigar smoke I began to wail. And that pretty much sums up our relationship.

Family lore has it there are many secrets Grandpa John never revealed, just verbal nods or a shaking head accompanied by statements like, "You don't mess with old John," or, "Dziadek had his ways." The oral history was passed down, and today I know only these few details: He had told my father of his time in the Prussian army, vague stories of money he brought with him to America, and a German luger which my father kept hidden among his tools. Generally, what I recall of grandpa, from my own young experience to the stories told to me by my mother, is that he was a bad sort, ill-mannered and dangerous. He once reportedly tied up his wife, Antoinette, and forced her to swallow whiskey, in his alleged words, "Because she needed to learn how to drink." This all occurred before the era of domestic-abuse call centers and women's support organizations, a time when men from the old country treated their wives and children like property. Looking back, I think he was an authoritarian, like some politicians today.

A few weeks after grandpa's burial, at school we were to have a "Show and Tell" day—what we know of now as a good way to keep the kids occupied with stories, while letting the teacher relax a bit and monitor the children's developing social and interpersonal skills. The concept was that we should bring something unique to school and tell a story about it, concentrating on its design and construction, use, or even its provenance. That day I brought an alabaster box that my father had acquired during his service in the U.S. Air Force where he was stationed in Agra, India. Like a prize-suite model on *The Price is Right*, I showed off the small grayish luminous box to the class, gesturing to the strange flowers carved into its lid and the diamond-like pattern on its sides. I held it aloft so everyone might see it better as I explained that it was made of alabaster, a rare and often translucent stone that was used for many objects in the Taj Mahal, the elaborate tomb building built for the emperor Shah Jahan and his favorite wife, Mimtaz Mahal who had died in childbirth. I elaborated at length with an aside about how in those old days men generally had more than one wife. I also noted

## Dead and Buried

that the actual sarcophagi in which they are buried are entirely alabaster. The class sat in stunned silence. Was it the details about my father's war service, or was it the information about death in India? Or could it have been the multiple wives detail? I don't know, but as I recall it, my teacher smiled nervously and said something like, "Why thank you, Jimmy, for that interesting story." A week later my mother was called in for a parent-teacher conference to discuss appropriate interests for a boy my age and for my fourth-grade class. Looking back, I suppose it would have been better at the time if I had brought a rock from our back yard to Show and Tell.

As the years progressed, I could not escape the idea of death. My family would attend numerous visitations and funerals of old neighbors, great aunts, former employers, old nuns, and I would go along as well, not necessarily because I knew the deceased, but because my parents wanted to ensure I didn't "get into trouble" at home, alone. I had a habit of rearranging entire rooms to realign the Feng Shui. At one visitation I noticed that the funeral home itself bore our family name—Baran Funeral Home, our eponymous brand. My father explained that his cousin, a son of his father's brother, also named John, had established this business on Central Avenue in Chicago when it was a heavily Polish and eastern European neighborhood. After my father walked away to talk to some old acquaintance, my mother made a point of explaining that this was "the Baran side of the family," and indicated with a wave of her hand that they were not to be trusted. She was quite adamant when she added, "When I die, you better not send me here. I don't want these people handling my body. I can go to Ewald's. There, it's settled." Ewald's was the funeral home used by my mother's side of the family. Generation after generation of Kashubians had been buried through Ewald's on Southport Avenue, just a few blocks north of the Kashubian-built Roman Catholic parish, St. Josephat's, where every family wedding was held.

My father and I visited the Baran Funeral Home many times for no other reason than so he could talk with his cousin John, the funeral director and owner. The men, in their late 50s, were both Masons and seemed to have a lot in common. Always the curious child, on one of these visits I said I was interested in learning more about the business, and John, my father's cousin, introduced me to his son, yet another John, who was about 30 at the time, and he took me for a tour of the whole building. He showed me the main visitation room, and the smaller, secondary viewing room, which could be opened up to the larger to make an even bigger visitation room—for dignitaries and other important people who expected hundreds in a gathering for last respects. Both had plush carpet with a vine pattern, ornate velvety wallpaper and heavy cream-colored damask draperies. The sofas and chairs were French Provincial, with a painted off-white finish. And the pink-lit torchieres really set the mood. Then there was the coffin showroom, organized, as you might expect, from the cheapest budget styles (displayed in uncomplimentary lighting, usually sitting on the floor), to more expensive models mounted at an angle on the wall, with warmer light on them, and finally the grandest solid wood model, displayed on a catafalque complete with a silk floral tribute. Although I was just a kid, I understood the marketing approach—when people need to make decisions at a hurried, emotional time, they usually spend significantly more than they should.

"But where does the real work happen," I asked. The younger John apparently did not understand my question, so I got more to

## Dead and Buried

the point. "Where does the person get done up?" And with that my cousin took me to see the embalming room, discreetly located at the very back of the building, its double doors hidden behind beige drapes leading from the hall, with another set of double doors leading to the back drive where an anonymous white van sat parked, at the ready. Here I saw the porcelain embalming table, complete with hand-held sprayer and drain, bright lights above, and I asked, "Where does the blood go?" Cousin John answered, "To the sewer, of course. We don't save it." *Heavens*, I thought, *directly to the city sewers?* My imagination wandered for a moment on that detail. Perusing the room, my eyes settled on the smaller steel and tubed equipment lying next to a large glass bottle. I was especially interested in the workings of the "arterial tube," "autopsy aspirator," and the "cavity fluid injector," as I would learn they are called. I did not find any of this creepy or weird. "Do you have an extra one," I asked, pointing to one of the instruments, "one I could take home?" Cousin John softly replied, "No, we really don't, and it wouldn't be a good idea for me to let you have any of these." As a consolation prize, he did offer me a small brochure from an instrument manufacturer. I thanked him, and rejoined my father in the front lobby, excited about all the things I had seen. When he asked if I'd had an interesting talk with cousin John, I nodded eagerly and said, "Yes, very informative." I had made my decision, and I was going into the family business, I felt certain. Our name was already on the building, so why not?

At our next Show and Tell, when my teacher asked for volunteers, my arm shot high almost automatically. It's a bit of a blur to me now, but I do recall showing off a few of the photos of various instruments in the embalming equipment brochure, and discussing the great tour I had of my cousin's funeral home in Chicago, and then announcing that I intended to join the family business and become a funeral director when I grew up. In the unusually quiet space of the room there were a few uncertain smiles, some fidgeting and a look of tearful horror on one girl's face, and then some loud laughter from a couple of the boys. My teacher rose to her feet, "Jimmy, I am speechless," and, looking for a quick change of topic, "Thu-thank you for the presentation," and an overly cheery, "Now why don't we all have an early recess this morning?" My classmates escaped through the door swiftly, chattering away about kickball. The next day my mother was invited to yet another parent-teacher conference.

Months after Grandpa John's funeral, dejectedly concentrating on my lessons—having been overlooked several times for the Show and Tell presentations, I lost interest in moving into grandpa's old bedroom, but I didn't forget about wanting my father to spend more time with me. As fate had it, he would not have the time. As mother retold the story years later, "Your father was no man for having children. He just didn't care about kids." While dad was a disinterested, hands-off father, what he did put energy into at the time was flying, and on weekends he would take private pilot training lessons. And then of course there was his habit of Seagram's 7 and 7-Up, or ginger ale, or Coke, any mixer he might have on hand. By the time I graduated from high school my father was a full-on boozer with a private pilot's license, and flew Cessna single engine four-passenger prop planes. He even flew to the city where I was attending university, just to visit me. I suppose in his way he was trying to bond, be involved in my life. Too little, too late, I think. By this time, I had moved on, my feelings no longer hurt, in college

## Dead and Buried

and living on my own, fatherless almost. My dusty disappointments with him settled in the past, I was of an independent mind, a free spirit, with no need for continual parental supervision or conversation. Later on, by my early 20s I had my own secrets, stories I did not need to share with him.

In the years that intervened between grandpa's death and the time I finished high school, I adapted to the lack of fatherly attention. I made friends with my first bicycle, a bright electric blue with a banana seat, large reflectors, and high handlebars. I would ride ten or more miles a day, up and down our neighborhood streets at first, then farther afield. After graduating from the eighth grade, I upgraded to a metallic purple Schwinn 10-speed with racing seat. By now, I cycled around possibly twenty-five miles a day, across freight train tracks, across multi-lane busy roads, along river and creek trails in the Chicago Forest Preserve which was, really, a forest with beautiful trees that offered a feeling of freedom, tranquility, of being transported to another place.

I also took piano lessons. When I was 11, my father bought an old Baldwin upright for one hundred dollars and we kept it in grandpa's old room, now called the music room. I practiced every day after school and quickly made progress. The piano was an escape from parental supervision. I explained to my parents that I needed privacy in order to practice, and this shielded me from raised voices and confusing discussions in the basement where my parents often spoke after my father came home from work. By my second year at the piano I was in my teacher's studio recital and played a short Sonatina. By 1977 I had received the Early Bach Award for playing fifteen early Bach compositions at a Piano Guild U.S.A. audition. I was destined never to choose a predictable or simple career, and at this point, in high school, I thought it might be better to become a professional pianist than to pursue the funeral business.

But death had transfixed me at the age of six. My fascination was not unhealthy, not creepy, just a deep curiosity. My grandma, Mary, had died suddenly, heart attack they said, and I could not wrap my head around it, did not understand. I saw my mother's grief, how she wept in the car as we drove home from St. Joseph Hospital in Lincoln Park, my father silent in the driver's seat, eyes fixed on the road. I had wished that I could do something to help at the time. For days I could hear mother's tears, her gasps through her bedroom door, around corners, and I kept quiet, gave way for the heavy air in the house. I was not to go to the funeral—a sitter was summoned to supervise me, but I had yearned to go, to see my grandma. I still did not really know, did not understand the finality it meant. Unlike today, where children are ubiquitous in places they don't belong (in my opinion)—in restaurants, on airplanes, at the office; in those days, small children did not go to many events with adults.

Mary Samp, my maternal grandmother, had lived on Janssen Avenue near old St. Josephat's church. The whole neighborhood was Polish Roman Catholic, and I remember in grandma's house the carved crosses, the painted ceramic Jesus with his heart exposed, wrapped in thorns, a crown of thorns on his head, and a dried palm frond held behind it against the wall, so real to me that I was fearful as I gazed upon it, the hand-colored china like real flesh. As soon as we arrived, I would dash upstairs to grandma's flat, the door wide open, and after a quick hug I tugged her faded apron with the small blue-and-yellow flowers and led her to the kitchen. Her refrigerator was different from ours, and I al-

## Dead and Buried

ways wanted to see what she had inside. She called it the ice box, and I couldn't open it myself, so she did, and I could only reach the bottom two shelves which is where she kept the fruit, usually apples that I would grab and immediately start to chomp, juice running down my chin. Apples were my favorite treat. "Don't you feed him, Dolores?" grandma would ask, and my mother, embarrassed, would reply, "Of course I feed him. He's always hungry." My mother recalled her pregnancy and the fact that she could only eat apples for nine months. "It's the strangest thing," she told me one day, "but maybe that's the connection—why you like apples more than anything else." I still recall those visits to grandma's house, cousins running back and forth in the yard, chasing each other, climbing trees and eating grandma's apples, then the long goodbyes and the drive back to our house.

My grandma Mary is buried in St. Adalbert Cemetery, in Niles, along with many of my ancestors. Each funeral cortege winds its way on the same solemn route from the Ewald Funeral Home on Southport Avenue, northward via Elston, then down Milwaukee Avenue until the city buildings, so close together on narrow city lots, thin out at the suburban border. The names on the grave stones looked odd to me then, foreign, difficult to pronounce: Dahme, Pionki, Tutak, and my mother would take me by the hand and point at graves, walking down an entire row in the cemetery, telling me here rests an aunt, an uncle, her father, her favorite aunt, Stella. It turned out we were from the Pionki line. The Pionkis came from Poland in the late-1800s, settling in Chicago, the number one destination for those émigrés leaving Warsaw and Kraków. As I take my place in the line of my ancestors, I often wonder if any of them were like me—if they played the piano or

45

another instrument, if they enjoyed reading, and if any of them were gay—and what their lives might have been like.

Over the years we attended many family funerals—uncles and aunts. As I got older the funerals of cousins joined this solemn procession of loss—all taken suddenly, and we were left with a quiet stillness. After some of the funerals there was the luncheon, in old-world Polish style, at Przybylo's White Eagle (only a true Pole can pronounce the name) on Milwaukee Avenue, where the home-style menu was brought out on large trays by Polish waitresses: pierogi floating in butter, Bigos—kielbasa on a bed of sauerkraut, Mizeria—cucumber salad in sour cream sauce, oven-roasted chicken with paprika, cabbage rolls, buttered noodles, roast beef, mashed potatoes topped with butter. If the family was in the mood for it, a bottle of Seagram's 7 whiskey was offered to each table for the toast to the deceased. No one eats like this today. Now a funeral buffet is light, airy, maybe some fish, a paté, some fresh fruit, a white wine.

By the time I was 16 and a sophomore in high school, most of my friends from childhood had moved away, families relocated for a father's work mainly. But my friend Teri lived a block away, and over the years we had spent many summer days together, walking up and down the block, spending time in my back yard, then walking back to her house, talking about all sorts of things, our homes, books, what kind of puppy she wanted, what it was like having so many brothers. She was the middle child, and the only girl, with two older brothers and younger twins. She had a sense of independence, was a free spirit even. On a cold January night she and her four brothers died in a fire at their house. The event still gives me a chill, makes me pause to remember their faces and that catastrophe for our town, our neighborhood. It

## Dead and Buried

was on every news broadcast the next day. The shock and loss left a gaping hole somewhere in me that made me feel like I couldn't breathe, because I could not speak the words intended for Teri. There was a vacuum of silence.

Years later, I drove back to Brookfield to see the old neighborhood. The stately elm that stretched out its athletic branches upwards of eighty feet tall and wide still stood in front of our old house on Monroe. Dutch Elm Disease had skipped this lucky tree. Teri's house was there, remodeled and painted a different color, the fire long forgotten. A few trees had been cut down and new trees planted, mainly maples. It was still very much the same place. But it felt different, the context had changed, like a new photograph taken and pasted over the first, it had forgotten me and so many of us. Nearly fifty years have passed since that terrible night. The painful loss is distant in time, and the memories are quiet now.

At the beginning of my senior year in high school, my friends and I had big plans. I was going to be rooming with my friend Tony, a very popular guy in school, what we today would call an influencer, and we were planning to go on the History Trip to England over Christmas break. Tony saw in me what others did not, and thought I was a star. He said I was going to do great things, "I just know it!" he once pronounced, as if he had seen it in a vision. He had a talkative, upbeat—manic, even—gusto for life and people, and included me in all his plans. The fall term at Broadview Academy had just started, and on September 18, 1978, while I was practicing piano in the chapel, with just one spot light illuminating the piano keyboard, the main doors of the chapel were unlocked and flung open, the lights systematically turned on, one row at a time, until the room was fully lit. Within a few minutes our school principal rushed in and distractedly brushed past me, saying, "Keep playing whatever that is, it sounds good," as everyone gathered. I had no idea what was going on, but as the room filled I calmly continued playing Bach's "Jesu, Joy of Man's Desiring," which I was preparing for a future school concert. He then just stood at the podium, erect, like a stake driven into the ground. When he opened his mouth to speak, it was with a dry crack. The news came as a shock, like being punched in the stomach, and a shudder spread visibly like a wave through the crowded chapel. Some of the girls broke down in sobs. Tony was gone; he had died. We had been laughing on the phone just the week before, and now he was dead on that sunny fall afternoon—the news eclipsing the previously beautiful day. The emptiness in my stomach returned; I was speechless. Somehow a dull numbness attached itself to me, and to many of my friends, and lasted the rest of the fall term.

In the early years of my funeral-going, there were elaborate floral tributes at the Ewald Funeral Home for the two-night visitation, or wake, and these would be loaded into a flower car—a custom-modified Cadillac with open back, really a fancy pick-up truck. The cortege would circle its way to old St. Josephat's church for the mass, gloved pall bearers carefully moving the coffin from hearse to church under a canopy of dappled sun filtered lovingly by shadows of elm, ash, and maple leaves from the surrounding trees. The mass usually had everything—a priest, deacon, altar boys, incense, communion, all set to organ music if the family requested it. The memory summons the fragrance of chrysanthemum even now. Then the cortege made the hour-long journey to the cemetery, and once inside the gate, wound its way to the grave, where a green outdoor carpet was laid out to cover the exposed earth, on which

## Dead and Buried

sat two rows of chairs where everyone gathered for the Committal. Nowadays, it's done quite differently, abbreviated. Maybe a one-night visitation with perhaps one or two floral sprays, or no funeral home visitation at all, followed on the next morning by the brief mass (if at all), a rushed trip to the cemetery where the final committal is done economically, almost too quickly, in an open-air "chapel" with orange indoor-outdoor carpet. After a reading from the Bible and the Lord's Prayer, a brief announcement is made: "This concludes our services today. The family would like to thank you for coming." All this as the uniformed cemetery workers quietly, yet not unobtrusively, mill about in the background. Does anyone even know how this speech sounds, how the anonymous logistics come across? It must be what funeral directors are told to do nowadays—be efficient, get the job done quickly. Time is money. Frankly, the services are not concluded until the committal to the earth—*"earth to earth, ashes to ashes, dust to dust."*[2] If you linger just long enough after the first few cars drive off, you'll see the flatbed truck with its heavy hydraulic arm drive up to the side of the chapel, then lift the burial vault in which the coffin has already been placed and set it down on the steel truck bed. It's not a very gentle scene, it's awkward actually—a shock to my sensibilities.

I intend to be buried after mass at the church, with choir and organist, the priest to accompany my remains to the cemetery for the Committal. Shortly afterward, a lunch buffet will be served and, hopefully, good humor will prevail, people coming together as we do in good times and bad, guests mingling and reminiscing over a life lived one way or another, with memorable lifetime events, travel, and achievements nodded to, smiled over. With any luck, those gathered will tell funny stories about me and have a good laugh.

And then the world keeps spinning, time moves ever-onward, night will fall as surely as the dawn arrived. Life and everyone I knew will go on.

As years slip past like sand through our fingers, the succession of deaths has become a litany of saints, having transported the living from our lives to the other side. The grief held back all those times in the past builds up like a procession—tragedy heaped upon tragedy, layer upon layer of loss—so that each subsequent death becomes harder to bear, stays longer on the memory, calls back to mind the deaths of long ago, unrecoverable losses, conversations abruptly ended, nothing more to be learned from these loved ones. The next death will be the most unbearable. And suddenly I'm aware that those left, myself included, stand at the head of the queue, on the edge of time itself. When I was a child, time moved so slowly, waiting for the school year to end was an eternity. *What happened? Where did time go?*

Gone is the ancient grandfather, demented and mean, in God's hands. Dead tragically young is a friend from high school, what might have been had we been more compassionate and trusting of each other? Gone now, the Iron Lady, Margaret Thatcher, whose hand I shook and who talked with me at length. Departed from this world are two of my favorite professors, Tella Marie who coached me at the piano, and Eric Bickley who effortlessly and elegantly taught me and so many others the art of film. Both of these astounding people opened my eyes, my mind, and expanded my life. While I'm at it, I must admit that growing up, I didn't see my parents as inspirational, but after reflection, looking back from the distance as if at sun glistening on a sea, I can tell they were inspirations in their own way because they just got on with life, solved problems, put

## Dead and Buried

food on the table, and taught me to be a gentleman. Gone now, and I'm unable to thank them appropriately from a new perspective.

Those inspirational people were people I knew well, daily associates, family, celebrities, and friends. There are also those whom I barely know, the man with whom I exchange the peace during mass, the neighbor who might die with no one there for comfort, the accident victim on Lake Shore Drive seen from above as the police and ambulance crew clear the scene—we don't know the time and place. My mother once told me, "Never speak ill of the dead," and it is advice I've not always taken to heart. But as I mature, and as I remember this, I let go of former grudges, not necessarily forgetting but at least forgiving with the hope that others, too, might forgive me. I don't know which death comes next, or whether it is next week, next year, or in a decade. None of us know. Death always comes like a thief, when we do not expect it.

As I remember their names, I find comfort in the words from the *Book of Common Prayer*: "Rest eternal grant unto them, O Lord: And let light perpetual shine upon them. May their souls, and the souls of all the departed, through the mercy of God, rest in peace. Amen."[3]

# My Family Tree

As you glide along Lake Shore Drive on a clear evening, the city is magical, glimmering, the glass of high-rise windows shimmers with excitement, with possibility. On a moonlit night the city is like an anchored ship in harbor, and the light soundlessly glistens in silvery-gold reflections off the water. The perfect accompaniment for this scene is Claude Debussy's "Clair de lune," with its gentle opening chords, then, as the moon rises the tempo becomes more urgent, and animated notes like points of moonlight refract and dance across the waves. The traffic hums along, echoing the sea. These buildings were not here when my great-grandparents arrived in Chicago in the late 1800s. This was not their neighborhood when they lived here. But as a child, when I first cast my gaze upon this cityscape, I was fascinated, excited and eager to make this my home.

Before my time, Chicago was the place of Upton Sinclair, Carl Sandburg, Willa Cather. By the time I started circulating in the city's culture, it was the domain of maestro Georg Solti, whose golden baton led the world-famous Chicago Symphony Orchestra from 1967 until his death in 1997. The CSO, under his direction, recorded Beethoven's Ninth Symphony, which is still the benchmark recording of that famous work—thought of by many as the historic zenith of musical composition. Today, Riccardo Muti heads the orchestra. I met the fine-art and fashion photographer Victor Skrebneski, who worked with such icons as Andy Warhol, Bette Davis, and Diana Ross. He had the genius to create black and white images of nude models for the Chicago International Film Festival, and, repeating this theme, created jaw-dropping ad campaigns for luxury jewelry brands using clever makeup and lighting to highlight the gold and gems worn by attractive nude models with Aphrodite hair and Adonis muscles. These were some of the interesting people of Chicago who gave the city its creative luster, its magnetism. Their example convinced me this was the right place for me.

I loved walking and cycling in Lincoln Park, and walking up and down Michigan Avenue, or as I liked to call it, Avenue Miche (pronounced with a French accent)—it simply felt cosmopolitan, international. With work contacts, I enjoyed lunches at L'Escargot, a French restaurant that was located in the Allerton Hotel, where the room was quiet, patrons well-behaved, where white tablecloths touched the floor and lunch was served by a silent waiter, with Mozart playing in the background. Now gone, it remains only a fond memory of time past—the way things were done, properly. Nowadays, some restaurants on the Avenue are avoided—by me at least. Their hyped names, their claims that famous basketball stars dined there—it's a magnetic draw to the unattractive side of city dining: tables just inches apart so you'll literally bump elbows with strangers. There's the self-described socialite talking about her plastic surgery; there are the overserved, loud patrons spinning tales of their latest merger or acquisition to someone half their age; and I still

## My Family Tree

recall the over-perfumed woman two tables over braying about a son who, according to her, "Just got a job with the CIA!" (I promise I'm not making this up.) Those who know the Avenue's restaurants know to avoid the tourist traps and the wannabe displays.

I still walk the Avenue—what's left of it. Crate & Barrel moved, replaced by a much-too-big coffee house that charges six bucks for a croissant. Cole Haan is gone. They once carried a line of Italian leather shoes, but quality slipped and prices went up—a precursor to shrinkflation. Now their brand is made in southeast Asia and China, and it's available only online. Gone too is Kroch's and Brentano's, the largest book store in Chicago. You could request a book at the sales counter, and if they couldn't get it, it was out of print. I would spend hours browsing there. Today it seems there are no book stores whatsoever on the Avenue, an alarming sign of the times. We do have a number of cell-phone stores, though. *So, this is what it's come to.* The trendier retailers (I don't need to name them) all seem to have 24/7 police guards parked just outside. And Water Tower Place, that great, gleaming indoor mall, now is less than half occupied, a victim of another sad trend since the Covid-19 pandemic. Yet the city stands tall, still strong. People will continue to come.

Chicago is also the city of internationally known mayors. There's Richard J. Daley, who led the city with an iron fist from 1955 until his sudden death from a heart attack on December 20, 1976. Somehow, I'll never forget that day—the Daleys were a part of our lives. Then there's the charismatic Jane Byrne, who served as Chicago's first woman mayor from 1979 until 1983 and who made the city more welcoming to the LGBTQ community when she ended the police practice of raiding gay bars—more than ten years after Stonewall. When these mayors held press conferences, the city paused, every news outlet was there, and people listened.

I go to the Art Institute and the Field Museum. In 1977 the Field hosted its first blockbuster exhibition: Treasures of King Tutankhamun, which more than a million visitors saw. My piano teacher and I drove there at 6:00 a.m. so that we could stand in line to guarantee that we gained entrance early. Speaking of Field, the family is interred at Graceland Cemetery located at Clark and Irving Park on Chicago's north side. Walking through that park-like place of rest is like a stroll through history—Ludwig Mies van der Rohe, Daniel Burnham, Louis Sullivan, Allan Pinkerton, Potter Palmer, William Wallace Kimbal, Marshall Field—these architects, city planners, hoteliers, piano builders, department store founders and builders of Chicago are all buried here. Speaking again of Marshall Field, his famous department store—a model for Selfridges in London—still stands, though now it's commonly called Macy's (and we pray its doors remain open). In the golden age (and even into my early adulthood), Marshall Field & Co. had it all—you could go there for everything—clothes and shoes for the entire family, furs, fine perfumes and accessories, housewares for the kitchen, a whole floor was dedicated to bed and bath, and another floor was furniture (most of it actually made in the U.S.). I still have a wool overcoat from Italy I bought there thirty-five years ago, and it still looks like new. Fields sold quality—quality that endured. Chicago's famous cultural centers, artists, emporiums, and my experiences here have enriched my world and inspired me to look beyond my immediate surroundings.

I had thought until recently that my American heritage—my being so overtly American and more locally Chicagoan—was all I needed to complete my sense of place in my personal historical

## My Family Tree

journey. Digging a bit into family history, I learned that I am a Pomeranian.[1] Not the breed of dog, clearly, but a descendent in the ancestral heritage of those who were born and lived in Pomerania—"Pomorskie" in Polish—a geographic area situated on the southern shore of the Baltic Sea in northern Poland. I find the Pomeranian facet an interesting conversation starter, intriguing, with possible aristocratic implications. Originally ruled by Duke Wartislaw I, the Duchy of Pomerania was established around the year 1000 and lasted until 1637. In the 19th century, Pomerania became part of the Prussian empire. Fast forward to 1990 and beyond, and Pomerania is just another part of Poland, proud and independent again after Russian occupiers finally left in the 1980s.

My mother's ancestors lived near Gdansk until the late 1800s, when everyone in one branch of the family—the Pionke family—emigrated to the United States, all of them. The family is said to be of an old line of nobility, but sadly one whose titles have long been invalidated, forgotten, now useless and irrelevant. During my childhood I often imagined, fantasized really, that our family was abducted from our rightful place, Tsar Nicolas style, and that if the circumstances were corrected we would be ruling a small country, perhaps with a surname that included Saxe-Coburg. We instinctively felt we were born to the Tyrian purple, yet we were somehow displaced. I imagine my family history by way of wishful memory, a dream-like vision of my ancestors and the age-old lands they once occupied. How different the world was over the span of centuries and the distance of cultures and miles.

My mother told me stories about our history, that our ancestral line was from the smaller tribe of Pomeranians known as Kashubians.[2] They were agrarian, farmed the land, tended orchards, and raised sheep among a variety of other activities. Very few Kashubians owned the land they farmed or where their sheep or cattle grazed. Life was not easy in the 1800s, but for Kashubian people life got a lot more difficult under Prussian rule starting in the mid-1800s, when the Polish language was outlawed from use in public and in churches. Roman Catholic Kashubs were targeted because the Prussians wanted the land, and the Kashubs had few resources, little money, and most did not own any land, so, of course, they had no power. From the 1880s to 1900 Prussian authorities helped arrange transportation (whether negotiating steep discounts or even paying entire fares) for Kashubian people to leave their homeland and emigrate to America. I suppose this was a softer, nicer form of ethnic cleansing, where they didn't actually kill people—a bit like the modern-day disgruntled southern governor ordering that people be transported to Washington and New York, Sacramento and, ironically, Chicago, where thousands of immigrants came in the 1800s and early 1900s.

Like many migrants today, my ancestors took what little they had (blankets, a tablecloth, clothes, a photograph or two, crucifixes, prayer books, a few kitchen utensils, pots) and made their way to Hamburg where they boarded ships headed to New York. Émigrés came in entire family groups, and some even in entire villages. The main destinations for Pomeranian Kashubians during this time period were Canada, the United States, and Brazil. The American groups settled in small towns in Wisconsin and in Chicago. The Chicago group settled in the Lincoln Park neighborhood and established a Polish Roman Catholic parish named St. Josephat's on Southport Avenue in the late 1800s. The church building that stands on the site today was built of stone in 1902 in the Polish

## My Family Tree

Cathedral style. Times change, and today Lincoln Park and the parish of St. Josephat's are no longer a Polish stronghold. But at least the church still stands, a silent reminder of those who built it.

My maternal great-grandparents arrived in Chicago sometime between 1880 and 1890, during a wave of the Kashubian diaspora from Poland. At family Christmas parties and summer picnics, my mother and aunts often reminisced about the old days and how their family came to this country. Upon first hearing this oral history, I was informed that we were not just Pomeranian, but Kashubish, from a tribe of people who spoke their own Polish dialect and were so tightly knit that their entire family moved to the United States at the same time. It was fascinating if oddly irrelevant to me at the time. The one verifiable date I know is October 19, 1892, when August Pionk was granted U.S. citizenship in Chicago. Their Polish names today sound foreign, distant, ancient, anchored in history, an age apart. Great grandparents, August Pionk married Augustyna Antonina Piwka, and Michal Samp married Matylda Sychowski. Later, my maternal grandparents were born in Chicago—the first generation to be born in America. All these ancestors are buried in St. Adalbert Cemetery in Niles where they must occupy an eighth of an acre. To put my life in context I recall their names, the places they lived, and try to understand their circumstances. To honor them, to keep them with us, their names must be written and spoken as if a litany of saints. And I wonder as well if any of those ancestors were lesbians or gay men. Their lives would have been very different from mine today. That thought sobers and surprises me, how I am a part of this family where in the later 20th century we understand the importance of living our full truth. A hard realization for me, the subject of that coming out, but how hard it surely

59

would have been for any one of them, my distant aunts, uncles, cousins in history.

Constricted by their place in the world, language and educational status, in the early 1900s my family had little. They had little or no gold, little or no savings, no fine art collections, no real estate, and—more importantly—no connections, no real chance to become managing partners, executives, or doctors in private practice. Like today's immigrants, though, they had basic skills, were eager to learn, and were even more eager to feed and house their families. Eventually they set up small corner stores: dry goods, the butcher, the tobacco shop, the sweet shop, and there was also a druggist and a funeral home, all in walking distance to St. Josephat's church. Most of the men worked in the nearby manufacturing businesses—a drum factory, a lamp maker, the Kimball piano factory, a bicycle factory, and a printing company, to name a few, jobs that were task-based and did not require advanced language skills. Workers just needed to know how to get to work, get there on time, stand in one place and know what to do when things were put in front of them. And this is how they put in a full day's work. Repeat, get paid, maybe even advance some if the "big boss" liked them. The men, mainly, were the workers. The women almost always stayed at home, bore children (at this time, babies were born at home, not in a hospital), cooked and cleaned, did the laundry in the bath tub (I still have the washboard my mother was given by her mother). Repeat again and again and again. It would take two or three generations after their arrival in the U.S. for their progeny to hit educational and financial success as we consider it today. The imagination reels.

My maternal grandfather, August Joseph Samp, Sr. married Mary Marie Pionke on October 18, 1916, and in the years follow-

## My Family Tree

ing they had nine children. They lived at 2427 N. Janssen Avenue in a second-floor apartment. Grandma Mary and her children's names appear on the 1940 U. S. Census page for this neighborhood. Mary's children, these second-generation Americans, decidedly had fewer children than their parents and grandparents. Once our people were more established, children went to Catholic school, then some attended high school, World War II interrupted lives, and after the war many had the opportunity for job training. Incomes rose, and one by one couples moved to larger homes away from the Janssen Avenue neighborhood, which had been the locus of family life for perhaps fifty or sixty years. Gone was the idea of having eight or nine children. Most of my aunts and uncles only had two children. My generation in the family includes eighteen cousins in all, a small extended family when compared with the extended family of past generations.

Grandma and Grandpa Samp always lived on Janssen Avenue, just a block north of Fullerton, and Grandpa Augie walked to his job at the Greenview Manufacturing Company. My mother Dolores was the second of their nine children. She was born in the midst of the Spanish Flu pandemic of 1918-1920. The Great Depression would come in 1929 and last until the end of the 1930s. For those who had it hard before the Depression, it would take even longer for them to recover. During this period work was difficult to find, wages were low, and for those without real estate, ownership in factories, law firms, banks, or corporations—my relatives included—times were very hard.

My mother, who grew up in that Polish Roman Catholic neighborhood, recalled that many of the neighbors had large families at the time. My grandmother Mary came from a relatively small family—only six siblings, all girls—Stella, Martha, Rose, Cecilia, Augustyna, and my grandmother Mary, all born in the second-floor rear flat in a brick house that still stands, located at 2433 N. Janssen Avenue. At the turn of the 20th century, expectations were different from those we have today; then, a family of eight or ten would live in a two-room apartment—and they were content. Now, if children have to share a bedroom, or if there's only one bath, it's a tragedy. In 2019, a popular house-flipping show called *Windy City Rehab* aired an episode about this very house.[3] As the footage rolled and the host talked about this and that, I saw the unmistakable ramshackle apartment of our aunt Rose. The landlord never did fix up that place. It looked horrible. By today's standards, it was unlivable. The building should have been condemned long ago. But how remarkable. Cousins called, we reminisced, we told stories about our ancestors—and how aunt Rose's apartment was on TV. If aunt Rose was still here, she would have many stories to tell us.

My mother was close to that aunt Rose, a character, a talker, friendly and gossipy—always laughing. But aunt Stella was even more special. Stella would often take my mother, Dolores, and her older sister on field trips, shopping, to the lakefront, on walks in Lincoln Park to the statue of William Shakespeare and to the zoo. Aunt Stella had always wanted children, but for some reason did not have any. So, she and her husband Frank would take the girls and treat them to new clothes, shoes, lunch out, and experiences they normally would not get to enjoy.

Similarly, grandfather August's family was relatively small. Six siblings again: Mary, Anna, Joseph, Theresa, Helen, and my Grandpa August. His sister Mary had twelve children. And this is how the family expanded, growing exponentially in Chicago.

## My Family Tree

The Lincoln Park neighborhood of the first half of the $20^{th}$ century, where my mother grew up, was a walking neighborhood, and very few people owned cars. To get around, there was the Fullerton Avenue street car, later replaced by the Fullerton bus, to take residents east to the lakefront or west to Ashland Avenue, then to Elston and beyond. Nowadays, if you don't have a car, how can you possibly be expected to get to yoga, pick up the children at Latin School, and hit the Whole Foods? I suppose you'd hire a car service! My mother told many stories about her childhood—how she would take turns with her older sister—to do the shopping when their mother Mary was busy with a newborn or with laundry. There was a butcher shop only a block or two away, and across from it was a bakery, then there was the tobacco shop where they bought pipe tobacco for their father, and the sweets shop where for two pennies the girls could get genuine licorice pieces to take home and enjoy. Greenview Manufacturing, where Grandpa Augie worked, is gone now, and since the 1980s townhouses stand in its place. There was Ernie's Department Store on Fullerton Avenue, where the staff encouraged each of the girls to take home what they liked, try it on, then return it if they didn't like it, or pay for it if they did. All the business owners knew everyone from the neighborhood, and all the children were almost like one family. And at Southport and Altgeld stood the Ewald Funeral Home, which played a central part in family history until my mother's arrangements were handled there in 2008. After her funeral, Ewald—the last of the family-owned businesses in the area—closed its doors permanently, like so many small businesses, a victim of gentrification or a success story, depending on your perspective.

As August and Mary's children grew up, found jobs, and then got married, most moved away from the old, familiar neighborhood, which, by the mid-1960s was getting rather tattered and run down. One aunt eventually moved farther north to Niles. Another aunt moved far south with her husband, to the Archer Avenue area, a part of Chicago with a large Polish population. Yet another aunt moved to Pulaski Road, named for American Revolutionary War hero Casimir Pulaski. My parents became disillusioned with the city in the mid-1960s and decided to move to the suburbs. And so, the extended family grew apart. We saw each other less frequently. We were less involved in each other's lives. We made great effort to spend time together at weddings, graduations, our family's Independence Day picnic, birthday parties, and finally, funerals. But never again would we have daily or weekly visits, as things had been in the 1930s and 1940s on Janssen Avenue.

Times were changing.

It was sometime around the Polish Revolution of 1905-07 in Russian-controlled Poland, when my paternal grandfather, John Baran, could no longer bear the living conditions and decided to leave for *Ameryka*. While the 19th century was a time of upheaval in many places, with wars both short and long, localized and international on the European stage, by the early 20th century Poland was predominantly under the control of Russia. Daily life was disrupted, the Polish people felt their country was in hopeless chaos, and by this time they were basically living hand to mouth, beaten down in body and spirit. John Baran was born in 1880 in southern Poland, otherwise known as Lesser Poland, and lived his early years in a two-room unheated house—picture a barn with dirt floors and no indoor plumbing. This building was located in the tiny hamlet of Zagórzany. It had two little rooms—one for the family and one for the cow. There was a stream nearby for drinking water and for bathing. The family raised chickens that roamed freely in the surrounding meadows and forest with its pine, oak, and ash trees. Grandpa would recall that when his mother was ready to cook the evening meal, he was sent out to catch a chicken, which he swung at arm's length in a rotating fashion until the body detached from the head, blood spurting. The still-warm bird then was tossed directly into boiling water over an outdoor fire. If a mother prepared a meal in this way today, either the Health Department or the Department of Family Services would come to investigate. Next to the house stood a large pear tree that offered shade and fresh fruit in summer. These are the scraps of memory from grandfather's recollections before his death in 1971.

In the first decade of the 20th century, Grandpa John emigrated to the United States aboard ship along with two of his brothers. Other than what I've written here, almost nothing is known of their upbringing, youthful adventures, or education prior to their arrival in Chicago. The only background detail we know is that Grandpa John served in the Prussian army. Our Polish surname, Baran, means that the ram is our family's namesake. From conversations and witnessing the way Grandpa John behaved, I was able to glean that he came from a line of people who believed that women and children were property—and the husband and father did with his property what he wished to do. John married Antoinette Tutak, whom he met in Chicago, and whom he would divorce after claiming she was a risk to the lives of their children. They had five children—my father, my *tatka*—Frederick, then Joseph, John, Leo, and Marion. My uncles Joseph and John both died as infants, an unsurprising occurrence at that time in history. I never knew the other siblings, Leo and Marion, though they came to grandfather's funeral service, uninvited and unwelcome, for they had not lifted a finger to help out with grandfather when he became "difficult" as mother put it, senile and demented, setting the house on fire, requiring that the police and fire department be summoned. Looking back on this, it is clear he had dementia—or his second childhood, as some would call it—but there was no medical diagnosis for this at the time.

My father often said his siblings were useless, "All they want is money! Where's the money?" This statement often signaled a long sermon on the topic of good-for-nothing relatives, especially if he'd had his usual two or three Seagram's and 7-Ups. These stories came up many times through the years, and I felt dubious about these tales. Marion and Leo, my father's siblings, were described as selfish and unkind. Still my father insisted, with a dismissive wave of his hand: "They are worthless. They only show up when they know there is money to be had." In fact, when Marion visited us on the day of grandfather John's funeral, my father would not open the door when she knocked. They had not visited us, or grandfather, in the five years he lived with us, so they were not welcome now.

Where or how Grandpa John came into his money is a mystery, though family lore tells me he came into money while he served in the Prussian army. Shortly after his arrival in the U.S., and early in his marriage to Antoinette, they owned several apartment buildings and a tavern on Elston Avenue. Later, John would have more success with his last tavern, named the Silver Moon, on Diversey Parkway, which closed its doors in the mid-1960s when his health declined. But in the early years of the twentieth century, Chicago was a city of immigrant communities, tightly knit, where people could live most of their lives without going past the edge of their

## My Family Tree

native-speaking area, and grandfather was able to capitalize on this community by offering good booze and developing a regular clientele. At the time, Chicago had Ukrainian, German, Italian, Irish, and Polish neighborhoods, each with their own taverns, bakeries, general stores, small grocers, sweets shops, butchers, dry goods sellers, barber shops, churches, and, of course, funeral homes. Apparently, people came to the United States from abroad, hoping to create a new life, but kept their long-standing grievances with foreigners whom they didn't like, and chose to segregate themselves. It must be a part of human nature, because this system keeps repeating itself, generation after generation.

In 1965, with encouragement from Grandpa John, my father purchased a house in the Chicago suburb of Brookfield, which at the time was a quiet, friendly town of mainly middle-class factory workers, their homemaker wives, and mostly wild, free-running children. There was probably a lot of day drinking among the women. The 1950s red brick cape cod in which I grew up on Monroe Avenue is still there. My father had a job at Western Electric in Cicero, where his expertise in radio and meter workings and repairs kept him in demand—work he learned during World War II when he was stationed in Agra, India, serving there to keep Allied radio communications reliable, and this qualified him in the 1950s for a post-war training program in the expanding field of telecommunications. Western Electric was to become part of the Bell System, and then evolve into AT&T, which later morphed into Lucent Technologies—probably among the first American corporate names to be more about branding than actual product. He remained there until retirement, at which time his pension payments were actually more than his salary had been, as the company had grown, its stock doubling at the sale of various divisions. He kept every pay-stub, neatly stacked on a shelf in the basement pantry, kept on one side, just in case of audit by the IRS. Over the years this pile would end up about two feet tall. In retirement he enjoyed his hobby as a private pilot, flying Cessna single-engine planes.

As a traditional gay man, I have no children to whom I might pass along my name. My family tree ends with my husband and me. Casting my gaze across the past, I realize my unique American life, complete with the choices I have been able to make, the experiences I have had, would not have been possible without my ancestors' emigration to the United States. I take my place in the line of these silent sentinels, with hope that my life paints a portrait of fulfillment, actualization, enjoyment, a vision achieved that, while unimaginable in past generations, in my time has become a light shining both over the past and toward the future, illuminating each of us as valuable and crucial beings in our human family.

In the fullness of time, Lake Shore Drive will be rebuilt, and new buildings will rise on this storied shore of Lake Michigan. Many lives will be lived here. I was always spellbound by this stretch of road as a child, and now find my home here. My life weaves into the continuity of this place in our ever-evolving city. For now, I am blessed to gaze upon this shore, the harbor, and the almost-endless lake beyond—a glorious and peaceful scene that to some never changes, yet to me it's always new, with sun rising, clouds in their ever-changing painterly patterns, and that silver moon. And the lake still shimmers under a cloudless sky; silvery-gold reflections of moonlight soundlessly dance on the water.

# The Epiphany

I had a secret when I was four years old. I didn't have a vocabulary to explain it; no word came to mind. I just knew something, something very private. And instinctively I also knew I couldn't tell anyone about it.

On a summer afternoon, as my mother and I boarded a Chicago Transit Authority bus on Diversey Parkway near our home in the Lincoln Park neighborhood, I noticed the man high above me in the driver's seat. His well-tanned, strong legs were at my eye level. My heart skipped a beat; I became short of breath—dizzy for a moment. After paying our fare, mother turned to move down the aisle, and I waved and smiled at the driver. He turned and smiled too, as if to say, *What an adorable child*, and likely thought nothing more of it.

That moment stayed with me for days, weeks. I couldn't get that man's thigh out of my mind. And I knew I couldn't tell my mother; I couldn't ask anyone about this newly important idea that consumed me. I just had to let the thought exist. *Why was that thigh so interesting, anyway?* The thought made me nervous, and my imagination reeled, keeping me awake at night with excitement and curiosity, nervous vibrations going through me.

## James Philip Baran

Several years later, my family had by now moved from the city to a leafy suburb far from the diverse influences of urban life. When we picked out the house, I described it as a house in the park. It had large pine trees, a lush grassy lawn in front and in back, and it was quiet, very quiet. I became friends with a particular boy in my class, Jack. We hadn't really talked much, but our mothers knew each other, so we found ourselves together after school one afternoon, and began a friendship. I was about seven, and we were in first grade. Our families lived about two blocks apart, so we often walked to or from school together. We had a lot in common, both our families were Polish and our birthdays were close. In the summer we rode our small bikes and played ball in the street. In the winter, we got creative, finding games we could play indoors.

I took it upon myself to clear out a small storage room under the basement steps that led to the laundry and my father's work room and used old rugs for the floor and my grandmother's old drapes to cover the unpainted walls. I moved an old ottoman and chair into the small room and pronounced it my playroom. When Jack came over on a winter's day to play, I showed him the room and we took to spending our after-school hours just relaxing there, playing with an old typewriter I had found in my father's work room or leafing through *National Geographic* magazines and books. Of course, boredom ensued, one thing led to another, and one day we decided to compare penises. Just like that. At the time, we were both unimpressed and moved on to something else, back to *National Geographic* perhaps, and never mentioned it again. We were just curious boys learning about ourselves.

Weeks later, it was another cold, windy day with heavy snow falling. School was closed for some February holiday—a long-dead

## The Epiphany

president's birthday, most likely. I was bored, having gone down the list of my usual at-home play activities: building a puzzle, playing a record on my orange 45-rpm record player, tagging along with mother as she loaded the washing machine, going into my room and jumping up and down on the bed until she yelled for me to stop making noise, and then just lying there on the bed, staring at the ceiling. As a child I liked to explore new things every day, something our family doctor called hyperactivity, which sounded good to me. In the summer I was usually finding secret passages in the bushes, through the pine trees and lilacs that dotted our suburban back yard, climbing our old apple tree, and taking my bike on long rides through the nearby forest preserves, along the creek that fed into the Desplaines River. But on this winter day I felt confined, cooped up, a prisoner like some unwitting stooge who got caught in a crime and was punished by not being allowed outside.

After I had eliminated all the usually interesting play sites such as my closet, my sister's closet, the basement storage room with its shelves of canned goods and spare light bulbs where my father had carefully hidden his sexual technique books from even the cleverest explorations of a child, I finally realized I had not yet played in my parents' room. I crept upstairs. While exploring their bedroom I discovered another small room, mother's dressing room, and in it her walk-in closet.

I had never seen such a large closet, a whole person or two could walk right in, it was that big. Lined with cedar paneling on the walls and even the ceiling, it smelled fresh, like outside. I was developing a strong sense of curiosity, and I was easily charmed by new and different things. As I peered into the cedar-lined closet, I saw that there was a larger space toward the back, and thinking it might make a good playroom, I wandered in—dug my way in, actually, because mother's cast-off dresses and shoes covered the floor. I decided I'd do a bit of cleaning as a surprise to help her with the housework, so I started with the floor, taking out the dresses that had fallen, folding them, and clearing some floor space. I had never seen such clothes before—strapless dresses made of shiny-smooth material with voluminous pleats. Perhaps this was where I first learned about color, pattern, shape, and the feel of fabric. I also found in the general debris of cast-off items a pair of sleek, polished boots that looked identical to the ones I had seen Nancy Sinatra wearing on *The Ed Sullivan Show* when she sang *"These boots are made for walkin'."* By now, I was really excited, Nancy's song running through my head.

    I rummaged through old socks that needed darning, old shoes that I'd never seen before, new shoes still in boxes, furry pieces of animals that looked like fox and mink with heads still attached that were somehow preserved and harmless. I set these aside for some yet unknown purpose. I tried to find the perfect group of playthings for this winter day's imprisonment.

    After sorting through the clothes and discarding wrinkled summer shorts in bright flowery patterns, yellow and orange belts, and odd-looking lace-covered hats that frightened me, I discovered something of a calming color: a gray, silky smooth dress that had no visible means of support, no way to hold it up. And I thought how strange it was, why it was even here in mother's closet, because I had never seen her wear such a garment, nor even my sister. I thought it odd, and wondered why anyone would wear something so difficult to hang on one's body. I decided it must be a costume for a play.

## The Epiphany

So, I tried it on, still thinking how unlikely that anyone would want to wear something like this. At the last moment, I added the go-go boots to complete the look. I had to hold the bodice up with my hands and drape most of the gown over an arm in order to walk in the gray dress, it was so ill-fitting. And as I stood in front of the mirror across from my parents' bed, surveying myself top to bottom, I decided it was a most unattractive costume, and was about to cast it off and look for other items to play with. I must have been in that room for over an hour, and my silence in the upper reaches of the quiet house probably sounded suspicious to my mother, because to her silence always meant the child was up to no good. Before I was able to change back into my regular clothes, my mother entered the room and stopped in the doorway, having quietly searched the house for the silent deviant child who was always playing with things. When I turned, our eyes met, and I will never quite forget the look on her face: no sound escaped her lips, but her mouth was wide open as if to scream, eyes bulging, a stack of bath towels and sheets falling from her arms to the floor. It was a look of shock, as if her brain could not compute the reality of what she was witnessing—the early development of the drag queen, or at least a queer child.

It's still a blur to me, and I don't recall it very coherently, but in one swift motion she tore the dress from my body, accompanied by a calm and firm statement—half spoken to herself, I think—"*No, this is not going to happen to me; you are not going to do this to me; no son of mine is going to wear a dress ...*" and on she went, nearly hysterical. I had never seen her like this before. I tried to explain my logic, now sitting on my bum in my underwear, that I was only interested in it because it was so strange, it looked like nothing I had ever seen before, and I wanted to see how it was possible to wear such a thing. She wasn't hearing any of it. To this day, I don't know what became of that wicked grey dress. I was told in no uncertain terms that under penalty of banishment, being sent away, I was never to put on my mother's or sister's clothes again. I shrugged, "No biggie, mother, I just wondered why anyone would wear such a thing."

The topic was never discussed again. And I silently agreed that my curiosity should be kept to more boyish things like transportation—trucks, bikes, cars, planes, and trains.

\* \* \*

A few years slip by, and I am older, 11 now. Grandfather died in 1971, and the following year I began taking piano lessons. It was late spring or early summer, I recall the season because it was warm when the movers brought the heavy upright Baldwin, an ancient thing—in fact, so old the mahogany was black with a crazed varnish, but it was in working condition. A refined woman who taught music and was a member of our church took me on as a student. I was a quick study at the piano, learning the key signatures, scales, and simple Bach preludes. As I quickly advanced, even playing the Special Music selection at our church now and then, my mother, who had initially thought it a fad, a passing fancy, became much more enthusiastic about my piano playing.

On one Saturday evening, after I finished practicing my Bach preludes for the day, mother turned on the television because a famous pianist was going to be on *The Ed Sullivan Show*, and mother wanted me to hear him play. She had mentioned that strange-sounding name before, and said that, "Really, you should play like him."

## The Epiphany

From the living room sofa, I watched silently as a surreal scene unfolded: the pianist made his entrance onto the stage, lights coming up, silver candelabra on the mirror-encrusted concert grand, glittering coat over his shoulders, a ring on every finger. Before he even sat down to play, I knew something was terribly wrong. *No, this can't be, this can't be*—I kept repeating to myself. I sat there, stone cold and horrified, a sweat breaking out on my scalp, my mouth dry as if stuffed with cotton balls. My father, who had come upstairs from his work room/bar at mother's insistence, belched and grumbled something in disgust and got up to make another Seagram's and 7-Up. He did not return.

By the end of Liberace's performance, I still did not have a vocabulary, no word for this came to mind, but I knew instinctively that I couldn't discuss it with my mother. Certainly not with my father. I felt like I did that time with the bus driver. This reawakened awareness was unsettling to me, because I knew deep inside what it meant, even though I didn't have the words for it. What I knew about it upset me, and I thought, *No, this is not going to happen to me. I am not going to turn into that. I am not going to become the Liberace of Brookfield.* There must be a better example, someone else, because surely Liberace and I are not the only ones. After years of television-watching and magazine-reading, still I had found no examples of what I was looking for all this time. Well, there was Charles Nelson Riley on *The Hollywood Squares*, but I couldn't be sure about him. And Paul Lynde was clearly in the running— he was so quick-witted, nonchalant and funny in a limp-wristed, head-bobbing kind of way. I then saw Truman Capote on TV, the dramatic, caricatured personality, the languid movements, Kabuki-like gestures, and that horrible feeling returned: *No, No, not again. I can't be like him. This cannot be the way it's going to be.* I lay awake nights asking the ceiling why there are no good examples of this thing I am. Where were my role models? And this dearth of examples struck me as odd. In recent years, more and more children and adolescents have found confidence in their identity because they've seen themselves reflected in young adults in TV shows or in books and magazines. Maybe this is why uninformed and paranoid authoritarian politicians—former playground bullies now grown up—are so eager to legislate to stop any discussion of sex or gender in classrooms. Are they actually dumb enough to think that the mere act of discussing reality is a grooming tactic invented by invisible elites to indoctrinate youths into, what, I don't know, being tolerant? It's too bad people are this stupid. All they have to do is ask the question, "Hmm, why don't straight people wake up gay after they see a drag performance?" and they'd understand it doesn't rub off.

But back to Liberace on television. Somehow this man was really popular, and I had no idea why. I had banished him from my mind when, several years later, the horror returned again to TV. This time, "Mister Showmanship," "the man with the candelabra" walked across the stage in a long cape, and as a wave of applause ended, he played a Burt Bacharach medley, arms flailing elegantly at the end of each phrase. My mother would request my presence on another occasion when Liberace was a guest on some other television show, when he arrived on stage riding in a Rolls Royce and wearing a white fur coat. My mother would comment, wishful almost, "I wonder why he's still single. He could have any one of the women in that audience," and my father would clear his throat, growl and huff as he got up to leave the room, off to the bar. I won-

## The Epiphany

dered how she could not understand, and I kept my cards close to my chest, still a bit uncertain. Sometimes mother would say, wistfully and with a big smile, "Oh, you should really play like him." I was always horrified by this, embarrassed really. I did not want to dress in such a conspicuous way or be so outrageously noticeable. I recalled mother's reaction when I tried on that dress when I was younger, and I wasn't interested in repeating that scene. Nor did I want to play a medley of "Strangers in the Night," followed by "Hello Dolly," finishing off with the "Beer Barrel Polka," an incongruous and frankly hideous combination, each section punctuated with arpeggios, egregious glissandos, trills where none were necessary, arms flying heavenward with lace cuffs dancing, a crystal candelabra vibrating on the bass side of the piano's music desk. I wanted none of that. Well, to be honest, the candelabra might be nice, but really, the whole scene was ridiculous. And that kind of costume would have created a real coming-out parade.

What I did want was to play Bach with precision, Mozart with sensitivity (bringing out Wolfy's playful side in the melody), and Brahms with the gusto and romanticism that only Johannes himself could invoke. And so, I immersed myself in music. It was an escape. I was in a different world when I played, and as I perfected my scales and Bach preludes I didn't have to think about those alarming images of Liberace and why I was so put off by them.

* * *

About four years later—I was 15 by then—my sister Bernie invited me into the city to stay over on a warm and sunny June weekend. She had a lovely apartment on the third floor at 522 W.

Oakdale, what one might call a Greystone, just east of Broadway in Chicago's Lakeview neighborhood. Her roommate, Jane, was a sweet woman, and I thought of her as another sister. We went to dinner, orange roughy was on the menu, a fish I had never tasted, and it was served with sliced oranges and mixed vegetables, a spread unlikely to be had at home. My sister let me have a sip of her wine when the waitress was not looking.

Bernie and Jane's apartment had three bedrooms, so I had my own room that weekend, right at the front overlooking the street below. I sat near the window, gazing out at passersby, cars going hither and thither, and I imagined myself living with my sisters, getting a job downtown, taking the number 151 bus through the park and south to the Loop, making my own way and living free of the bondage that the suburbs had come to mean for me. The girls were so modern—they wore bell-bottom jeans or slacks made of floral-printed fabric, loose linen blouses, flowery jewelry. The apartment was furnished with bright orange rugs in the living and dining rooms, a teak dining table with four orange director's chairs, and a modern brown-and-orange chevron-patterned velvet sofa. This was high interior design then, mid-1970s. The kitchen was spare, but I knew that because my sisters went to work every day they surely ate out all the time, so there was no need for cookware and spices. The bathroom was sparkling clean and tiled all the way up to the ceiling. From their apartment's décor to the neighborhood itself, I immediately felt at home.

That Sunday I didn't want to leave. I had already decided this was my neighborhood. Before driving me back home to the stifling suburbs, my sisters took me out for brunch, something else that was new to me, breakfast and lunch combined, very *au courant*.

## The Epiphany

On our way to the restaurant, we stopped because there was a disturbance, something going on in the street. Jane pointed out that it appeared to be some sort of parade heading north on Broadway. Buses and trucks appeared to be crammed with men and women. Everyone was shouting and waving their arms. Music I had never heard before was blaring from speakers mounted in the bed of a pickup truck—decidedly upbeat music with bass like a heartbeat, a celebratory theme. I heard someone saying it was Diana Ross' new song, "Love Hangover," and the words echoed and were lost amongst the shouts.

Just what was this, I wondered. A protest? A celebration? It almost seemed like both. It certainly had a different feeling—not at all like the July 4th parade in Brookfield, with the Kiwanis group and the Rotary Club float, with a sea of White people watching. I heard someone scream *Gay Power!* and a whole truckful of men and women, Black, White, Hispanic and young—a group I easily could have fit in with, passed us by, still chanting, *Gay Power, now!* They continued up the street, raising their arms and their fists. On the next truck there was more dance music playing, and there were men kissing, women hugging, and the growing crowd along the curb cheered them on, smiling and raising their arms high, waving. It was magical. Could it be that I'd just seen my own reflection? Were these people just like me?

*Woooo! You show 'em, You go! I'm with ya! Gay power!*

Bernie and Jane looked at each other with knowing, proud smiles, then at me. Turning to face the scene, Jane announced—as if surprised—"Well, look, it's the gay pride parade." And just then, my life started to make sense—one smile, one shout, one kiss at a time.

# All in the Family

Those were the days. It's a slogan my mom used often, wistfully recalling a past no longer present, such as for example the way banking was done in the 1940s, where you went into the bank and they greeted customers in person. "I want my money handed to me by a teller—the way it's supposed to be done. None of this ATM business," she would insist, jaw clenched and shaking her head, with a quick dismissive wave as we walked past the cash machine and into the bank lobby. "Gosh, those were the days." Or grocery shopping, where you'd go up to the butcher counter and ask for a five-pound sirloin roast and the butcher hauled out what must have been a 150-pound side of beef and asked, pointing, "Would you like it cut from here, or here?" Those, indeed, were the days. Not like today where the butcher counter is staffed by a tattooed 20-something who gestures toward the beef section and mumbles through piercings, "This is what we have."

Those were the days. Honestly, I laughed whenever mom said this. I myself always looked forward, always interested in what life would be like when I was a year older, or when I went to high school or college—the imagined road wide open ahead of me, visible through the windshield. In the 1970s mom would talk every day to each of her six sisters. There was no voicemail then, and call waiting hadn't been invented yet, so if one or other of her sisters were on the phone she'd get a busy signal and have to keep dialing—endlessly. I could hear her in the kitchen, "My finger is going to get sprained if I have to keep dialing. Jimmy," she'd shout, "call your aunt Evelyn for me, please? I just can't dial anymore." We had one of those black wall-mounted Bell System telephones. When it rang, it caused such a clatter, it could wake the dead. The thing practically shook itself off the wall.

After doing the round robin of calls with sisters, my mom would finish the laundry and start dinner. Lunch was always something simple like a sandwich and fruit, but dinner was a production. Any night of the week, my dad wanted meat and potatoes. If mom made something like spaghetti or lasagna—at my suggestion—dad would take one look and bark, "What the hell is this? What kind of food is this? Dago food, that's what it is. I want meat and potatoes, got it?" And the offending meal would be eaten in silence, with me the only one enjoying the food. The next night we would return to beef roast and boiled new potatoes, because dad wanted "real" food—like in the good old days. Or it might be pork chops and boiled new potatoes. Some evenings we had mashed potatoes just to shake things up a bit on the vegetable side. On a really special occasion we'd also have carrots or beets, even broccoli or squash. When I was ten, I didn't like any vegetables, least of all potatoes, but I'd eat the meat. When I asked to leave the table, mom pointed to my plate and said, "As soon as you finish your potatoes." But by then they were inedible, cold and dry, so a battle of the wills ensued. But once I took two or three small bites, mom would relent

## All in the Family

and say, "Okay, you can go now," waving me out of the room.

At ten, in 1971, growing up in a quiet town like Brookfield, Illinois, there wasn't a lot for a kid to do. We certainly had no iPads, no streaming service, so a child's imagination was an important asset. When I acted bored and sat on the sofa staring out the front windows, my mom would say, "Go outside and play—use your imagination!" School was hell with unruly and undisciplined kids screaming and throwing things, so I looked forward to not being there whenever possible, enjoying my quiet walks home and the peaceful hour or so before my dad got home from work. My father, Fred—or, when he was speaking with authority, more likely shouting—became "Professor" or, if the topic was religion, "Bishop," nicknames my mother teased him with from time to time when he was pontificating in a jovial mood about this topic or that. He had joined the National Geographic Society in the 1950s, so we had an uninterrupted collection of their magazines to read and from which to learn about the world. Since he did not finish high school, he believed that reading was a way to teach oneself about different cultures and places, and *National Geographic* was a great educational resource.

Like most families, we had a television and a stereo, books and board games, and I had my bike, so I usually spent most of my free time outside riding around town, exploring the paths in the Chicago Forest Preserve, on the Brookfield to Riverside stretch of trail. On weekends my parents expected me to stay home or accompany them on weekly shopping trips into the city to the grocery and bakery. Stop & Shop was the best grocery store in the area, and that's where we went. Then we'd go to some small local Polish or Jewish bakery for pastries, bread, rolls, and cookies. My mom's favorite bakery was Kaufman's Bagel Bakery on Kedzie, near Wilson, on Chicago's north side. They made the best chocolate chip cookies, large and soft, almost like a cross between cookie and cake. I still remember their rich chocolate fragrance and soft texture.

On Saturday night, after getting home from the shopping and other errands, and after mom put away all the groceries and dad retreated to the basement for his Seagram's and 7-Up, we would often have a light supper of cheese and crackers, fruit and fresh pastries. Afterward, it was TV time, and my mom usually tuned in to the slapstick antics of Harvey Korman and Tim Conway on the *Carol Burnett Show*. Other shows we enjoyed included *The Jeffersons*, *Maude*, and eventually *The Golden Girls*. There was something simple about these shows, and they offered a sort of reflection of our evolving culture in each. Carol Burnett showed us how to laugh at ourselves. Carol became Mrs. Wiggins or the Charwoman, and Harvey Korman—in drag—became Mother Marcus, a full-figured Jewish grandmother. They had high ratings, and the shows always got great laughs. Ironically, no one ever tried to shut down the *Carol Burnett Show*, or accuse the show's creators and stars of being a threat to children. It was just good, *harmless*, humor. The Jefferson family gave us an example of Black people going into business and succeeding, with plenty of funny scenes, a foil to all the bad news about actual job opportunities and life for the average Black family of the time. And Maude was the alter ego of the housewife, authoritative, all-knowing, ready to prove her husband wrong at a time when men ruled the house. Although fictional, these characters on TV showed us an alternative, humbling, informative, and often funny way of seeing ourselves. Through comedy, they imparted wisdom.

## All in the Family

The show that hit closest to home was *All in the Family*. The resemblance between the TV show and our own living room was uncanny—it was as if Norman Lear had come through our house and said, "Yeah, this is what I want." There was the console piano, the television, the two different chairs for Archie and Edith, likewise for mom and dad. But the most significant thing was the physical resemblance between my parents and the show's main characters. My mom, ever the optimist, humming a tune while wearing a flowered house dress and apron, looked and acted a lot like Edith Bunker. My dad, drink in hand, didn't just resemble Archie—he could pass as his twin, complete with the same ideas about race and religion. When he got started on something, it was best to just let him rant and not interrupt, much the way Edith acquiesced to Archie. To this day, I am thankful for most of my teachers, because they inculcated in me concepts that helped me think for myself, and I was able to understand the world beyond my dad's racism and paranoia.

My parents didn't finish high school, because their lives were interrupted by the Great Depression, and they needed to help their families by working. Like Archie Bunker, my father had a blue-collar job, and he worked in a factory in the early years of the technology age. As with Edith, my mother was the homemaker, but beyond the TV character my mother taught me principles of honesty and integrity—she didn't need a college education to understand the difference between right and wrong.

Like the Bunker house, in our 1950s suburban cape cod there was no dishwasher, and certainly no ensuite bath in each bedroom. Our family had just one car, which was only used for grocery shopping or family visits on weekends. We had no laptops, no iPads, no smartphones. Yet somehow we managed to live contented lives, took care of all our responsibilities without the use of apps and without being tethered to devices all day. Imagine what that was like.

In the early 1970s I tuned in to the TV shows along with mom and dad because, in a nutshell, I had nothing else to do—all my friends were with their families on weekends, and my friends and I usually went bike riding on weekdays. Over the years, in my still-childish way I had found joy in exercising my vocabulary and reading skills, and it occurred to me that by replacing lines in a poem or song—as long as the edit had the same number of syllables, accents fell in the same places, and even rhymed—then the parody would not only respond to the original content, it would add an often ironic or hilarious meaning. This would always cause my family to think, "Surely that's not the way it was written, or is it?" So, now, with my new interest in music, I would sing along at the beginning of *All in the Family*, changing some words to alter the meaning—the subversive, harmless habit I carry with me into adulthood. When they sang the line about a car that "ran great," I was ready with "gee, we oughta segregate," touching an idea that made my dad raise his glass and mutter, "Boy, you don't know how right you are," as he continued to watch, nostalgic for a time sadly in the past, the natural order now somehow upset.

Then there was *Maude* with Beatrice Arthur's sassy, ironic, omniscient tone and great delivery where she set everyone straight about women's rights, welcomed Blacks into her sitcom living room, and even supported gay rights. Looking back, these positive references to what would become the LGBTQ community took too long, yet she was ahead of her time. I could see Maude's comments

## All in the Family

left my parents speechless, too confused or reticent to add their own commentary, so I held back. It was still too early for me—still a kid—to assert myself.

I grew up in that now-distant, all-but-forgotten past, the 1960s and 1970s—what Gen Z must think were the dark ages before social media. Back then, the very idea of sending money via a phone would have been preposterous—instead, we mailed a check. But during that time, things were clear-cut, or at least you could differentiate between fact and fiction more easily. At that time, and even into the 80s and 90s, we could rely on news presented by professionals who had studied journalism and who vetted their sources. Today, instead of reading actual news, many people go to social media—with its inherent disregard for facts—entranced by anger, lies, distortions, and misinformation. They've fallen for it, duped by the slick messages on their devices, thinking, "If my friend liked it, then it's gotta be true. And look how many 'likes' it has!"

Times change, I'll admit. We went from a nation and economy that built and manufactured things (machinery, cars, appliances, books, telephones, sheets and towels—hard consumer goods) to one that reads spreadsheets, designs apps, creates "content," draws up mergers and acquisitions. Just try to find anything made in the U.S.A. today, and you'll see what I mean. Pundits (not reporters) talk in bullet points crafted to convince one half of the population that the other half is the enemy. And the corporate overlords at Google and Meta are watching, tracking every click, recording the demographics—ready to sell this data to the highest bidder. This mass insanity has to stop. It's no wonder, then, that in my father's time he thought being an auto mechanic or a funeral director were great careers; they were practical and provided needed services. If

I had told him I was planning on becoming a "content creator," he would have said, "You must be nuts," and he'd have been right.

During the 1960s and 70s my parents mainly voted Republican, but more importantly they listened to facts no matter who delivered them, and then voted for the candidate with common-sense goals, not for a candidate promising revenge. When Nixon—the guy they voted for—was investigated and then resigned, they applauded and said, "They should lock him up. The criminal!" Incidentally, our news broadcasts—on the five channels we had—consisted of verified facts (as compared to today where, in one example, a "news" outlet settled a lawsuit for $787.5 million because it actively was involved in broadcasting known lies).[1] My parents respected the local school board, left teaching up to the teachers; they admired institutions of higher learning, scientists and doctors who told them how to live healthier lives. And they firmly believed in the separation of Church and State. In those years, when someone in Congress was caught in a crime, or even just doing something unethical, they were often ousted—by their own party! Now, we see daily examples of elected legislators undermining government, lying, and stoking violence among our citizens. It's true that when I went away to university and came home with some new ideas—my own ideas—about politics or job goals, my parents would say, hands lifted toward the ceiling, "Send him to college, and *this* is what we get back?" with a dismissive shake of the head and a hint of disappointment. Yet they still accepted me, respected that I was able to think for myself and make my own decisions.

And I'm thankful I developed critical thinking skills. Not to disparage my father, but if I hadn't learned to think for myself, I'd be referring to some of my fellow citizens by a very bad word,

## All in the Family

and thinking yet another group has total lock-down control of the film and entertainment industries. If I had followed his vision for my success, I'd have become an auto mechanic or an assembly-line worker. There's nothing wrong with those jobs, but as I became better educated, I differentiated myself from my family and relied on my own motivation and ideas to take a path to success in ways that align with, or result from, my particular artistic creativity.

As I matured and followed my academic and cultural interests, I drifted away from my family. It was easy to remove myself from family situations because I was living far away, attending college. When aunts and uncles invited me to birthdays or other parties, I politely, sometimes nervously, declined because I knew the badgering I'd get when in the company of family: "Jimmy!"—they all called me that—"Where's your girlfriend?" If I had answered, "You mean boyfriend," the party would have come to a crashing halt. Or they'd ask, patting me on the shoulder, "Jimmy, when are you getting married?" I knew they meant no harm—they were just reinforcing the norms they grew up with and those traditions they themselves perpetuated. But I didn't want the family spotlight on me; I feared excessive scrutiny. I had not formulated a good response to those repeated questions. I never did have a quick wit with which to impress; I wasn't a fast talker, and couldn't deflect direct questions. I'd be terrible under cross-examination. And as time slipped by, I graduated from college and finally started a working career. By then, I suppose it was just accepted that I would only be seen in the family circle at weddings and funerals, the busy young adult living in the city. My regrets are that I lost touch with cousins, aunts and uncles, for no other reason than my fear of rejection for being honest, sharing my immutable self with them. What might have happened had I come out to the broader family when I was a sophomore in college? I don't know. But based on my family dynamics, I thought I made wise choices at the time, decisions that protected me from scrutiny while shielding my family from facts too difficult for them to process, too difficult for me to explain. I chose not to make waves. I was closeted, suppressed out of fear of rejection—rejection by parents, cousins, aunts and uncles. I was lost to many of these relatives and we still remain apart, our lives having evolved in different ways altogether. And today, all my aunts, uncles, and both of my parents are dead. Since our lives grew apart, it's quite impossible to bring them back together.

I can still hear that fond statement as only my mother could say it, with a slight smile and a glance into space, as if looking into the past itself: "Those were the days." I'm glad I grew up during that time of the 1960s and 70s. I'm also glad that I was allowed to have my own adventures, explore books, seek out facts without every moment of my childhood being policed or by being disciplined for—or being blocked from—reading materials that interested me and helped nurture the person I was to become. The lack of queer-oriented reading material for children and adolescents at that time didn't prevent me from becoming my genuine self—that fact only made it more difficult for me to adjust and eventually find my vocabulary. But I still found myself. My life took a path influenced by my environment, my creative spirit, my hope for adventures and travel, my interests, the books I read, the teachers who taught me, the programs I watched, the friends I had, and the family experiences I lived and took part in. Whether my parents wanted to raise a gay son is anyone's guess, but they did, and I celebrate that.

# Love for Sale

It has been said that you can never really go home again once you've been gone a while. With curious and hopeful anticipation, though, my family tried. The fateful trip would open the eyes of both of my parents and change their minds forever about the family tree.

It was the summer of 1978. I would be a senior in high school that fall, but a several-times-removed cousin was to be married that August—Hanya, daughter of my dad's distant cousin Leokadia. And so, travel plans were made with the help of my parents' travel agent. We needed professional travel advice because we were to visit the old country, Poland—hard core Eastern Bloc still under Russian control—where my paternal grandfather was born and grew up.

Poland was new to us, and yet very old. This destination was far, not just distant in mileage but a place where life was still lived in a 19th century sort of way. Cows grazing, a horse pulling a hay trailer, men wearing tattered black or dirty gray clothes, a woman in the kitchen baking rye bread every day and boiling beet soup for dinner—these were the scenes I saw that summer.

Zagórzany was a small town then, and it was no easy feat getting there. Located in southern Poland, the nearest commercial airport at that time was at Kraków, but as there were no direct flights there, we flew into Warsaw, our first stop in Poland. Reaching our final destination would be an adventure.

Zagórzany hugs the curve of the Moszczanka River about a two-hour car ride southeast of Kraków. At the time we visited, it was a haphazard sort of place with no town center. Today its population is around 2,300.[1] We could have gotten there from the Warsaw airport in about five hours if we had rented a car, but my father was never one for doing things in a logical way. He decided to hire a taxi.

The road trip turned into a 24-hour hell-ride, one that left us shaken and unsure about why we decided to make this trip. As we set out from Warsaw, the driver took us on a scenic journey through hills and towns. The car, a small Russian sedan, was older, maybe 1960s vintage, and with the weight of four people as well as our baggage, the suspension was overly taxed and the rear axle broke. Cutting our losses, we unloaded the trunk, and my father paid the driver with American dollars. The man appeared to bless us as he backed away, bowing, hat in his hands, giving passers-by the idea that we were dignitaries of some sort.

As we stood there, at the edge of the road, wondering what to do next, a bus approached. My father waved and the bus stopped. How convenient, what a relief. Things would get interesting now, as it seemed everyone on the bus knew each other, and they were going to Kraków on some religious pilgrimage to Cathedral Wawel, the famous medieval stone church in which the Polish royal family and other important Poles are buried. On the ride, however, it

## Love for Sale

seemed that some of the women in the group had plans for my father, at least for his money which he had flashed as he paid the bus driver when we boarded. A bleached blonde near the front of the bus offered my father the seat next to her, and a sort-of happy hour ensued. While they passed cheap Polish vodka to my father with encouraging talk and lots of laughter, my mother and I could only find seats near the rear of the bus. Because she was brought up in a Polish household, my mother could understand the language, even though she could not speak it very well herself, and she overheard what she thought was a plan hatched by two nefarious-looking men seated just behind us. The basic gist was, according to my mother, that they coax us off the bus, rob my father of his precious American dollars, and beat us up. As we approached a busy town, my mother got up and yelled to my father that we needed to get off the bus. In the confusion of raised voices, the bus driver pulled over to the side of the road and stopped. My father paid the bus driver to watch as we unloaded our bags from the cargo area and walked to a hotel situated across the road. Safely inside the lobby, my mother explained what she had overheard. My father made light of it because he never worried about anything.

As we settled in at the hotel, we learned that we were in the town of Kielce. We also learned that on July 4, 1946, in what today is known as the Kielce pogrom, forty-two Jews were murdered—after the Holocaust and after World War II.[2] At the time of our visit, thirty-two years after that terrible event, I was struck by how bleak and grey the town was, the people ashen-faced, as if knowing an evil presence lurked under the surface and in the very air. We could not overcome our unease that evening, and a quietness settled on us. Recalling it today, I understand that—in our own time—while we may think a battle or war is over, there are still people around us ready to kill, easily set to violence by misinformation, lies, or fear.

On the way down to dinner that evening, I noticed that my mother still managed to look elegant in her understated way, and she tried to be cheerful. She wore a pink and white foulard dress with a modest, rounded neck line, and its hem landed just below the knees. She always wore Cobbies, a brand of sensible loafer-style slip-on with a two-inch heel—just high enough to qualify as a woman's shoe, but low enough to be good for walking. She completed her ensemble with a light-weight wool, three-button coat in a jaunty yellow and white, modern checkered weave pattern. My father, meanwhile, wore his simple grey suit trousers, plain white dress shirt, completed with his vintage-1940s red tie, a tie he wore all his life. I was in my uniform of the time: khaki trousers and a striped rugby shirt, with white tennis shoes. Our entrance in the hotel restaurant was like Liberace going on stage. Our collective fashion sense, while conservative and understated at home, stood out in Poland. Without intending it, we walked in like we owned the place—conspicuous, brightly attired Americans. We decided it was best not to walk around the town that evening and to leave first thing in the morning. Turning to the menu, which had been presented to us by a matronly woman wearing all grey, we saw nothing recognizable or appetizing, and in the end, my father ordered for us—Polish rye bread with butter and some sausage and sauerkraut dish that I thought inedible. At 17, I decided I was now on a diet.

The following day, after a breakfast of more rye bread and butter, my father made sure a relatively new taxi was summoned. After the thwarted kidnapping and robbery attempt on the bus, we found a driver willing to take us the final stretch of our journey, my dad's

## Love for Sale

negotiation skills on full display as he flashed an American fifty-dollar note, his gold upper incisor glinting in the sun as he smiled. It turned out to be a hot day, and we sped along the bumpy roads with windows wide open. By the time we arrived in Zagórzany, it was mid-afternoon, and we were tired, sweaty and disheveled. We pulled into the farm driveway, two uneven dirt and gravel ruts that provided a vague path up the slight hill, and stopped in what would be called a courtyard if it had been in a more elegant setting. Here, however, this was a square area about 100 feet in each direction, scrappy grasses and patches of dirt in which chickens roamed about clucking and pecking, bordered on one side by the house, then the barn directly opposite, and a small square building no larger than a phone booth half-way between the two. We would soon learn that the small structure was the unvented outhouse—the house itself had no indoor plumbing. A well sat about another 200 feet up from the square, with a hand-crank and a metal bucket attached to the end of a rope. My mother's first impression was simply to frown, and to quote Bette Davis, "What a dump."[3] My initial thought was that we'd never make it through the month, what with no shower or toilet. Where would we bathe? We didn't expect the Four Seasons, but, frankly, we did hope for a bath tub. In the end, we were thankful that my mother had the foresight to pack eight rolls of toilet paper, for there was none to be found in the outhouse or in the house itself. My mind only reeled as I thought of how our relatives handled the necessary cleanup. This was my first cultural crisis. Whether it was our clothes, the food, or the amenities we expected, the cultural differences were stark. It was our second day in Poland, and already I felt uneasy, as if there had been some misunderstanding and we had made a mistake.

## James Philip Baran

The actual house was another adventure. Built sometime in the previous century, all the rooms were connected to one another in a sort of daisy chain arrangement. The entry was to the kitchen, where we passed the faucetless wash basin defined only by its sloped metal frame with a piscina-style drain that literally dumped the sink water into the ground below the house. From the kitchen, we walked into what would be called the primary bedroom, most likely due to its desirable adjacency to the kitchen, and in this case without ensuite. That bedroom led to another bedroom, which in turn led to yet another and another. None of these rooms resembled a living room or dining room. There was just the kitchen and a series of bedrooms. In all, there may have been six rooms built around a large ceramic heater. In the kitchen a wood-fired burner and an oven were connected to the heater, and a smooth ceramic tile wall jutted into each of the bedrooms from the center of the house. The only way to take a bath was to fill a large metal tub that sat in a corner of the kitchen—just like you'd see in an old Western—with boiling water from the stove along with water from the well. A single bath would require at least six trips to the well. I learned that summer how to take cold sponge baths—outdoors. Making our adjustment feel even more strange, we soon realized there was no phone, no television, and not even a radio in the house. Talk about a crisis: where were we to get news? In today's lexicon, we were literally "off the grid."

We arrived in mid-July, and our cousin's wedding was not until mid-August. Settling in, I entertained myself with the young calf I found in the barn, helping out by making sure his feed trough and water bowl were full. His mother was named Marlena, a large, reddish-brown, mild-mannered dairy cow that pleased herself by munching grass near the sunny south side of the house. Marlena never made trouble, but when she wandered across the road or into neighboring farmland, one of our cousins would be summoned to round her up and lead her back home. Watching Marlena was a highlight of my summer, along with feeding the young, nameless calf. As the days wore on, and I got to know the calf better—he seemed almost glad to see me whenever I popped in to feed him, so I chose a name for him. He was to be Benji. And he was a handful, hungry always, but a joy to spend time with, watching him munch on grass and grains.

After our arrival, during the first two weeks of our stay, we took interesting day trips to other towns, villages, and cities. We toured Gorlice, Nowy Sącz, and spent several days in Kraków—a deep dive into our cultural roots. The highlight of that visit was our tour of Wawel Castle with its large state rooms and the very interesting crypt with its many coffins. I swear, someone could shoot a good horror film there. We also took a day to find the place where Grandpa John grew up. My father spoke Polish, so he took the lead in this effort. He talked to his cousin, Leokadia, and then to neighbors, asking about the location of the old Baran house, where the Baran clan had lived at the turn of the century. It only took a few hours, and after a few conversations my father felt we were on the right track. We walked down an old deeply-rutted path now grass-covered from disuse, on and on we walked, probably a mile or more. Along the way, we encountered an old crone carrying a burlap bag of sorts, hunched over—just like a character in a movie. My father spoke with her for a few minutes, and with a crooked finger she pointed in one direction down the path. The forest was dark, with tall trees, oak, elm, ash, pine, and only patches of sun broke through the dense, leafy canopy. We stopped at a place where we could see the vague outline of a rectangular foundation, about twenty feet long and perhaps ten feet wide, a slight rise in the grassy earth defining the outline of the old house. Next to this was an old pear tree, and my father decided this once was the house. Grandfather had spoken of a pear tree many times, recalling that he could reach out a window and pick pears as a child. Now the tree was perhaps twenty feet tall with a thick, gnarled trunk, and small pears were visible on its branches. Father picked a pear to take back home, hoping to plant its seeds in our Brookfield yard. It was the first time I observed my father expressing any sentimentality.

About a week before the wedding, activity around the house increased to a nervous bustle. A sort-of freelance baker was hired to make cookies, pastries, and cakes. The oven was hot from seven in the morning until at least five in the evening, and then Leokadia would bake bread. All that baking made the house hotter than it was outside. By the time the big day arrived, there were at least thirty loaves of rye bread and perhaps twenty kinds of cookies, and treats such as Faworki (thin crisp Angel Wings with powdered sugar), Kolaczki (filled with prune, strawberry jam, or sweetened cream cheese), plus an enormous two-tiered white-frosted wedding cake adorned with small pink flowers. All the baked goods were covered with a fine mesh material to keep the flies at bay.

About three days before the wedding, we were moved into the most secluded bedroom in the house, since we were guests of honor from *Ameryka*. Every other room was cleared of furniture and scrubbed, its windows washed, and its floors swept and mopped. Long tables were brought in from around the village, some of them no more than saw horses with boards nailed on top. Chairs were brought from all the neighbors' houses. The rooms were all connected by removing the doors and hanging ropes of fresh flowers strung with bright paper cut-outs of stars and other shapes. Candles and Vodka bottles were placed on every table. It was about this time I noticed that Benji had gone missing. Had someone left open the gate to his pen? Marlena was still grazing in the meadow, but the young calf was not to be found. When I asked my father about Benji, I only got a confused answer: "I think your calf wandered off to another farm; I'm sure they'll find him."

Guests started arriving two days before the wedding. They were put up in the barn or at neighboring houses. One woman in particular was a buxom, bleached-blonde about my mother's age who went by the name Ivana. She brought with her a girl who was a few years younger than I, perhaps fourteen—a sort of mini version of herself, equally blonde. It was nice to have someone near my own age, except for the fact that none of these people spoke a word of English. I had no one to talk to except my parents. And then no one bathed. The classier relatives just splashed perfume or cologne to mask their overripe body odor.

The pre-wedding party began a day before the actual wedding. Meals were casual and eaten outside, with one's hands and often without a plate, reserving the nicely decorated tables in the house for the wedding-day feast. A few musicians showed up—I never did find out if they were hired or if they just happened to be passing by and joined the party, but they were welcomed joyously. The vodka was poured generously, especially for my father who, again, flashed American currency. With all the people, and all the booze, my mother was getting concerned. I was only getting bored.

That first night of the party, I thought I'd make myself useful, so I volunteered to keep the water flowing at the kitchen sink by running every half hour to the well, sending the pail into the water far below, and then slowly turning the crank and hauling up the full bucket. There was some drama when, instead of slowly lowering the bucket into the well with the crank arm, I just tossed it down into the well and let the crank spin like mad. Of course, with my luck, the bucket and the rope itself tore loose from the wooden crankshaft at the top. A neighbor was summoned whose athletic son literally repelled into the well using a rope and anchor system he cobbled together and brought up the bucket and rope to be reattached.

As more and more guests arrived, the group became increasingly loud and agitated, fueled by the vodka I'm sure. It was a hot evening, and after dinner I took a walk around the property to take the air and try to cool off. On my way back, as I passed the barn, I thought I'd seen light coming from inside, so I stopped to take a look, thinking someone had found Benji and brought him back. I surreptitiously peeked through the wide crack in the barn doors. No Benji in sight, but what I saw was like a frolicking Fellini scene: a short man ran chasing a tall laughing blonde—both of them naked, her breasts bouncing as she pretended to be fleeing from his grasp. Another couple were sitting on the edge of the barn's loft—naked as well. Still others were walking about, "cruising" as we might say today, not settled into couples yet. And all I could think at that moment was that these people hadn't bathed.

I went back into the house and reported to my parents what I had witnessed. My mother was shocked, mouth agape, and shook her head. "You just stay away from them," she told me, continuing, "Like animals—in the barn—sex—they can't help themselves." I

## Love for Sale

could almost see her imagination reeling as she spoke, while applying her evening ritual of face and hand creams. Later—almost out of the blue—continuing her line of thought, she added, "They have no control—and these floozies, no wonder—the way they're dressed, it's a sin." My half-interested father, counting his money, only replied, "What are you going on about?" Things started to add up in my mother's mind. She had seen Ivana take my father aside to talk. Quietly, my mom demanded to know what that woman meant by talking secretly with my father. He calmly explained that she was inquiring about my age, gesturing toward me, the 17-year old son from *Ameryka*, whether I was single or married. My mother was appalled, eyes bulging: "Shameless hussy, is she some marriage broker? How dare she try to arrange a marriage—and to my son." And then, putting on her cotton sleep gloves, turned to my dad with, "Don't tell me she offered you money!"—as if she divined a secret pact. Caught off-guard, my father laughed with a shocked shriek, his guilt exposed in a wordless pause, that gold incisor visible again. But then he regained his composure and went straight-faced. He explained, "It's harmless, really, she's just looking for a way to get her daughter a better life," noting that yes, in fact, she had suggested they work together on the plan, and that with her daughter married to me, the U.S. would have to let her become a citizen. They both ignored me as I asked, meekly, "Do I get a say in this?" My mom, hands on her hips, head shaking and defiant, pointed directly at my father as she did whenever her decision was final, and told him in no uncertain words, "Over — my — dead — body!" *Someone's on my side! There will not be a double wedding!* My mother went into a kind of crisis mode, wringing her hands, mentally calculating what this would cost me, married off at 17, forced to work to support a young wife with sights set on a glamorous American life, my future college plans derailed, cut short for the sake of an immigration marriage. Mother's calculations didn't stop there, with me, but extended to her and father, who, by her estimates, would end up supporting the parents and grandparents of the girl if we went through with this plan. She was having none of it. My mom had always been an overprotective mother, but this time I was not only thankful for her intervention, I was relieved.

On the day of the wedding, my parents decided we should take a tour of the town, a way to get out of the way during the final wedding preparations. We visited the local Roman Catholic parish church, now festooned with fresh flowers and more of the same colorful paper cut-outs that were in the house. We also stopped at the cemetery, where we saw graves of several ancestors. One grave in particular stood out because it had a gable-style leger stone resembling a roof over the entire grave along with a tall cross at the head. I pointed out that the cross looked new, that the grave cover stone looked old and brown with some cracks, while the cross was very clean. My father's cousin Leokadia explained—with several genuflections—that the original cross that rested atop Piotr Baran's grave was struck by lightning. *Really? What are the odds?* We also learned that this ancestor, Piotr—Peter—had lost his mind in some sense, well, how can it be explained? After all, in rural Poland in the early 1900s there were no social workers, no psychiatrists or therapists to help the locals work through whatever issues they may have had. There were no emotional support hotlines, no AA, no Sex Addicts Anonymous. Back then, in rural Poland, you just lived, you beat up your spouse, argued with neighbors, ate, shit, and then you died. Nobody cared if you had addictions, paranoia, or depression.

## Love for Sale

The story about Piotr going mad, losing his mind, was memorable. My mother often reminded my father that perhaps that was where his own madness originated, in that rustic village in southern Poland.

That afternoon after the wedding ceremony had concluded, the entire church procession walked—danced, really—back to the house, where we all filed in and took seats. The bride and groom walked into each room to receive hearty congratulations, and vodka shots were served with gusto. When Hanya and her new husband came to our table, my father—clearly the patron of the day—handed them a crisp one-hundred-dollar bill and congratulated them in Polish. The whole room rose to toast my dad, singing a traditional celebratory Polish song: "Sto lat, sto lat, niech zyje zyje nam," which translates roughly to "Good luck, good cheer, may you live a hundred years!"[4] The vodka flowed all evening. After two or three rounds of booze, my mother and I started to wonder about the wedding dinner. In a short while, the gourmet meal was served by the caterer and her assistants. Indeed, this was the best meal we'd had since our arrival in Poland a month prior. The main course was a real treat—caramelized pearl onions, baby peas, and small herbed new potatoes attractively surrounding tender cutlets, with a delicious wine reduction sauce to the side. Always a finicky eater, I inquired, "But what is this meat, it's so tender." My father spoke Polish to another guest, and after some translation he told me it was veal. "It's delicious," I said, adding, "I've never had this before. Where does veal come from?" At first, there was an awkward hesitation, then my father stuttered, "Well, um, … ah, hmmm, let's see, uh … it's from a young calf, that's where I think it comes from." My mother, savoring a mouthful, glanced sideways at me, trying to smile. My breath was

103

knocked out of me, and I practically shouted, "Don't tell me! Not Benji!" Once I realized it was the sweet calf I had befriended—*I even helped fatten him up*—I was overcome emotionally, sick even. It was our first edible meal in Poland, and I couldn't eat another bite.

A week later, we arrived home, and my mother nearly kissed the ground—she was that happy to be home, where running water and a tiled bathroom awaited. My parents, each in turn, could be heard in that bath, sighing luxuriously in the warm water of a porcelain tub. In my weekly phone calls home over that next year, I followed the tales told in a series of letters from the Polish cousins—letters with a theme: money. Money was needed for appliances, for a new car, for an apartment, and then—inevitably, for a baby. Perhaps those distant relatives saw us as their lifeline, a connection to a better life, a better world. Maybe my father knew he could not sustain our Polish clan. He never spoke of them again. I don't know what he may have written to them, what he said, but eventually their letters stopped coming. And our cord to old Poland was cut forever.

# The Journey of Coming Out

I've always loved travel. Whether it's by bus, train, car, ship, or plane, the vehicle hardly matters. The journey from one place to another always seems magical to me, an adventure that captures the imagination and offers new experiences. When I consider a journey today, ocean liners like Queen Mary 2 come to mind, or British Airways flights to London. Journeys to Europe, Asia, Mexico, and Egypt flash in the imagination—distant places that offer once-in-a-lifetime opportunities to learn about and appreciate other cultures. Today, we have Google Maps, Siri, and Trip Advisor if we need help with our route, advice about what to do or see, and recommendations or critiques of innumerable establishments. I often wish we had had social media in the 1980s when I was approaching adulthood. It might have made a difference at an important time in my life—in the fall of 1980 when I journeyed by plane with a paper ticket and no phone, with two trunks in the cargo hold, to Tennessee, or what is referred to in today's lexicon as "fly-over country."

My destination was a small college town east of Chattanooga, close to the Georgia border. I was an outdoorsy young person, and the geography and terrain of southern Tennessee were big attractions for me—Lookout Mountain, Ruby Falls, the hiking and camping options in the area, bike trails, the beauty of the majestic outdoors—all these things appealed to me. I didn't think for a moment about the people themselves at my destination—what they would think of me or what they themselves would be like. After the disappointments of my academy years, I had an optimistic outlook and expected college to offer a new, more accepting environment. I thought I'd find new friends and a rewarding college life. How naïve I was. Trip Advisor would have come in handy back then and would have helped me avoid the most harrowing experience of my life.

The journey I've dwelt on in memory started with that trip, but ended in me standing up and walking out of a church, leaving a denomination that has—in my life—become a hate group. I often thought I was just in the wrong place at the wrong time, and this is certainly partly true. It took me forty years to cast off the traumas inflicted by people who live by the ideology of fundamentalism, and I now have confidence in my experience as the basis for the story of my journey out of the Seventh-day Adventist church. I'll be clear: I did not abandon my faith or God. I took a detour into what was for me the darkness of fundamentalism, but I eventually escaped.

My coming out journey is closely associated with my rejection of the uninformed judgments and shame cast upon me by intolerant people, or maybe they were just people too afraid to question the beliefs they'd been taught. Coming to terms with my immutable self was not a simple act—especially in a denomination that prides itself on being an arbiter of who belongs and who does not, who is included and who is excluded. I didn't put on one of mom's pearl necklaces one day and announce dramatically to parents and the world: *Grab your boa, get your castanets! I'm gay!* That wasn't me. Accepting

## The Journey of Coming Out

myself and leaving a destructive, all-consuming, narrow-minded religious group took time and strength. Similar to the leadership in authoritarian countries like Russia or theocracies such as Iran, certain religious groups claim that homosexuality is an aberration, a willful choice, or refer to it as if it were a disease like leprosy. The prejudice and bullying by conservative Christians can be like some survival-themed game where the strongest, best-connected influencers/bullies join forces to target a weaker person—someone on the margins—to cast them out. The bullying tactics are perfected over time, and those bullies never back down—an idea that might make a good authoritarian political slogan. And if they're lucky, the victim of this constant barrage of mean-spirited name-calling, criticism, and ridicule will commit suicide, or at least leave. It's a vicious sorting system that offers no space for diversity and which, in my opinion, is no Christian approach to life. I was in dangerous territory, but as I began my first year of college I didn't realize it.

I finally came out when I was 21. By today's standards, I was a late bloomer. Nowadays young people have good role models in media, in government, in books, and on television. Maybe that's why so many on the so-called "right" in high political office are eager to craft legislation to erase our visibility in the public square and in books, to take us back to some long-lost idealized past where gays were invisible and didn't stake claims to our rights.

I

Looking back to the time I was four or five, I showed all the signs of a budding queer, and indeed my journey had begun. I recall having a near-encyclopedic knowledge of Motown's female vocalists, an uncanny ability to memorize comic skits by Lily Tomlin, a desire to see all the films starring Elizabeth Taylor and Marilyn Monroe, and a keen eye for furniture arrangement. In hindsight, the writing was on the wall. When the Supremes were guests on *The Ed Sullivan Show*, I went on stage too, following the choreography perfectly and singing along to "Stop in the Name of Love," imagining the spotlight on me as I snapped my fingers, holding an imaginary microphone. My parents, meanwhile, stared in surprised humor, unsure of how to react—*what a precocious child!* Then there was the time I saw Ike and Tina Turner on TV—I instantly became a backup singer. And I thought that if I couldn't do that, I'd still do something original, something unique. As a child, I knew I was playing at things, that I was not grown up yet, but that when I did grow up I'd have to have some kind of career. Within a couple of years, I went through a period where I would only wear velvet, but by then it was the 1970s, so that was okay.

I'll admit it—I was the weird kid in our neighborhood, probably in the whole town. I was the child sitting on the front porch singing "Love for sale" as passers-by quickly moved on down the block, shocked smiles spread across their faces. When relatives visited for our annual Independence Day picnic, I'd have the front porch set up as a stage, record player ready, and when cousins drove up I'd turn it on, playing the Supremes' "Come see about me," and doing my dance routine to greet our guests. After lunch, I'd lead my younger cousins in a conga line from our back yard onto the front sidewalk and down the street, "Boom! chick-a-boom, chick-a-boom," we pranced around the block—a kick to the right, on the beat, then a kick to the left—and so we congaed, neighbors no doubt thinking this Fellini scene was better than TV. Then we'd play parade, where I led the group down the middle of the street it-

## The Journey of Coming Out

self, hoisting our American flag high above my head, drumming out a Sousa march rhythm with improvised vocal kazoo backup. We didn't need iPads or smartphones when we were kids—we invented our entertainment. An apropos soundtrack to my childhood would have been Aram Khatchaturian's Waltz from the *Masquerade* suite.

When my family visited the homes of aunts and uncles, I would initiate new adventures and what my mother called "monkey shines." On one visit to my aunt Rita and uncle Stan's house, while the adults were having coffee and cake in the living room, I led my younger cousins on an expedition through the back yard. There, in the center of the yard, we found a dead tree—long dead by the looks of it because there was no bark on it, no twigs or leaves. Four of us surrounded this tree, and then—succumbing to temptation—I gave a gentle push, and each of us in turn gave a push. This went on for quite some time. The ground surrounding the roots gradually opened wider and wider until—with one heavy shove—the entire tree fell across the yard and into the neighbor's property with a loud crash, crushing aunt Rita's roses in the process, all four of us laughing with shocked glee and running to hide. Uncle Stanley—Stosh as he was known—rushed out of the house, fist in the air, and yelled at us, "Hoodlums, goofy kids! When I get my hands on you—!" Aunts and uncles came out to see what the ruckus was about, martini, coffee or a glass of wine in hand. In the end, Stosh calmed down after another uncle of mine pointed out, "It was dead anyway, Stan. Look at the bright side, now you don't have to hire a tree service to cut it down!" Everyone laughed. The adults went back inside for another piece of cake. All was well. Except on the ride back home mom told me, "I know it was you. We can't take you anywhere without something big happening."

## James Philip Baran

Perhaps it was my personality, my interest in the music created by Black musicians, macabre movies, or perhaps it was a fear of the "Other"—regardless, I was so unique I didn't fit in. My efforts toward acceptance were thwarted by my own originality, apparently, when all I wanted was to belong, be a part of the group. By the fourth grade, I was being harassed in public school, called names, bullied. It didn't help matters that I had memorized the lyrics and dance moves to the entire repertoire of the Supremes and the Temptations and would lead sing-alongs during recess. *Maybe that's what started the bullying!* I was ten years old, and one evening when my father came home from work I told my parents I wasn't going back to that horrible S.E. Gross School. I explained the bullying, that some mean boys followed my friends and me home, throwing stones. Under normal circumstances, my parents would have said, "You obviously did something to cause this," but now they took me very seriously. I was given an early dinner and told to go outside and ride my bike. They sat up late that evening planning for my transfer to a new school. They granted my wish, and the next day I did not return to Gross School. Instead, my father phoned the principal and lectured him about how certain boys in my class behaved like animals. He took the day off, and the next day too, to drive around the area and find a new school for me to attend. Today this would have been an easy Google search followed up with a few phone calls, perhaps a downloaded PDF application and an electronic funds transfer from bank to school. But back then it was very time-consuming. By the next week, I was placed at West Suburban Seventh-day Adventist Day School in Broadview, a ten-minute drive from our house. My parents were assured that West Suburban was a good school, and that its mission was to develop good Christian character.

## The Journey of Coming Out

Smaller than Gross School, West Suburban SDA was arranged on one level. The yellow brick, flat-roofed building had a central hall that ran the length of it with three or four classrooms on each side. Boys' and Girls' bathrooms were at the end of the hall where a large addition housed a gymnasium with girls' and boys' locker rooms at the south end of the building facing the local Adventist Church. On the other end of the building there was a large open field where we played flag football, softball, four-square, and the best game of all—tetherball.

I entered West Sub in the 5th grade, and our home room housed both 5th and 6th graders, divided straight down the middle, two columns on each side of the room. When our teacher had lessons for one grade, the other group had in-class assignments or study time. We broke for recess twice a day, once in the morning and once in the afternoon. We all brought our own lunches, and the school provided a small carton of milk. I usually had a bologna sandwich with an apple or banana, or a Twinkie on Fridays as a treat. Other kids brought PB&J sandwiches or rice cakes with marshmallow spread. *Now that's health-conscious!* When I asked my mother if we could buy those items for my lunch, she looked at me and said, "You're not going to be eating that—it's all sugar!"

It was in this 5th and 6th grade classroom where I took great pleasure in the reading skills sessions and history lessons. I tried to get along with everyone, but I didn't feel like I fit in. There was a strange boy who sat next to me, Samuel. He was a repellant, malodorous boy with some sort of skin affliction, greasy with large scabs and red, pus-producing sores which never went away. He would pinch me when no one was looking. He would wipe his scabby arm across my face when the class was paying attention to the teacher as he wrote on the chalkboard. He was creepy, corpulent, and repulsive. He had an older brother, a cute, athletic guy named Stephen. But they were both a bad sort. I imagine that today these brothers are possibly serving long sentences supervised by the Department of Corrections.

It wasn't enough to just let me go to school here. As the year marched on, mom and dad decided to become Adventists, taking me with them to church and the baptismal tank. At Camp Meeting we were paraded—the new converts—across the stage, me in my stylish beige and brown two-piece Yves Saint Laurent boy's suit. I tried to tell them I was unsure about this move, that, really, I preferred my Saturday morning time with Bugs Bunny and Wile E. Coyote over church services, but my objections were overruled. The connection to this denomination would turn out to be a significant wrong turn on my journey, and I didn't have either the authority or the ability to correct my course at the time.

Gross School was bad, but this place turned out to be a different sort of bad—religious bad. Soon enough, I found out that many of my fellow students were wolves in sheep's clothing. Our home-room teacher came up with some discussion game or other—Advanced Show and Tell?—where he asked us each in turn to tell about our family history. In the course of telling my story, I mentioned that my family was Polish, and this solicited gales of laughter from my classmates. Quick shouts of *Polack* followed. It was quickly becoming clear that these malicious misfits were hell-bent on labeling me the outsider. I wondered what was wrong with my classmates, so judgmental, so jeering and unfriendly, feral almost. Our teacher had no control over them. They didn't seem to laugh at the Italian kids, who often had a history of verbally

## The Journey of Coming Out

dramatic parents. They didn't laugh at the Swedish girl in class. And they didn't laugh at the kid from Kentucky with the rope belt. I began to feel as if how selective they were in who they targeted was some game where I didn't know the rules, because it made no sense. My trousers may have been a tad short, but they were still a fashionable shade of green. My classmates, so eager to point at someone, called them "high waters," with another shrill cascade of laughter.

The taunting and jeers didn't stop. Looking back on it, I suppose children are children and—not knowing any better (and, *more importantly*, not being corrected)—they parrot the prejudices and ideas they learn at home, as the apple doesn't fall far from the tree. I did not know why this was getting worse at my new school, yet I felt embarrassed, as if maybe this was somehow my fault. So, I took it. I sat back and let it happen, quietly reflecting on what might be wrong with me, that surely something was wrong with me, looking in the mirror to see if I could find it, every day feeling less confident. One particularly mean girl in my class laughed—brayed, really—calling me Rosebud one day, Femalon the next, the nickname embarrassing because I felt I knew what it meant underneath the letters and syllables. *How could she tell? Was it written on my face?* Everyone seemed to enjoy her sassy ingenuity, which they supported with another chorus of hysterical laughter. Then there were a few of the boys who offered occasional sideways whispers of *faggot* and *fairy* when I passed them in the hall. With each taunt about the way I walked, talked, or dressed, a majority of my class would add other wisecracks or jokes about me, loving that they had their own outcast, the "Other," the person who distracted them from their own shortcomings and problems.

James Philip Baran

I dreaded the moment when the teacher left the room for a bathroom break, because this is when the violence started and these children not only threw taunts but actual objects in my direction—pencils, empty food containers, shoes. I imagine they learned their prejudices and bullying from parents and pastors, their Pathfinder troupe, and from the peers they associated with in the church community. My class itself was, to me, a hate group, only at the time I had no vocabulary to describe this. Apparently, there was no one willing to correct these children's anti-social—and anti-Christian—behavior, how it went against church teachings, the core idea being that we all are supposedly brothers and sisters in Christ. Even the pastor's daughter, Jeena, whom we all thought the coolest girl in class, turned out to be bigoted, in my opinion. In school, she was a bit of a nonconformist, even laughed at the church, so I thought she was an independent thinker. Her joker personality blossomed later at academy, but so did her bullying tendencies. Still, I thought she'd turn out to be more good-natured and accepting one day. I was often gullible, easily duped, in those years. In adulthood, we reconnected on social media, and there I learned she had only gotten worse, with uninformed, absurd views about democracy, far-fetched, unproven claims of a corrupt Biden administration, and then homophobic and racist posts. Intolerance is the last straw for me. Personally, I find it impossible to carry on a reasoned conversation with someone who has blindly accepted conspiracy theories and proven falsehoods; I am dumbfounded by their unwillingness or inability to accept fact, and in turn I have no way to relate, no way to respond to their fantastical statements. I can imagine what a reasonable politician might think when confronted with anger and outright falsehood—these things derail a normal conversation. Since

## The Journey of Coming Out

I'm not a social worker, and I realize it's impossible to talk sensibly with a person disconnected from reality, I blocked her—removing a toxic individual from my life. I have to admit, there is one good thing about social media—you really do learn about people's character, or lack of it.

Puberty and adolescence set in, and we started to grow up, some faster and some slower. I became more comfortable in my body, accepting that I was a bit different, and decided it was just too bad that some people couldn't see my good qualities. I started respecting myself, making a checklist of my qualities and strengths. While I wasn't an actual athlete, I liked basketball a lot, but broke my glasses twice in one month, so I was forced to give that up. I was quite good at volleyball, and I enjoyed softball, tetherball, and on some days just the rush of wind in my ears while on the large swings that our school had on the grounds. As for my fascination with Motown, instead of taking up rhythm and blues, I channeled my musical interest and talent into classical piano. By my second year of study, I showed signs of talent and performed in my piano teacher's studio recital. By the time I was a sophomore in high school I had received critiques and accolades from judges in the Piano Guild U.S.A. I was enthusiastic about the piano and driven to study harder.

After elementary school, I attended the Adventist boarding school, Broadview Academy, set amongst the corn fields of rural Kane County and composed of a chapel and administration building, cafeteria/laundry building, gymnasium, and girls' and boys' dorms built on an almost treeless rise above the corn. In the winter, you really felt the wind. This school's marketing slogan was "character above intellect," and where, once more, there would be harassment and bullying, a clear sign to me of some people's poor character. I learned to ride it out—confident that it would get better, and that in adulthood things would be fine. This latter fact turned out to be true, though it felt like an eternity getting there. After I came out, I took the time to phone Adventist business headquarters in Silver Spring, Maryland, to request that they remove my name from all records and ensure I was not inadvertently left on the membership roll. I wanted nothing to do with what I saw as a hate group. I received a letter of apology for the ways I was treated at the academy from the former principal after he learned that I cut ties with their church, and as I held that letter I wondered, amazed, as to why he was so concerned years after the fact. He had showed no concern at the time, while the bullying and name-calling were going on. But back in high school, my insulating tactics included keeping mainly to myself, applying myself to reading and long practice hours, and eating lunch and dinner alone while the wise-cracking Hinsdale cliques sat across the dining hall laughing hysterically about this or that. There would be many occasions when members of those small packs would embarrass or try to humiliate me about my clothes or the way I walked or talked. I'd silently encourage myself with, "What does not kill me makes me stronger."[1] I stood tall and finished high school with these kids, and at graduation weekend I realized that most of us were misfits in one way or another.

After my experiences at Broadview Academy, I took a year's break before starting college. In addition to the work experience and income, I learned more about the world outside the shelter-prison of parochial school, saw people outside the context of fundamentalism, and my generally overprotective parents gradually gave me more freedom. I hadn't yet learned about survival and personal dignity, though. I hadn't learned my lesson. As if I hadn't had enough, still looking for acceptance I went to yet another Adventist-run institution—a bad decision and another wrong turn on my journey. It has been said that hindsight is 20/20, and I would eventually learn that if you're gay, at all costs you should avoid small towns.

## II

There are many small college towns like Collegedale; but since I actually lived in this one for a while, I can fairly accurately describe this particular place. When I enrolled at Southern Missionary College in 1980 the town was rustic, secluded, off-the-beaten-path. Surrounded by hills and forest to the west that created a natural barrier between Collegedale and Chattanooga, the clearing where the college sits is a sort-of valley, not unlike the expanse of land in the film, *A Return to Salem's Lot*,[2] about a town inhabited by seemingly nice people who turn out to be very different from how they appear. The humidity and rain were stifling in Collegedale. The architecture of the main campus buildings was like that of Tara—well, modified Tara—updated colonial-style buildings designed to inspire dignity or anchor the campus with a historic Southern plantation-like appearance. My memories include musty classrooms without air conditioning that smelled like chalk and mildew, an administration building with lurid bright green carpet and, once more, the odor of mildew, overpowered now and then by the smell of soy- and gluten-based sausages wafting from the cafeteria. The dormitories were like those at most schools, shoeboxes piled upon shoeboxes in which the students slept and studied. In the men's dorm the showers were dark and mildewed, with shower poles mounted between floor and ceiling, spray heads that shot razor-like streams of water that seemed intentionally designed to strip your skin.

And finally, we get to meet the people. Believe me when I say that the United States is really like a dozen different countries—because people can be so culturally opposed and different-minded from one another, even quite prejudiced against people from other parts of the country. Frankly, I wonder why there hasn't been a war here, started by people who hate diversity. Some Americans, as I would learn, don't seem to understand how our government was designed, repeatedly referring to "our Christian country." *Wait! This is not a theocracy*, I thought to myself. I tried to explain that the United States, technically, is not a Christian country, but is in fact a nation free from adherence to any one religion so as to protect everyone's individual freedoms, that we respect everyone's religious choice.[3] A few of my fellow students recoiled when I said this, as if I were a heretic. One acquaintance actually said, "I guess that's what they teach you people up north." At first, I found this situation humorous, a result of being sheltered or misinformed, but at that time I couldn't imagine a willful rejection of fact. So, I undertook a personal mission to share in an open-minded dialog with my fellow students to show that we have more in common than not. I'll be the first to admit that I was naïve. This was going to be a challenge. It seems clearer to me now that once people get indoctrinated in certain ideas, then even solid, vetted, confirmed evidence won't change their minds.

I admit I'm no social worker, nor am I a psychologist, but still I'm able to think and attempt to formulate a psychological theory about what makes fundamentalism a vortex of fear and even hate.

## The Journey of Coming Out

It is my understanding (and also very well-described by Wikipedia) that religious fundamentalism includes a "tendency ... characterized by the application of a strict literal interpretation to [sic] scriptures ... along with a strong belief in the importance of distinguishing one's ingroup and outgroup, which leads to an emphasis on some conception of 'purity' ... [and] an unwavering attachment to a set of irreducible beliefs."[4] Keep that in mind as I describe my experiences.

While I was in Collegedale, I often heard people say with great pride and heads held high that they are "in the world but not of the world." Ironically, though, many adults here have retirement investment plans, own real estate, and drive foreign luxury cars. These folks are "of the world" in my opinion when they advertise that their music school is "all Steinway" (now *that's* a luxury brand!). Members of the denomination also work for gainful companies that generally rely upon their own denomination for sales—food service companies that manufacture meat substitute products aligned with the vegetarian diet, book stores that carry strictly those narrowly-focused books, DVDs, and magazines written and edited by members of their ingroup. The book covers and illustrations I recall from the 1980s show man/woman couples staring from a mountaintop toward the sun beaming through a distant cloudbank, children with pets, with the occasional Asian or Black character thrown in to show variety. To me, this is one method by which they groom their youth. To me, this is what indoctrination looks like, although I didn't understand the concept at the time. It is a place where administrators, staff, and pastors successfully mold young people into religious purists, and cast out the unclean "Other," with exclusionary sorting tactics perfected by religious pride, a checklist of appropriate/inappropriate behaviors, and an almost-predatory hunting instinct.

## James Philip Baran

In my recollection of this college town, many students glide along sidewalks high on some imagined or cultivated sense of purity or superiority. And I know, because I was one of them. In a vivid way, the town is like Stepford, that fictional place where the wives are submissive and everything is rigidly in its place—except what I'm describing from memory is my reality from the time, not a stage set. Everyone here is straight, or at least they better look like it, and believe me, people are watching. At least someone, someone of influence or authority, is watching. Whomever it may be, they seemingly surreptitiously watch others closely for any sign that they may be different, so that they can point out anyone from their outgroup. The observations are nearly always about appearances—a style of dress, a manner of sitting or walking. *There! There's one!* The targets of such scrutiny are often quietly shunned, avoided.

The students, for the most part, are in neat couples—boy/girl—and if not, they are coaxed into couplehood and with any luck married by 20 so they can properly bring forth new members for the denomination. Since everything appears to be neat and orderly, it takes a while to realize there is a nefarious dark side to this Dixie, where appearances matter most, where judgments are cast, branded like some scarlet letter. When I enrolled there in the fall of 1980 I didn't know that darkness would cast a pall over me. At that time, I was one of the Stepford youth, hypnotized by the gleaming smiles, grills of braces straining teeth into perfect rows, assured that I was among the chosen—the remnant.

From my experiences and observations, it appears to me that ardent fundamentalists feel compelled to exert some control over the lives of *other* people, and are fixated on *others'* private lives

## The Journey of Coming Out

to an unhealthy degree, with matters concerning sex, apparently, being of chief importance. My first semester English composition class was going painlessly, but my teacher's essay assignments always seemed to be looking for our lives' secrets behind our grammar and punctuation. She asked us to "tell about your upbringing," or had other ways to pull personal details out of us in writing. While professors in public schools might give the same direction on an assignment as a way to kickstart a student's creative storytelling process, in this highly monitored and protective environment I felt sure my words would be carefully watched, analyzed. In today's lexicon, I felt certain she was phishing for information. I crafted my essays creatively, making sure I ticked all the right boxes to show I came from a good Adventist home.

That first year at Southern (1980-81) went fairly smoothly, although I became aware that I was, in fact, being closely watched. I was only 19 at the time, yet some people seemed overly concerned that I was not dating or engaged—as if this should have been my primary goal at college. One of my music teachers took me aside one day and told me bluntly, with a touch of hysteria: "I don't care what you do, just get a girl—*any girl*—and be seen with her. People are talking." This made me feel emotionally threatened, blackmailed. One thing that still disturbs me to this day is that unhealthy obsession with sex, or the appearance of it—policing what goes on between *other* people, and even pushing them toward marriage. This would be funny if it weren't alarming. At the time I felt like saying, "Hey, hold on a minute, my parents didn't get married until my mom was 28 and my dad 32—*like normal people*." This happened over forty years ago, yet I remember it as if it were yesterday; it's burned into my memory. In that instance, the sanctity of my free will, personal choice, and my privacy were violated. Did I really do something wrong by not having a regular girlfriend? Did I break the rules? And if so, who wrote these rules, and where were they recorded? I was perplexed by this outrageous demand, and I wondered why my social life was such a concern to so many people.

Up until that time I had not given sex or relationships much thought, but I saw that now I was forced to dwell on it. If I wasn't going to fall naturally into a nice boy/girl couple for everyone to see, the authorities would harass me until I met their demands. I had thought, from about 16 or 17 on, that the sexual attraction thing would just resolve on its own, that it was nothing to worry about—that one day I'd simply meet the right girl. I had also observed a classmate in high school withdraw, her exit described as an "undiagnosed" illness; she was staying with an aunt for observation (so we were told), but we knew she was pregnant. With the implied shame of that settling on my mind, I realized I didn't want to be accessory to that life-altering situation. Among my closest friends I began to slowly open up. I never admitted being gay, because I had not developed a full understanding of what that meant, and certainly there were no examples of gay people in the media. Also, I instinctively knew that to bring up this subject would cause a scandal, unwanted attention. Instead, I just went about my business, which at the time was to do my coursework, practice piano and organ, and try to become the best me that I could be. In my mind, the sexuality thing would just spring into action in its own time.

Every day at this point, I was now aware that people—nosey people—were watching, wondering, and gossiping.

After a summer in California, spent with my sister and her friend Jane in San Jose, I returned to Collegedale for my second

## The Journey of Coming Out

year at Southern. Late that fall of 1981 a letter came addressed to me, a cheap mimeograph copy in blue ink. It closed with the words "Project Cleanup." This blackmail message demanded that I leave Southern as soon as possible, and that if I chose not to leave, then my parents, my home church, and the Seventh-day Adventist denominational headquarters would all be informed of my homosexuality. *All this because I didn't walk around campus with a girl on my arm?* Indeed, I continue to ask myself, why do these people obsess over sex? It's as if this is the only thing on their minds, consuming their imaginations. Oddly enough, they don't seem to worry about the fabric blends worn by their pastors or faculty. I trembled. I was offended. And I was afraid.

The so-called "Project Cleanup"—*perhaps it should have been called Project Coverup*—was probably a loose association of people around the college: a few teachers, staff, dorm monitors, including most likely the men's dean, and maybe a few trusted students, who perhaps met a few times to compare notes and compose a list of students whom, *in their opinions*, they thought did not belong, or whom they felt deserved certain labels. There was no person's name on the letter: "Project Cleanup" stood in the place where a signature would normally be if someone of integrity were sending a letter. These people had no evidence that supported their letter to me, except for their perceptions of characteristics they saw in my behavior that fueled their over-active imaginations. I was someone they wanted to remove in order to protect those they thought of as their pure young men from my apparently dangerous influence. More likely it was to keep up appearances, that everyone visibly must fit neatly into strict categories—the ingroup and the outgroup. In all honesty, as long as you look like a track star or tennis pro and have a girl on your arm in church, no one will ask questions. I was clearly different, though. I wasn't an athlete. + I didn't have a regular girlfriend. + I was in the arts. = Homo! Anyone could have added things up, and some apparently did. I felt wounded, damaged, threatened, spied upon, and it took a lot of time to rebuild my sense of value. After so much suppression of my own life, I'd almost forgotten how to stand up for myself.

I took that letter to the college's then-president, a robust, formerly athletic man who wore dark suits and ties, and leather dress shoes that befit his role as the lead administrator of this educational enterprise. I didn't make an appointment to see him: I simply walked boldly past his secretary's desk and into his office in the stately administration building. He was standing, his back toward me when I entered, and he swung around in surprise. I introduced myself, showed him the letter. I told him how hurt I was by it. He read it nonchalantly and passed it back to me as if he had seen it before—or at least as if he had better things to do at that moment. It didn't seem to surprise or bother him. I recall him saying something like, "We will just have to wait and see what they have to say." I interpreted his response as a way of telling me he wouldn't deal with it, but more alarmingly that he was possibly involved. So, I turned to the only person I could trust—my self—and considered my options. I was hurt, terrified, in a state of panic—I went into survival mode. At 20, no one should have to go through this, yet it was happening to me. Needless to say, I left at the end of that term.

Looking forward, all I could do was chart a course that would prevent further pain, especially to my parents. This situation would have devastated them, and I wanted to prevent that. I didn't want to make waves. I was still living in fear, a fear fostered by the fundamentalist beliefs I'd been taught. At the time, I may have been inexperienced and sheltered from a lot of the world, but I had heard stories of conversion therapy,[5] a form of psychological and physical torture that conservative Christians force upon their gay children under the code words "Christian family therapy," "reparative therapy," or "sexual reorientation therapy." The names of these so-called "therapies" often shift, and thereby deflect any critical analysis of what, precisely, the so-called "experts" are doing in these places as they "treat" minors. One good question I'd like to ask any one of their "experts": Has anyone tried conversion the other way around—you know, tried to convert a straight person into a lesbian or gay man? Perhaps repeatedly show scenes from the TV series, *M\*A\*S\*H*, with Corporal Klinger in drag, or make them watch that great black and white film, *Some Like It Hot*, where Tony Curtis and Jack Lemmon dress in drag to escape the mob. The answer would, clearly, make null and void their very argument for "reparative" therapy in the first place. But profits need to be made, good Christian parents are suffering, and fundamentally they don't love their children with the unconditional love that Jesus offers us.

While I was at Southern, a close friend told me of his experience in conversion therapy. This friend described his time in one such place in Alabama, marketed as a religious "retreat" or "therapy center," and where he was battered emotionally, psychologically, and physically until he ran away. As he told it, the administrators took his personal property, his identification, money and wallet. Then, over several weeks they forced him to sit in prayer groups and discuss his "sins." By this time, he was so emotionally and psychologically degraded and torn down, he simply fled, ran away, and found someone to help him get home. It's a similar story to that told by Garrard Conley in his book, *Boy Erased: A Memoir*. Another friend of mine shared the story of his father telling him, "You're gonna change even if we have to beat the fag out of you." *Now there's Christian compassion!* Even then, while I was not completely sure of my sexuality, I knew it was not possible to change a person's physiological-psychological personality and attractions. Again, all anyone has to do is look at it the opposite way around. A person's mind-body wiring is simply the way it is, and you can't enter a few keystrokes into an onboard hard-drive to create a new personality. It shocks me to this day that with the official statements from the American Psychiatric Association[6] and American Psychological Association[7] that people still can't understand—in fact, refuse to accept—the reality that some of us are simply gay, and that this is a perfectly normal, natural expression within the spectrum of human sexuality. This inability, or refusal, to accept facts crosses over into other areas of life; just recall how people faced the Covid-19 pandemic, refusing to accept scientific facts and medical recommendations; observe how people still refuse to accept verified facts about an election. I think there's a reason for this, but I can't quite put my finger on it. I do think it is a type of mental illness or cognitive disorder rooted in an inability or refusal to accept facts. I'll put my trust in the psychiatric and psychological associations, with hopes that they study this phenomenon. And frankly, the FBI should investigate it as well, because, as I see it, that way of thinking—refusing to accept facts—is a potential threat to our government.

Over time I built my own protective wall and reinforced it by not talking frankly with my parents about my experiences in Collegedale, and the reasons are simple: my own fear of rejection, and

## The Journey of Coming Out

also because they would have been deeply hurt, their own religious beliefs and life experience shaken to the core—all because the word "gay" and its implications presented ideas outside of or beyond their own experiences. My parents grew up in a different time, a time when no one, apparently, ever talked about taboo subjects, homosexuality probably at the top of the list. They didn't know any gay men or women, so they had no way to relate to the topic. Even an open discussion of sex—of any kind—was not part of their upbringing. In a conversation before her death, my mother told me the story of one of her sisters approaching her just before that sister's wedding, curious about the basics of sex, things that could have been easily explained had her school offered a sex-ed class. Conversations around this topic apparently didn't take place in the 30s, 40s, and 50s, and these conversations never came up in our own house in the 60s and 70s. I suppose we were just expected to learn it all on our own, on the street, from magazines secretly passed among children.

My parents and I had danced around the subject of sexuality a decade earlier when we were watching some television variety show. I had been studying piano for just over a year when, one evening, my mother called to me from the living room, "Jimmy, come quick! You should hear this man play. Honestly, you should play like he does." Taking a seat in front of the TV, I noted the floor-length fur, the mirror-encrusted piano, the rings, and gritted my teeth. I had sat there quietly, a strange realization settling in over me like a dark cloud, understanding that this Liberace character was, up to that point, the only example of my people I had ever seen. My father, walking past the living room with his Seagram's and 7-Up, ice cubes clinking like Martha's in *Who's Afraid of Virginia Woolf?*, grumbled in disgust and said, "He'll get what he deserves"—and I understood the angry, phobic subtext of his comment. No wonder I was suppressed, closeted. No wonder so many of us were afraid. If there had been more positive role models of happy, normal LGBTQ+ people on television, in the news, in magazines, then we'd have come out of hiding much sooner. Today there are good role models for LGBTQ+ people on TV and in books. (Maybe this is one reason for all the brouhaha and quickly written Republican legislation recently, to legislate what books and what words cannot be used in classrooms. Could this be a plan to keep children and adolescents from understanding who they are, or a plan to prevent most students from being taught about tolerance?) In retrospect, it's not that I didn't want to tell my parents; it's that I knew this situation would challenge their faith and their view of the world—conversations I was not ready for. And I was being practical, too—they were paying my bills at the time. I imagined my life on the streets, sleeping under a freeway overpass, and decided to keep my mouth shut. Begging for food and bathing in a stream was not my idea of living. In hindsight, though, I know now that my parents would never have abandoned me. But I wasn't sure of that then.

After the initial shock from that anonymous blackmail letter, I shut down emotionally. I carefully considered my options, and then—like a general in the military—planned my extrication. I drove home with a few acquaintances for the Christmas break, and quickly found a new university to attend, applied and was accepted. Because there was no Wikipedia, no Google, and there were no college web sites at that time, I had to walk to our public library and peruse the latest copy of *U.S. Colleges and Universities*, an index of all higher learning institutions, their curriculums, and the costs to attend. Brown was not accepting new students mid-year, neither

## The Journey of Coming Out

was U of I, so I settled on Illinois State, whose administration welcomed me with enthusiasm. I drove with my dad to Collegedale a couple days after Christmas, and when we arrived I told him: "Keep the engine running—we're not staying long." I hurriedly packed my books, clothes, sheets and blanket, threw everything in my two trunks and loaded the car. In my last stop before leaving town, I tossed the room key over the monitor's counter at the Taldge Hall main entrance without saying a word to the glaring guy. No official ever attempted to contact me afterwards, and I remained in touch with only my closest friends.

Driving north beyond Chattanooga, I felt safer as the odometer advanced, crossing the miles between past and future, the steady hum of the car's engine calming me. After a few days at home with my parents, my father drove me to Normal, Illinois, where my new university life awaited. There, I blossomed and grew up in a more democratic, collegial environment, and I became who I was meant to become. The busybodies were left behind, the spying ended, my personal privacy sacred once more. No one even asked me why I wasn't dating. Gone was the undeserved shame; gone was the unwarranted embarrassment. I was now just another normal college student.

Like a series of accidents, fights and injuries, life in fundamentalism left scar tissue, echoes of pain, unnecessary shame, and these leftover ghost effects made themselves real in that I could no longer play Chopin's Aolean Harp etude, could no longer listen to this or that piano sonata—almost any music I had studied while in Tennessee became an aural-memory trigger for pain and stress. Some psychologists study the relationship between music and memory, and research has shown there is a link.[8] Over the following few years, I gave away most of my collection of sheet music, partly as a way to close a chapter in my life—cast away the old, and open myself to something new. I didn't attend any churches, either. Moving on from the traumas of fundamentalism—being labeled "different and therefore dangerous," and forcibly put into the undesirable "outgroup"—I lost interest in formal church attendance.

### III

After forty years, when Collegedale was a remote memory, a news story in early 2022 about a student there caught my attention. This individual had come out via social media as nonbinary, causing a stir. I read the article with interest because, deep down, I was hopeful that there had been progress at the college and in the denomination. But hope is easily crushed. The article indicated that the student had met with the university's "senior advisor for sexual integrity" who said that the university was working on "updates to the Sexual Integrity Policy."[9] The first red flag I see is that there's someone, either in the administration or perhaps an outside consultant, who oversees "sexual integrity." (That obsession with sex! What about citizens' rights to privacy, the First Amendment?[10]) So, let's talk about integrity for a moment. *Merriam-Webster* defines this as "firm adherence to a code of especially moral or artistic values."[11] In my opinion, moral and artistic values are subjective and can, therefore, hold different meaning to different people, but more importantly, that the code is adhered to by the individual who chooses to follow it—not enforced by the authorities who wrote it. The second red flag I see is that the so-called "integrity policy" apparently has to be updated because of the coming out event. In my opinion, the authorities overseeing this policy get to update and define its scope and meaning, and therefore frame the

## The Journey of Coming Out

context and justification for intolerance of anything outside that particular definition.

Turning to scientific fact, in the 20$^{th}$ and 21$^{st}$ centuries scientific data proves, and the respected therapists and doctors of the American Psychiatric Association and American Psychological Association all agree, that homosexuality is not a mental illness or disorder, not a matter of choice, yet still, fundamentalists willfully refuse to acknowledge this reality. Holding their bibles, they assert that lesbians and gay men—and now these new, scary things: nonbinary and trans—are all sinful, willful rejections of the will of God. It's my opinion that those folks are going to hold steadfast to uninformed notions about sexuality and sex, because if they were to change their official stance there would be a lot of explaining to do—they would have to admit they had been wrong.

While I was still trying to blend in, I went on several dates with young women—I was willing to give it the old college try, plus I had been ordered to do so. These young women were ready and willing to get physical. After some experimentation, I knew that the hetero thing was not my cup of tea, and I diplomatically parted company with the latest girl I was going out with. To me, the very idea of sex with a woman was utterly foreign, an offense to my sensibilities, abhorrent—I had the same reaction to it as a typical straight man might have if someone casually suggested to him that he consider sex with another man; I was repelled. The feel and taste of lip gloss, the scent of grape bubble gum, and the feeling of long nails and hair spray made my skin crawl.

In the 1980s, at Southern Missionary College there was a secret world, a hidden community, and I'm pretty sure it's still there today. During my time at Southern, I had to get up quite early, around 4:00 a.m., in order to fit in a busy day of music practice, work, and classes. I regularly witnessed several young men gathered in the communal shower room quite obviously displaying their erections, stroking themselves gently. This happened often. At first it confused me, but then what was going on gradually became clear. Still, I was reluctant to participate because I was unsure of myself—I lacked confidence and was afraid these guys might be setting a trap. Gay men existed in that rigid religious environment before I attended, and I am sure they are there today.

After growing up, or perhaps after maturing past rigid and intolerant worldviews, I've learned a few things, and one of them is to be honest, to face facts. It's a shame that not everyone can do this. Gay and lesbian people live everywhere in the world. Too many people want to argue about this, and too many people in government want to make our lives difficult, and even wish to erase us. Lesbians and gay men, as well as bisexual, trans, and nonbinary people are everywhere, in every country and in every community. These are simply facts.

While it took another ten years before I worked up the courage to explain to my parents what it means to be gay, my healing had begun. While I had been getting D's in religion class at Southern, I was on the Dean's List in the more democratic university in a northern state, earning nearly all A's in my classes. I would graduate with a bachelor's degree in Music, a minor in English, and then go on to complete a master's in English. In my work life, I had a job in marketing, I was a writer, an editor, a designer and art director, and was in charge of a magazine production department. I was a speaker at conferences and events, and served on the board of an industry group. In a nutshell, I was a success. What makes me most proud, however, is being married to one man with whom I share a healthy, affirming decades-long relationship, a stable life with shared interests in travel, music, literature, art, and culture. I am a proud member of the diverse LGBTQ+ community and living proof that gay is good and perfectly normal.

## IV

That's my coming-out story, my memories, my observations, and my opinions. It may be enough to know this history, these experiences. But more important for today's battles to defend democracy and our LGBTQ+ community, I see in my own history that a deeply disturbing religious-political partnership seems to have evolved over the past forty years between conservative Christians and the Republican Party. The intersection where the two meet is, on the surface, about defending conservative values, but beneath the surface—in my opinion—this partnership is dangerous for our democracy because it fosters intolerance: intolerance of debate, intolerance of the education system, intolerance of science and fact, intolerance of anything outside of strict "one man/one woman" relationships, intolerance of diversity.

In 2023 alone, the list of proposed anti-LGBTQ+ legislation surpassed 650 bills (a higher number than any previous year). The primary goal here seems to be to "force LGBTQ people out of public life."[12] Conservative Christians have apparently become political actors and are involved with—or at least agree with—governments that create anti-LGBTQ+ legislation. If nothing else, the silence on this topic from Christian denominations is alarming. In 2023, the leadership of the Seventh-day Adventist church appeared to support the government of Uganda in its legislation designed to imprison—

and even to kill—anyone who identifies as LGBTQ+.[13, 14] It's the kind of thing that might be done in a theocracy. In my opinion, if that Ugandan law remains implemented and unchallenged by the international community, then certain religious leaders may possibly use that as a case study to influence legislators in the U.S. to draft similar legislation. I've thought about this from both a religious and reasonable-person perspective, and I can say that if I one day learned that my own denomination supported draconian laws like the one in effect in Uganda, I would formally—and vociferously—object, withdraw my support, and leave. Why? Because I have a conscience.

Here is further evidence of authoritarian legislation designed to clamp down on diversity and the rights of LGBTQ+ citizens. There are the ongoing book bans in Republican-run states, banning any book with LGBTQ+ references or role models, banning use of the word "gay," banning discussion of sexuality and gender, and even banning discussion of the Holocaust.[15] Now that's a subversive way to indoctrinate students: remove or limit educational resources that might enlighten them; forbid them to read vetted, factual materials that might help them become tolerant and well-informed. Then there's the so-called Parental Rights in Education Bill (misleadingly named, because parents already have rights surrounding children's education) that makes it illegal for teachers to discuss sex, sexuality, or gender with students.[16]

Similar to the ways I was singled out, separated, and targeted as the "Other" in my experiences in fundamentalism, in my view today's Republican party operatives often try to do the same thing. Many Republican politicians appear to seek to divide us, separate us into ingroup and outgroup, Us and Them, using hot-button issues to mark our differences and align the separate sides with Good or Bad.

## The Journey of Coming Out

What happened to listening, weighing pros and cons, compromise? Even in the years when Ronald Reagan was president, Republicans and Democrats lunched together, golfed together, and could be seen in public—together—at civic and cultural events. What happened to the camaraderie? What became of friendly dialog?

I think we've come to a point where we don't recognize one another, except as possibly the "Other." In the course of history, we've naturally sorted ourselves in categories like national origin, religion, political leaning, race, sexual orientation, education level, and the list goes on. Today, clever political operatives leverage those categories, their underlying motivations and fears, and craft rhetoric that makes us either good or bad (positive rhetoric to reflect themselves and their constituents; negative rhetoric to point to and label the "Other"—anyone in different categories, who—by implication—is undesirable or dangerous). Whether it's the result of fear, misinformation or misunderstanding, or some battle of "values," the escalation of negative rhetoric divides our people into Us v. Them. In my view, the results of this are visible in the disrespect and intolerance often on display in state legislatures and Congress. On this new political stage we're now seeing vitriolic verbal attacks akin to a Thunderdome[17] battle, where anything goes and the candidate with the most anger seems to win. In these optics, the players look undiplomatic, undignified, undemocratic, and oftentimes unstable—the polar opposite of how politicians should comport themselves, in my opinion.. The escalating battle of wills, misunderstanding and anger seems to increase intolerance toward differing ideas and is, in my opinion, authoritarian and leaning, step by step, closer to fascism.

The Us v. Them scenario is especially clear in both fundamentalism[4] and fascism.[18] Both are anti-democratic thought systems that shun diversity and sort people based at some level on the idea that "different" equals "dangerous," a misleading equation. In politics the scale runs from nonthreatening to increasingly violent: simple labels such as Democrats v. Republicans evolve into "honest" rural voters v. "menacing" city dwellers with the addition of carefully selected adjectives used to frame the "Other" as a threat. The well-crafted sound bites culminate in false descriptors that serve to elevate one group and demonize others as "decent patriots" v. "baby killers." By misusing—or weaponizing—vocabulary, authoritarian politicians, in my opinion, seem to want to divide us with fear and anger. Turning back to religion, the clever ingroup v. outgroup sorting argument becomes We = the Saved v. Them = the Damned. And then, of course, neither group may associate with the other for fear of being tainted by the "Other," so forget about learning something from people who are different. This system keeps people in separate boxes and enforces a circle of contempt. To be honest, I don't see a way out of this. Is it possible that the goal is civil war?

The way I see it, many fundamentalists and many Republican politicians construct their belief systems by being unreasonable, intolerant, and undemocratic—they seem to be unwilling to consider different viewpoints on many topics. They often speak in biblical terms, use hyperbole and histrionics to project what may be their own issues onto their enemies, as in labeling people "indoctrinators" or "groomers," when in reality they are the ones who indoctrinate and groom—by suppressing debate and independent thought within their group. Today, social media helps feed this insanity because it relies on automated algorithms to repeatedly serve users the same kinds of information they tend to follow in the first place. So, they don't get news from outside their ingroup. I imagine this may be a reason why Republican Attorneys General have sued the Biden Administration to block reasonable efforts to combat the spread of disinformation and falsehoods on social media.[19] I see it as a public disservice that some people apparently wish to block common-sense efforts to sort fact from fiction. And now we have technology that should alarm everyone: artificial intelligence, or AI, so those alternative facts—along with doctored or fake images—can be imperceptibly and undetectably crafted to alter reality, revise history, and influence people for political gain.

When I was in Collegedale, I was shocked to be in a place where the march toward authoritarianism was accepted, practically unnoticed by anyone. November 4, 1980, began with a quiet morning, a thin cool mist hung in the trees on the hillside. Classes had been cancelled so that we all might vote in the presidential election. School buses lined up to herd us to the nearest polling place, their diesel exhaust fouling the cool morning air. Before I was allowed to board, an older member of the faculty or staff threw his arm in front of the bus door, blocking me for a moment, saying, "You better be voting for Ronald Reagan." We had been told so often that our religious freedom was in danger if a Democrat was elected to the White House that we actually believed it. With fear and misinformation swirling in our minds, I'm sure most of the students voted for Reagan that day. I'm ashamed to say that I was one of them—I had been indoctrinated.

## V

The Bible is a religious text, one written and interpreted by fallible people over extended periods of time and subject to a variety of circumstances and agendas. It is not, by the way, a U.S. Government document. If laws were based on the Bible, our government would have to make illegal countless acts, such as manufacturing fabric of mixed materials (see Leviticus 19:19), and courts would be overrun with cases prosecuting people for eating pork or wearing pigskin gloves (see Leviticus 11:7-8). But these are lesser-known, inconvenient biblical rules. In my experience, I recall that many conservative Christians love to quote the Bible in a "gotcha" kind of way, proud of their ability to memorize verses taken out of context—Bible verses cherry picked and often used as weapons to degrade and dehumanize others. I'd like to remind those people that there is not a single word about homosexuality spoken by Jesus himself in the entire New Testament. Those people who, in my opinion, appear to want to maintain their ingroup's prejudices by not permitting historical research and dialog willfully ignore that the word "homosexual" was only coined in the year 1868.[20] I'm no theologian, but when I read Paul's writings (such as 1 Corinthians) I detect an underlying anger and outspoken prejudice in his words, and I recall that he was human, fallible. If we want to remain faithful to the exact words in the Bible, then we should heed the more-relevant texts that clearly lead us to look at ourselves, like John 8:7: "He that is without sin among you, let him first cast a stone …" (KJV), or, equally important, Leviticus 19:18, "… thou shalt love thy neighbor as thyself," and Leviticus 19:33-34, "And if a stranger sojourn with thee in your land, ye shall not vex him. But the stranger that dwelleth with you shall be unto you as one born among you, and thou shalt love him as thyself …" (KJV). Look around and observe how many of today's Christians do not welcome strangers or immigrants and ignore those in need.

I've often asked myself why I had to stumble through such darkness in the Seventh-day Adventist Church. And all these years later,

## The Journey of Coming Out

I wonder why the intolerance continues, why others have to suffer. Why is homosexuality—or any sexual expression or identity outside of strict one male/one female relationships—looked at with such fear and loathing by so-called Christians? I'll tell you: because—in my opinion—those who set the tone and the agenda for the denomination have become disconnected from Jesus' teachings and, in my opinion, are caught up in a system of thought that always requires the "Other," someone to be feared and excluded. I still believe, though, that there are some genuine Christians in the pews; however, those who rise among the ranks of leadership, or those who are in some sense the "gatekeepers," in my opinion, tend to be more hardline conservative, inflexible, and unwilling to look beyond their strict rules and exploited Bible quotes. A more accurate term might be "pseudo-Christian" for this group because, while they officially claim to be Christian and often use the name of Jesus, in practice they are intolerant of those who are different, lack compassion for those who are outside their standard, and generally rely on their religion to set themselves apart from, even above, other people. Christians, however, are people who possess "belief in the teachings of Jesus Christ."[21] Jesus' teachings center on inclusion, whereas exclusion seems to guide fundamentalist teachings. Another helpful reminder is that Jesus gave us only two rules to live by, and here they are: First, Love God with all your heart, mind, and soul. And second, Love your neighbor as yourself (see Matthew 22:36-40). Based on these instructions—*from Jesus himself*—authentic Christians will show compassion, forgive others, respect or tolerate those who are different, welcome strangers, and refrain from judging others.

My experiences in the Seventh-day Adventist denomination are nuanced. I've shared here the striking examples I've had of being targeted as an outcast, labeled, demonized and dehumanized by some, perhaps out of fear, or perhaps out of strict allegiance to official Church doctrines. But I've known a number of generous, thoughtful and compassionate Adventists, so I still believe there are genuine Christians in that church's pews. They're just difficult to find.

Exploring the theological implications, as I mature I've come to understand that an authentic, meaningful religious practice builds people up and brings people together, inclusively, and helps its followers navigate life in the world while respecting others, even those who are different from themselves. It seems to me to be a clear rejection of Jesus' teachings for a denomination to purposely break people down, judge, shun, and cast people out.

## VI

It's been more than forty years since I escaped what was for me darkness and danger in the Adventist Church, but the apparent rejection of Christian inclusivity and compassion seem to help maintain the status quo today. In 2022, it was reported that Southern Adventist University had a history of discrimination against Black people, when a researcher wrote that in the 1890s a young woman of mixed-race descent was not permitted to be taught in the same classrooms as white students.[22] Also in 2022, as I outlined earlier in this story, there were news reports that a student at that same college came out as nonbinary via social media.[9, 23] The reaction from administration, and quite possibly from the denomination headquarters, was almost immediate. Shortly after that news broke, the individual apparently was no longer enrolled as a student at that institution. This history is relevant because, in my opinion, these facts expose not just hypocrisy and failures at the administrative level,

## The Journey of Coming Out

but also cast light on an apparent effort to sort out the "Other" and limit diversity within the Seventh-day Adventist denomination and its associated businesses.

I came to the decision to leave the Adventist church in part because of how I was treated, but moreover because of what that experience taught me about the denomination—it's a place of intolerance and cruelty for anyone who diverges from a strict mold. The very idea that I am rejected by practitioners of a particular line of religious thought is all I need to know to realize something is deeply wrong.

After my departure, I did not concern myself with organized religion for a decade. Time helped wash away the unwarranted shame, the misguided ideas and discriminatory doctrines of fundamentalism. When I became aware that I was not welcome, I followed Jesus' guidance in the message of Matthew 10:14, and shook off the dust from my feet as I departed that place. When I went back into a church, it was one that was welcoming, compassionate, affirming and energizing. Now, I no longer feel self-conscious or judged for the clothes I wear, how I walk or talk, nor for whom I love. *At last, I belong!* Using today's lexicon, my "faith journey" led me to the Episcopal Church, a denomination that teaches that *all* are welcome at God's table, with our humanity, talents, gifts, and even our limitations. This may not be the place for everyone, but it works for me. The simple message I now understand is that God loves me, He loves all of us, and He asks us to build bridges with one another as a way to live our faith in the world, by accepting each other as we are, no prerequisites, no quid pro quo—like Jesus would do.

At the end of mass the celebrant or deacon charges us to "Go in peace to love and serve the Lord." This concluding directive reminds me to treat others I meet on life's road with the same grace, forgiveness, and compassion that God freely offers me. I have no way of knowing the journey, the starting point or, indeed, the ending point, for others' lives, but by offering kindness, acceptance, compassion, I serve to extend the hand of God to others. It sounds like a fantasy—beyond human ability—but it's really not that difficult: I just do unto others as I wish them to do unto me. I think it's called the Golden Rule.[24] If I act with a welcoming spirit, with compassion, and with a forgiving heart, I know others will do the same for me. Some days I succeed, on others I fail (and I know it), yet I keep trying. While I don't know the specific route of my journey, the stops I'll make, the people I'll meet, I do know this: in the long scheme of things, my journey is between God and me.

# Rumor Has It

I'm always wary of anyone who opens a conversation with, "Rumor has it …," and on a cold January day in 1982, it took me by surprise. I had just transferred to Illinois State University in the flatlands of Normal, Illinois. The winter landscape there is dull, and there are days when everything from the ground up is a flat gray—gray sidewalks, gray trees, gray skies, and if snow is on the ground it's usually bleeding into gray, with a dull gray light seeping through the clouds. I was encased as warmly as possible in jeans, sweater, hoodie, and my dark blue down vest as I waited in line at the Main Street AGA where I was gathering supplies for a long, cold weekend at the start of the winter term. Peanut butter, strawberry preserves, a large loaf of wheat bread, a few bananas, a quart of milk. Really, I was minding my own business. I thought I was doing a decent job of looking anonymous, blending in.

I hadn't noticed anyone behind me in the check-out line, so I was startled when some guy tapped me on the shoulder and said, "Rumor has it you suck dick." A sudden ringing reverberated in my ears, and my skin began to heat. The sheer audacity of it! This is the first thing some random guy—correction, *dick*—in the checkout lane at the AGA said to me on that dreary January day. "Uh, what? You've got the wrong guy, man," I said, as I turned around to face forward and set down my meager purchases on the conveyor—surveying my snacks to make sure nothing screamed fag. I thought my reply would end the exchange, but no, there was more. This guy insisted on pursuing the matter. "That's not what I heard," he added. Heads turned. By now, other shoppers stopped to listen. The cashier turned to face me. *WTF!* Well, I wasn't going to take this from a stranger. I told him, "You've obviously been talking to the wrong people, and they're referring to someone else." He was quick-witted, though, I'll have to give him that, and as he replied—trying to keep the conversation going, I realized he was interested, closeted, wanted to experiment, egging me on with, "You live in Manchester Hall, don't you? Fifteenth floor?" He had the right guy, alright. But not so fast, as I volleyed back with, "My cousin goes here, too, and we look like twins, so it's obviously a mix-up." I had had the last word. Relieved, I paid and left, sweating under my winter layers.

Don was his name, as it turns out, and he followed me right back to my dorm, which was also his—the now-infamous Manchester Hall, me on the fifteenth floor and he on the ninth with the other feral guys. I chose Manchester as my residence because of the one-block walk to the library, also only a block or so from the main campus quad, so it was easy to get anywhere on campus from Manchester. The fifteenth floor was designated a quiet floor, meaning that from eight p.m. to eight a.m. there could be no loud music, no running rampant, no screams, no floor hockey. The fifteenth floor was for serious academics, after all, students who read, wrote papers, did research in the evenings. The opposite could be said of the ninth floor where Don lived. On the ninth floor, mayhem was the only rule residents lived by. Whenever I visited my pal and secret crush, Craig, I noted there weren't any books in his room. *Study? What's that? Lights out? Never heard of it. Sleep? We can do that when we're dead.* This was the running attitude of the guys on nine. In a way, I admired them—so carefree, so *laissez-faire!* Between lunches where they showed off their live goldfish-eating talents and evenings running amuck on the campus quad, like scenes from *Animal House*, they were subdued compared to some of the trouble college guys can stir up today. Ninth floor versus fifteenth. The two were laid out exactly the same, but for the casual passerby, someone who, say, just randomly got off on nine, they'd think they were in another town, at another institution altogether.

We had no social media platforms on which to pose as influencers, and thank God we had no cell phones. I'm still amazed that I lived a relatively normal and fulfilled college life with no TV or iPad. I phoned my sister once a week and the same for my parents—from a land line. I saw all my friends by chance, running into them on the quad, in the library, or at Garcia's, the local pizza-by-the-slice eatery that had $2.00 pitchers of beer. Those spontaneous hellos and conversations were how we planned our weeks, just bumping into each other, so randomly and so magically. *Oh, there's a party this Friday on Cherry Street? I'll be there!* Now you need an app to see if anyone interesting is within 100 feet of you, surfing the hook-up apps like shopping for bananas, each person a product. *No, not him, oh God no, not that queen!* Such a waste of time the phone is nowadays—all chance, surprise, and magic gone.

\* \* \*

## James Philip Baran

A year or so ago, while on vacation in Mexico, we were taking an afternoon in the sun on our rooftop deck; my husband, David, was doing laps in the pool, and I was just lounging, hoping to get a base tan and enjoying the breeze. I noticed a couple of guys talking, casual chit-chat really, this and that, random topics. I wasn't really eavesdropping, but I could easily overhear their talk as it shifted from job responsibilities to the latest apps to speculation about the real value of crypto. They seemed an odd couple; one was unremarkable in every way, but the other was fit, noticeably so with full six-pack abs and a perfectly round bubble butt that sucked in the entire seat of his swim suit. This I couldn't help but notice as he rolled over onto his stomach to even out his tan. Even a straight guy would stare.

After a half hour or so, they were packing up their towels and lotions to leave, so I said hello just to be friendly—*they are people, too*. The usual, if predictable, brief conversation ensued: *Are you enjoying Puerto Vallarta? Where are you visiting from?* These two, quite pale, must indeed be from the north, and I was right, Bubble-Butt Boi announced they were from Vancouver. I shared that we are from Chicago, and Bubble Butt's immediate response was, "Rumor has it there's an excellent fetish community there." Wait. *What?* Had I heard correctly? I tend to refer to cities by famous landmarks—*It's called the Sears Tower!*—and cultural institutions such as the Art Institute, so I said, "Actually, Chicago is known for its world-class museums, shopping and universities." His confused frown indicated that, clearly, we were not on the same wavelength, as if to say, *Well! You're no fun.* I ran into him again that evening in the lobby of our building in *Zona Romantica*, and he popped up off his sofa as I passed, saying, "Hello, again, it was nice to meet you

## Rumor Has It

guys earlier," adding a shimmy while talking. I only smiled, "Yes, it was nice meeting you as well. Hope you have a great evening," as I stepped into the elevator. In another time, or another place, I might have stopped to talk longer, but really, I'll be honest, I'm married and not interested in some casual, spontaneous thing. I knew what he wanted, and I was not going to play that game. Besides, I was there to celebrate my birthday, and I wasn't going to let the evening get highjacked. Not that I'm an old stick in the mud, it's just that I have better things to do. Although Bubbles was cute, I will admit, and I'm sure he had a memorable time.

*   *   *

In London recently—for the Queen's funeral, actually, David and I were minding our own business and sitting quietly, looking out the window on the number 19 bus, headed from Piccadilly to Chelsea, a route on which we pass one great London shop or sight after another—the Royal Academy, Fortnum & Mason, landmarks, hotels, parks. On this particular September day, there was an old crow on board, sitting directly behind us, a real talker—a real expert, too—constantly uttering superlatives and broadcasting her opinions. At every moment of the journey she had something outlandish to say while saying nothing at all, and several times I thought, *that can't possibly be true.* Every five to ten seconds, as we passed this building or that, she'd alight, birdlike, onto a new topic. When we passed the Maille mustard shop in Piccadilly Arcade, she judged their product inferior, "I *never* buy *French* mustard—can't stomach the stuff." Her seat mate remained silent. *Well!*, I felt like adding, *I'm sure they're doing something right, since they've been in business for over 250 years.* Incidentally, it's the only brand I buy, so I can speak with authority on this one. (But I digress.) I don't normally eavesdrop, but her pronouncements were compelling—interesting in a funny sort of way, because her authoritative statements were just opinions, and often preposterous ones at that—as if she were narrating an alternative-fact travelogue. When we passed The Ritz, she whispered to her companion, "Rumor has it an earl poisoned his wife in a suite there. *The scandal,*" she shouted. I only smiled, stifling a laugh, listening more intently. She recalled having lunch there years before. The waiter had been kind but the food was inedible by her standards. I glanced over at David to see if he was hearing all this; his wink and smile told me he was enjoying the entertaining monologue. Then, as we passed the M&S mini grocer, our narrator pointed out how easy it is to pop off the bus and grab a few items then hop back on and be on one's way. *Well, that's just common sense,* I thought just then, as I recalled that we wanted to pick up cheese and wine before heading back to the flat.

On and on she droned, peppering the conversation with her neighbor with all sorts of nonsense, then declaring that her son was due in from Australia any day now, and what with him being with the *Foreign Office* (loudly emphasized) she could look forward to juicy stories about his work, a few insider tidbits about national security and, naturally, gossip from his network of contacts. I was waiting for her to comment—for the benefit of anyone within earshot—on her exact position in line to the throne when the bus entered the round-about to pass Wellington Arch. I could hear her disgust as she abruptly shifted gears to share her expertise on public art. "Just look at that atrocity, *there*"—now tapping loudly on the window with the ivory handle of her cane—"sticking up from the

## Rumor Has It

ground. *There.* What is *that* supposed to be, anyway?" Her presumed "atrocity" was, in fact, the understated New Zealand War Memorial, technically sixteen steel cross-shaped beams bursting from the ground all at the same angle. Her companion only nodded acknowledgement with a half-hearted "Mm-Hmm," or it could have been a muffled *"harrumph!"* And then, to answer her own question, the art critic muttered, head shaking, no doubt: "That's the trouble with the world these days. *No one* studies sculpture any more—they just weld." And that was it, her final judgment of the day—up to that moment, at least. The way she went on and on in her stream-of-consciousness, I could have listened and learned fascinating things all day from the unending litany of alternate facts and rumors. She was living and breathing evidence that there are all sorts of entertaining if not downright intriguing people in the world—she would have made a great talk-show guest. Her phone bill must be astonishing, and her friends—if she has any—very patient people.

Really, I thought it would be great fun to have a job with the *Times*, riding the number 19 around London, eavesdropping on important people's conversations, reporting the juicy details, fleshed out with hearsay, gossip, and rumor—an appealing, even glamorous if questionable, way to make a buck.

# The Graduate Student

As I lay there on the black asphalt road, listening to my breathing, I thought I heard a passing car and someone's voice—*were they talking to me?* Yes, they were. And here someone was helping me up to my feet. It was the police. Coming back to myself, I realized I had been lying on the pavement for an unknown period of time. Some start to the summer of 1984.

I had received my bachelor's degree that May, in Music with a minor in English. I had no solid job prospects other than house painting, so, not having a solid business-world option, I settled on graduate school and applied to the program in English. While I waited for an acceptance letter, confident that my academic record would result in one, I agreed to house-sit for a professor who was to spend the summer on the east coast and would not be back with his family until just before the fall term began. The house was comfortable, a 1920s two-story four square built of dark brown brick with a large front porch that had built-in limestone benches. It was a fine middle-class house for a university professor in those days. The couple were security-minded, and to protect their liquor and small fine-art prints wanted someone to keep an eye on their house for the summer, so it was rent-free. It's a no-brainer. How could I say no?

Professor Greene and I met casually, happenstance, at some graduate student event, and the conversation turned to summer, my plans, and that's what led him to ask if I was interested in house-sitting. Of course, I said yes. I was, after all, waiting for the fall term to start and would be around all summer. It turned out to be a sunny, dry, and hot season, with almost no rain, and the corn crops that surrounded our bucolic town suffered to some extent. With no formal plans on my summer calendar, I took up cycling again, having bought the year before a used dark red, Schwinn 10-speed road bike, slightly scratched but in good working condition, its gears smooth and its brakes tight.

I would ride every day to the library, sit and read in the cool climate-controlled lounge on the 4$^{th}$ floor overlooking the library's plaza and the campus quad, enjoying the leisure with which I was able to pursue academic interests for this season, using the summer to craft my own crash course on British literature and poetry, reading Virginia Woolf, Percy Bysshe Shelley, Samuel Taylor Coleridge, and other writers that interested me. In the afternoons and evenings, I usually biked south into Bloomington and spent time with friends who now, forty years later, cannot be found even with the latest social media technology. I recall the faces, the landscape, the oak, elm and maple trees, the sad cars of the day. One friend had a dark red AMC Gremlin, so you can imagine what our streets looked like, very dated from today's perspective, like some coming-of-age film focused on a 1980s senior class, filmed, as they always are, in Los Angeles. It is funny to me now, all these years later, how spotty memory can be, some details are forgotten

## The Graduate Student

while others are as vivid as if they happened only yesterday. I can still feel the wool carpet under my feet in that house, still see the sun pouring in through the living room windows, and feel the welcome summer breeze on the porch.

The house sat on Franklin Avenue just a short ride from campus. It was not unlike George and Martha's house in the film version of Edward Albee's *Who's Afraid of Virginia Woolf?*. It was decorated, architecturally, in the arts and crafts style, heavy dark wood moldings, windows on either side of the fireplace with divided panes and brass latches, green tiles surrounding the fireplace and forming the hearth area. The dining room had a large built-in china hutch with a buffet area, drawers and a central cabinet beneath it. Leaded glass doors guarded the upper portion of the cabinet which was intended for displaying fine china and crystal. These cabinets were empty that summer. There were practically no window coverings, so light poured in all day and into the evening. In the living room, where I spent much time reading on the plush white sofa, the main windows had the only window treatments in the house, black wooden shutters. I would adjust these at different times of day to either maximize or minimize the light.

Readying myself for English graduate work, I read most days while listening to the top musical artists of the day: UB-40, Tina Turner, Bryan Adams, Missing Persons, Kim Carnes with her "Bette Davis eyes," A Flock of Seagulls, and Men at Work. If I was in a classical frame of mind I'd dig out my recordings of Brahms' piano concerto number 2, Rachmaninoff's piano concerto number 3, Bach's Eighteen Great Chorales, or my ever-beloved Mozart, anything by Mozart. Regardless of what era it was from, I always had music playing. If the weather was inclement and I stayed in to read, I put on Bach's St. Matthew Passion to immerse myself in the comfort of rich harmonies and lilting melodies.

Friends would stop by, usually in the evenings, because in mornings they were either hung-over or going to work, and we would sit on the porch, or hang out in the back yard. In this period of my life I was not "out" as we say. I simply didn't discuss my sexuality in general. My close circle of friends knew, of course, for they knew everything about me, but I was still finding myself at 23. The teenage years were gone but not forgotten. I was an adult but still evolving into adulthood.

I had no boyfriend, and certainly no girlfriend either. Suffice it to say there was no significant other in my life at this time. I would be a late bloomer in that department. So as the summer settled upon us, I simply lived there, in that arts and crafts house on Franklin Avenue, reading, drinking wine now and then, eating when I felt like it, and biking to campus, across town for groceries and to visit friends. I was free on that bike in that summer of 1984. But circumstances change, disruptions occur.

That summer I felt out of place, in the wrong place at the wrong time, or as if I belonged somewhere in the future, and probably in another country. How did men meet each other, how did they identify each other as gay in a small college town surrounded by corn fields? That was my new conundrum. It's so easy now, people are just body parts with needs often falling into very specific types: Twinks, Bears, Otters, Bottoms, Vers Bottoms, Tops, you name it, all marketed like products with images sent directly to one's cell phone via the algorithms of Grindr, Scruff, and other apps. Thankfully, someone invented the smartphone, because this is apparently what it's for. Click a few times, and *Voila!* Just like

## The Graduate Student

that you've got fifty options from which to choose. But in 1984, finding a gay community—even a date—was a vexation to me. I searched the library shelves, checked the card indexes, and I never found one book to help explain how to find others like me. I often asked myself if something might be wrong with me. Oh, I knew about the 4$^{th}$ floor men's room at the library, and then the lower level men's room at Williams Hall, and even the small men's room just outside the modern, soundproof piano practice studios in a quiet wing of the arts building. I had actually been inside that one once, but was so shocked by the graffiti and, frankly, the overpowering stench, that I never set foot inside again. *Didn't anyone clean these men's rooms?* I was incensed to think that I'd have to find a boyfriend through a glory hole or underneath a stall wall. That scene was not for me. I believed that one day I would simply bump into Mr. Right, and that would be that. But the search gradually took hold of me, and that summer I was searching for Mr. Right Now!

I vicariously observed friends who apparently knew how it was done. There was Danny who posed as a world-traveler, who somehow always had a wad of bills in his pocket and seemed to have a new car every other month. He was a non-stop talker. Looking back, he was a real gold digger, at least that's the impression he made on me. We called him Chatty Cathy. And the smoke! Just yak, yak, yak between puffs off that Marlboro Light. It appeared to me that you had to be a real talker, and smoker too, to make friends and connections in the gay scene. Danny had a new boyfriend every two weeks, and he would move from Black to White to Hispanic, and then they would simply disappear, no drama, just gone. Same thing happened to him, just disappeared one day, probably fell in love with Ft. Lauderdale where he always said he wanted to live—in the warmth and humidity. I ran into him years later in downtown Chicago, literally bumped into him on the sidewalk. He looked much the same, though a bit pudgy with an overwhelming cough, and yet it was him, still talking a mile a minute, very gossipy, the older version of his former self.

Then there was Steve, a real social gadfly, smoked like a chimney, a queen, very swishy and effeminate. How he attracted so many butch/masculine guys on campus defied logic—he could have been a case study in a life skills course on picking up men. I swear he could have invented social media. He had the gift of gab, connecting and getting connected to desirable men. He always found out how much money guys had and hung around only with those who would pay for the endless vodka tonics he ordered two at a time at The Bar in Champaign-Urbana. I felt like the third wheel with these pals as they picked up guys wherever we went, while I sat there unnoticed, the apparent wallflower or fool watching their drinks as they made out. All I knew is that I was doing something wrong. Neither of them were very good role models, and, since I couldn't compete at their level, I spent less and less time with them.

My bike was my trusted companion, just as it was when I was a child. I took to riding in the evenings when the summer heat peaked in mid-July, and one evening found myself circling Franklin Park, near East Street and Washington, and as I rode, circling, I thought it curious that a small group of guys kept their eyes on me, watching intently from their bench on a particular corner—evaluating me, sizing me up. So, I finally got the courage to stop and say hello. They seemed alright, just a group of guys talking,

## The Graduate Student

and I gradually figured out they were all gay and this corner of the park was their summer hangout. As we talked, I got off my bike and leaned it against a tree and sat with them, the conversation turning friendly and interesting, as they were interested in who I was, where I was from, why they hadn't seen me before, that sort of thing. I noticed that as it got dark more and more cars started passing us, and it seemed these were the same cars, just going around the block. *Was it that difficult to find parking around here?* Then, one of my new pals told me we were "cruising" here. *Really?* It seemed to me we were just sitting and talking. I was afraid to ask, not wanting to sound dumb or uninformed, and I gradually realized cruising was slang for looking for a pickup. You know, sex. *Really?* I was intrigued and my heart started to race a bit, as this was all new to me. *Where had I been? How did I miss out on this?*

As we sat in the deepening evening, three Black men approached us, and things took a turn I never would have predicted, a turn that left a mark on me ever since that night. One man grabbed my bike, jumped on it, and I immediately lept up to grab it from him but was thrown to the ground by the other two. As the one rode off, the other two punched me in the back, the stomach, and the chest, kicked me in the face, kicked the back of my head—each taking turns. Every way I turned I was hit. While this was happening, my new group of chums took off, screaming like nelly queens. All I could hear after that was the scramble of footstomps and punches coming at me. Then a car came by, a horn blew, and the driver yelled something from his window which made the attackers run in different directions. All this happened in probably two minutes, and I was left lying there on the warm asphalt, bruised and bloodied with a black eye, a bump growing on my forehead, and a pain in both my chest and back that felt like several broken ribs.

I must have blacked out for a few moments. The police arrived, and as they told me en route to the hospital, it was some concerned neighbor, bystander, or other anonymous witness who called them. A report was filed, and I signed some papers, just what, I don't even know with my one eye swollen shut and my hands bloodied and still trembling. I was the victim of a hate crime, although that term had not yet been coined. Homophobic lower-class assholes, maybe, but most likely just guys who saw a bike they wanted.

After my examination at the emergency room, which involved painful contortions to get the angles right for the X-ray machine, it was declared I had no broken bones. Another type of X-ray scan was used, and this confirmed that there was no internal bleeding. A small miracle, I'm sure. I was sent home with ice packs and instructions for wound care. The police had kindly waited for me while I was being examined and drove me home.

The following day, I was visited by two plainclothes officers, and they brought with them several heavy, thick binders containing mug shots of thousands of men. The sad thing is they were nearly all Black. I was asked to page through the binders and see if I could identify my attackers. This task took hours, but the officers were patient. I have to admit that in the mug shots the men all seemed to have a similar look on their faces, degraded and angry, a look of defeat perhaps. I identified two of the three attackers, and the police completed their paperwork, which I again signed. They told me that these men were wanted for petty theft, among

## The Graduate Student

other things, and had been arrested just a few weeks before. After the police left that afternoon, I never heard from them again. And I was left to recover by myself.

Later that same day, one of the park bench boys stopped by to see how I was doing. I was surprised, unnerved even, because I never told him my address. Apparently, the police report was printed in the newspaper, so that if the attackers wanted to give me another beating, or worse, they could easily find me with my address printed in the local paper.

The weeks that followed were difficult to say the least. First, I couldn't drive my car, so I couldn't visit my parents. In fact, when I called them, I made some excuse about a summer course I was to take that prevented my visit—I was too ashamed or embarrassed to tell them the truth. It was so easy to lie back then, and so easy to lie to them, the shame of it follows me even now. All these years later, I recall a particularly appropriate line from an Agatha Christie book I once read: "Old sins cast long shadows," a sort-of proverb.[1] At the time, the worst part of my injury was that I could not get comfortable. The sofa was too soft for my back, the bed was even worse, so I tried the carpeted floor, which turned out to be the best option, flat and hard. And that's where I slept for at least a week, ice pack to my eye and forehead. The pain in my back and chest subsided within a week, and I was up and about again, though now I had no bike.

Once I was better, I felt I was at a turning point: a new year, graduate school quickly approaching (my acceptance letter had arrived), new friends, new classes, a new start. I stopped socializing with the Franklin Park guys, and at some point I landed a room in a house with close friends on Cherry Street near some freight tracks on the edge of campus. We lived in peaceful squalor, each of us left to his own devices. I had the front bedroom with windows that looked out onto the front porch and side yard. My friend Bruce had the sparsely furnished room just behind me, in the middle of the house. Our friend Rick had the room at the back, just off the kitchen, where he usually slept until noon. And another friend, Tim, used the screened front porch as his room. Bruce had a job in Bloomington during the summer. He owned a Buick Skylark convertible, a brightly polished red with a white convertible top, very sleek. Rick was in the English Department, though our paths never crossed on campus. Tim was studying some esoteric field like Sociology or Cultural Anthropology, I can't recall precisely. And I was taking graduate English courses including Modern British Drama and Nineteenth-century British Literature. I already had my sights set on a thesis on Virginia Woolf.

Each of us had our routine, kept our own hours, all quite separate. But together in the evenings and on weekends we made up a sort of madcap, laid-back, liberal and tolerant entourage of intellectuals who enjoyed a daily case of cheap beer, good music, barbeque, discourse about the state of the world, and some laughs. Our together time, in today's lexicon our Bro time, usually had a theme: food, music, and beer.

Being a man of words, and having gotten really tired of seeing guys almost effortlessly pick each other up in various campus men's rooms, I focused on finding romance through the newspaper and took out an ad. This required planning and patience. I rented a P.O. box. Once that was discreetly in my name, I wrote an ad that I periodically ran in the local paper. It went something like this: "GWM seeks same for friendship, good times, and maybe more.

## The Graduate Student

Please reply to P.O. box XXX." I then would check the P.O. box daily in nervous anticipation. In hindsight, what's most interesting are the responses I received. One responder was so paranoid that he asked me to place a photograph of myself in a shoebox and then place that shoebox under a specific dumpster in a specific alley at a specific time and date. I should have known this guy would be high maintenance. But I was up for the challenge and excitedly considered the possibilities. I followed the instructions, only slightly doubting that anything would come of it. When the candidate actually called me, I was surprised, and we settled on a meeting place for the interview, very "down-low," as guys would say in today's lingo. It turns out this man was in the U.S. Army, or maybe it was the Navy, I can't recall. We had an interesting conversation, but this led nowhere. He was so paranoid he couldn't even relax. I am not a social worker, so eventually I gave up on him. *Next!*

Another responder told me to meet him at a specific time, on a specific date, at a specific neighborhood dive bar, and that I'd recognize him because he'd be "the one drinking a Scotch and soda with a twist." When I got there, I milled around—there were quite a few people in the place, men and women. *A full bar, at 3:00 in the afternoon? That's pretty boozy!* I finally asked the bartender—a blonde with too much hair piled atop her head tied hurriedly and off-kilter with a ribbon—if she had made a Scotch and soda with a twist. She replied that there were at least three people drinking that. I wasn't about to approach three different people, and then ask them, what? *Did you reply to my ad?* Since no one even looked up from their drink, I walked out. This just wasn't the right time or place. I nearly gave up when one day I received a letter from someone who actually signed his name, Bill.

He gave me his phone number, too. *Wow, a brave one!* I picked up the phone and called. He turned out to be a perfectly normal guy, easy to talk to, simply dressed in faded jeans and flannel shirt, and we fell into seeing each other. We'd meet up at Garcia's for a slice of pizza and a beer, then head over to the cinema around the corner if there was a good movie playing, or we'd head up to his room at Waterson Towers. After a couple months, he mentioned that he was transferring to Western Illinois University, and after the Christmas break we fell out of touch.

Those college years were a time of transition into adulthood, and I just accepted change as easily as I might toss yesterday's paper, without any worry or care. We were young, our attachments tentative. People are people—they move on. "A rolling stone gathers no moss," as the proverb states.[2]

My acceptance into the graduate program in English included a teaching assistantship that paid a whopping four hundred dollars a month, barely enough to live on. But I loved every minute of my time in the program. First term I registered for three classes, each of which met for three hours one evening each week. Between sessions, we were required to read a book and write a critical essay about it, some interpretive study that focused on character, writing style, plot, usually with a goal of unveiling the psychological state of the author through his or her writing. Our American Literature professor promised to share with the class a randomly selected paper that we would discuss. This added suspense to the weekly writing assignments.

To be honest, I was completely overwhelmed by the second week of classes. In that American Literature class, one student wrote an essay that was well-argued, complete with references

## The Graduate Student

to critical theory, allusions to other works and authors, and an explanation of the novel's status among a number of great works of literature. By comparison, I felt utterly inadequate and childish in my short interpretive essay on Hester Prynne, the unwitting heroine/victim in Nathaniel Hawthorne's *The Scarlet Letter*. My paper's main argument was that when the work was written, as today, there were/are different standards of behavior for men and women, at least among certain groups. Too bad my paper went unnoticed—it would have enjoyed lively discussion on feminism and thwarted equality.

But as our professor extolled my fellow classmate's writing, he read directly from her paper. Then, from under the conference table he pulled a book, opened it to a page he had marked, and read aloud. Wow, it was exactly, verbatim, the same piece that my classmate had written. Confused for a second, not wanting to believe what I felt I already knew, it suddenly became crystal clear that she had copied an entire chapter from a critical essay volume about Hawthorne's works. The class sat in stunned silence as our professor slammed the book shut, his eyes daggers, lips downturned. He asked our classmate to join him in his office, and they were gone for at least a half hour. Those of us left behind sat nervously, quietly discussing plagiarism. Our classmate was never seen again, and apparently was dishonorably discharged from the graduate program. No one gets a second chance when the crime is so serious. It's a real shame that Congress doesn't work this way.

That drama over, I settled into keeping my nose to the proverbial grindstone and just did my best. Throughout those graduate-school years, I made sure I stayed on top of my coursework, reading the lengthy assignments, writing weekly critiques or interpretive essays. All except for one time. I had been deeply occupied in my British Drama seminar, spending hours every day for at least a week rehearsing my performance of Samuel Beckett's *Krapp's Last Tape*, so I casually ignored that week's assignment for my British Literature seminar, a reading of Emily Brontë's *Wuthering Heights*. I was, frankly, immediately uninspired by the narrative and couldn't get past the third line—so I set it aside. On the day of the discussion (I don't know what came over me—I had decided to keep my mouth shut during class), as everyone yammered on and on about "poor Heathcliff," I looked up distractedly from my Beckett performance notes and remarked, "I don't see what relevance a comic-strip cat has to this discussion." Heads turned. The sudden, shocked pause among my fellow classmates—along with a strange look from our professor—told me something was amiss. And then they all burst into rollicking laughter—even our professor, normally so quiet and dignified, threw her head back with a good chuckle. *What was so hilarious?* Clearly, the cat was out of the bag, and they knew I hadn't read the assignment. Momentarily humiliated, I joined in with the laughter, and the class discussion continued. Everyone, at some point or other, had skipped an assignment, after all. Over the remainder of the semester, my revealing comment became a sort of running joke: "Have you seen Heathcliff?"—one of us would ask as we passed in the hall—"I don't know where that darned cat went."

The following semester, in an advanced Shakespeare seminar, I suggested that we'd have great fun after class with an old British tradition: "Tea and Strumpets." I was in control of my non sequiturs now. The game was afoot, and everyone took turns.

## The Graduate Student

My friends of the time were a real support. I still remember their faces, their smiles, how effortlessly our lives intertwined, like brothers and sisters or members of a private club. Not everyone understood us, and still others didn't quite fit our exclusive gang. I referred to us as the New Bloomsbury Group, a designation appropriated from Virginia Woolf's literary and political circle in 1930s England. Our days passed in the splendor of reading and writing, deep literary conversations with professors, and library research where I could really dig into the books.

By Friday, we were burnt out on reading, so we were glad to attend another Graduate Drunk, the appropriately named English Department faculty and grad student mixer that was held at a different professor's house each week. We had a fine time, lots of laughter, and some heavy critical-theory conversations, along with the booze. These professors really let their hair down, literally. I remember our feminist literature professor, dignified in her two-piece suits or slacks and blouse combo as she presided over our class. At home, she was a different character, adorned with blood-red lipstick, she swanned through the room, barefoot in a caftan, Scotch in hand, channeling Elizabeth Taylor, *"Clink, clink ...!"* We had some good laughs with our professors at those soirées. One Friday, someone in the group excitedly told us that she had discovered gay Blue Jays in her back yard, and that she was planning on writing to the Audubon Society. Instinctively raising a hand, one of my classmates—obviously our resident ornithologist—pointed out that male and female jays are practically identical in coloration. "Oh, well, that's okay," came a cheery reply, "I'm sure there are gay birds somewhere out there."

## James Philip Baran

When a visiting writer was in town to give a reading, we pulled out all the stops. André Codrescu, the Romanian-American poet and cultural commentator, visited in 1986, and we took him to dinner after his reading. There were about ten of us who went to the local Chinese restaurant for Dim Sum, but what I remember best is André's good-natured encouragement of all of us gathered, who were, at least for a day, his humble acolytes. Such visits by luminaries, guiding lights to us, helped us envision ourselves in five or ten years, as writers, critics, or even radio personalities.

After an inspiring reading by a visting poet, and feeling very ambitious and wanting to break through my preconceived personal limitations, I threw myself into creative writing, a pursuit to which I had seldom dedicated any time. I was always the type of guy who thrived on life, I was a "do-er." The best times of my life were spent outdoors, not sitting with a writing pad working out iambic pentameter. Even then I believed that you've got to live and experience things before you can write a good story. Nonetheless I threw caution to the wind and registered for Advanced Creative Writing. (I didn't even bother to take Introduction to Creative Writing.) Tentative at first, I dove into the deep end when our professor assigned the sonnet. Fourteen lines with alternating rhymes, ten syllables or five beats per line—how hard can it be? My first English sonnet, with a humorous bent, was built on references to my old favorite playwright:

## The Graduate Student

To steal from Shakespeare is a crime. I'm told
the Feds will do me harm, and thus I take
no word or phrase from Shakey's page of old.
I only flounder in my mind and make
good choice of words that rhyme. But this and yet
no liberty with his dear text will I
enjoy. I know of ways my words to set
correct in place. And now I see, and sigh,
that I construct a poem in sonnet form
about a poem. I wonder, does this mean
I have performed a miracle, no norm,
or simply trod upon these feet so mean.
In either case, I feel that I disgrace
myself, Old Shakes, and you within this space.

Another, more difficult, assignment was the villanelle. This verse form captivated my imagination, and I gave the task my undivided attention. For what seemed like weeks I worked tirelessly, crafting villanelles. The trick, of course, is to find the right topic and select your words carefully because lines 1 and 3 must repeat throughout the poem and become the concluding two lines. My first few attempts were academic, technically correct, and, frankly, uninspired—simple exercises. But I finally found the imagery to make an interesting villanelle richer in meaning. It was fall, the leaves had mostly fallen, and on an unusually sunny and warm October day, with golden maple leaves skittering across the sidewalk and down the street, I penned a loose villanelle:

James Philip Baran

*A Tide of Winter*

I hear the leaves unleashed. I smell the frost
and want it to surround me with a tide
of winter. Close at hand, I feel my ghost
withdraw the heat within.
                      On many nights
I fall head-first through memories. And then
I hear the leaves unleashed.
                      I smell the frost,
a soul without a home. With stealth it comes,
yet flees before I seize one chance to taste
the winter.
            Close at hand, I feel my ghost
twist to find escape. But I have caught
him by the heart. Desperately he cries.

    With the leaves unleashed, I smell the frost
of centuries piled high. And then he tells
me that I must receive the cool thin breath
of winter close at hand.
                    I feel my ghost
dissolve, then join the ice that whispers in
my ear. And the flavors, mixed, are new.
Forever changed, they are reborn.
                        And still
I hear the leaves. Unleashed, I smell the frost
of winter. Close at hand, I feel my ghost.

## The Graduate Student

The creative writing seminar was stimulating. Difficult, too, in that it forced me to develop a better understanding of word use, definition, implications of words strung in a row, since when adjacent to one another, words gain nuance, imagery, and conjure overtones of meaning. Our poetry professor instilled in us an appreciation and respect for that craft. Today, I wouldn't be surprised if someone is developing a ChatGPT bot or app that will write poems for the lazy or over-committed student.

We did things the old-fashioned way in my college years—we used pen and paper, for starters. In my graduate school days, we luxuriated in vocabulary. And my collegiate comrades, my artistic accomplices, my poetic partners and I would take our word games out of the classroom and into the world. At parties (once a few drinks had been consumed) I often suggested we create Exquisite Corpse poems wherein four to six of us would each write a line to a poem in iambic trimeter, and as each new line was added the previous lines were concealed so that the next contributor would have only the immediate previous line to base his or her contribution upon. The resulting word mash-up was often quite impressive, nearly always sophomoric, with glimpses into our collective mindset. But, ironically, those short poems always contained some nugget of truth, nuanced meaning.

Over the course of my master's program, I studied British Literature, Modern British Drama, American Literature, Romantic Poetry. I also took every Shakespeare course listed in the fall and spring terms. I was a Shakespeare enthusiast, I will admit. He was, after all, the father of literature—to me, anyway. My friends and I had nicknames for him: "Old Shakes," "Shake N Bake," "Shakey," and "He Who Shakes His Speare!" Summers were reserved for the highly-anticipated and popular intensive seminar led by our graduate studies director. Each summer, the Illinois Shakespeare Festival puts on a handful of plays, most of them by the Bard himself, and the festival organizers coordinate with the ISU English Department to hold a high-level seminar. The class was one month long, with daily one-hour sessions, and we formed small discussion groups to continue our development of ideas surrounding the plays. These discussion circles often turned into drinking parties, because we would sometimes meet at Garcia's, where pitchers were just $2.00.

I attended several summer sessions of Shakespeare on Stage. Looking back at my essays, I realize that I was particularly drawn to presentations of prostitution, brothels, and the characters that inhabit these places. I wrote an essay, enticingly titled, "'Has she any qualities?': Marina at the Brothel," an analysis of how the virgin Marina, a spiritual creature, is treated by the hedonistic Bawd, who sees the girl as no more than flesh for sale, in the play, *Pericles, Prince of Tyre*. And if one essay wasn't enough, I also wrote "Virtuous Seediness: The Bawd in Shakespeare's *Pericles*," arguing the case that the Bawd wasn't all that bad, really, that if you looked at her from another perspective she was a practical business woman. My professor, at times, seemed dubious of my claims, no matter how well the text supported my ideas. Other favorite Shakespeare plays in those summer seminars included: *Taming of the Shrew*, *The Merchant of Venice*, *Cymbeline*, *King Lear*, *Macbeth*, and everyone's apparent top choice, *A Midsummer Night's Dream*, which is possibly the most-often performed Shakespeare play of all.

By the end of my first year in graduate school, I was high on life, on the exquisite experience of being an insider in the department earning good grades and fully ensconced in the bookish life

## The Graduate Student

of the college intellectual—I wanted it to go on forever. That summer of 1985 was hot, humid, and rainy. As usual, I was attending the summer Shakespeare on Stage seminar along with three or four close friends, and we formed a clique of know-it-alls. One play of the lineup, *King Lear*, was the focus of critical interest because of the ground-breaking decision to set it not in the period of ancient Britain but in modern-day Los Angeles, with the entire cast fitted out as two motorcycle gangs. Like Conan Doyle's Sherlock Holmes stories that translate surprisingly well into the 21$^{st}$ century (think of Watson blogging instead of keeping a journal, or Mrs. Hudson as a progressive, indeed *laissez-faire*, landlady instead of a cook and housekeeper), Shakespeare's plays generally can be translated into modern settings. Just change the actors' accents, perhaps make slight word-use changes, dress them in modern garb, and *voila*, it works. These plays are at once historical and also eternal, with endless possibilities for adaptation.

The Illinois Shakespeare Festival was held, then as it is today, at the site of an old country mansion, with a relatively good adaptation of an outdoor Shakespeare stage, similar in shape to that of the famous Globe in London, so that performances would have the intimacy and authentic flavor desired nowadays by directors, actors, and audiences alike. Opening night arrived, but instead of the clear, starred sky we had anticipated, a thunderstorm was forecast by the local weatherman. In cases of rain, plays at this festival are moved indoors to the climate-controlled safety and predictable space of the campus drama department's main theater, where actors and audience could stay dry.

As this was opening night, my entire seminar group had tickets to attend, and most of us had established a very tight, collegial if not downright party atmosphere amongst ourselves. For opening night's celebratory nature, we had to procure the necessary beverages that graduate and undergraduate students alike required. All these years later, I could not say whether we ate or when, but the party started around 5:30 at my apartment on Payne Place, a quiet, suburban-like street just a few blocks off campus. There were about six of us.

Money usually being tight, we had to get creative and combine resources. Since my friend Bruce and I owned cars, it fell to us to do the shopping. Just like any modern coming-of-age movie—think *Super Bad*—where everyone had a different request for alcohol: one girl wanted vodka, someone else wanted rum, most wanted beer. In the end, our money allowed us to get one 12-pack of beer and one bottle of Jaegermeister, which was on sale. Back at my pad, there were no complaints. We got out glasses and coffee mugs, poured the Jaeg in near-equal portions for everyone, toasted to our friendship, and enjoyed our drinks. As the performance was to begin shortly and we had to walk to campus, we divided the 12-pack of beer amongst ourselves, concealing cans in our jacket pockets. A play awaits!

As students, our tickets permitted us access to the upper balcony seating at the indoor theatre. Up the stairs we went, careful not to make a nuisance of ourselves with noise after our pre-show drinks. Once seated, we discreetly popped our beer cans and enjoyed a pleasing draught of Old Milwaukee, which was on sale at the corner liquor store. Or it could have been Pabst Blue Ribbon for all I know. Cheap, that was the main thing—it was cheap.

Now that the performance was underway, we were living in the moment, what with knowing the play, the costuming, all the entrances and exits, the whole plot itself nearly from memory. It was somewhere around Act II, Scene II, where Regan, Kent, Cornwall, Gloucester and all the servants are on stage when I popped my second beer can. The sound was not nearly as discreet as I had hoped, as it made that unmistakable loud *Snap!* which echoed around the theatre, amplified by the acoustical live ceiling. The "pop" visibly distracted nearly everyone in the theatre, some of whom arched their necks and looked around. The actors—ever the pros—managed to finish the scene and left the stage to enthusiastic applause. *Exeunt all.*

The house lights came up for Intermission, and we dashed from our seats. I realized only when opening that second beer that certain beverages are strictly prohibited in academic buildings, an offense punishable by, well, I don't know, but punishable I was sure. We left the building, self-conscious yet laughing, a moment in my grad school days that I'm hopeful went unnoticed. *Exeunt all!*

Our literature professor never commented. He must have known we were embarrassed and decided not to rub it in. But at future productions, he did say, "Let's just have a *sip* before the show." One might think we did not learn anything that summer, concentrating as we did on social hours, lunches, drink specials at local watering holes. But learn we did, and not just about Shakespeare's great dramatic art, not just about great acting and interpretation of the text, but about friendship and camaraderie. Higher education is a whole-being experience after all, something to be savored, lived, relished, and not forgotten.

# What's Love Got to Do with It?

I suppose I've spent my whole life in pursuit of love—love and beauty. I sense it in my appreciation of music. It's why the rich harmonies and heart-wrenching melodies of a Brahms Intermezzo stir my spirit; as do the simple abyss of Venetian water in a photograph by Alfred Stieglitz or moments on a ship at sea, considering the waves, the sky. There was beauty in the poetry I read by Samuel Taylor Coleridge and, differently, in that of Denise Levertov. All around me there were beautiful, fragrant, enticing moments, books, and interesting people. But love, well, that was elusive. Yet it seemed to me that others were in love, or in something that passed for it. Adolescent crushes hit me hard. In high school there were two or three guys my own age whom I found attractive, innocently so—like I'd feel toward a brother if I'd had one. I admired the complete ease with which they inhabited their own skin. Just sitting next to them was electrifying, and watching them play softball on the sun-baked field or throw paper airplanes across a classroom made me somewhat jealous. It seemed everything came naturally to them, like every moment was planned in their favor by the Fates.[1] But since I was unsure of myself, I didn't dare make a move. Pushed from my mind, the sexual idea would have to wait. All I knew for certain was *this* wasn't the place, and *this* wasn't the time.

My first memorable infatuation was with Magdiel. We were in high school, Broadview Academy—a fundamentalist boarding school. Macky, as he preferred to be called, was a wild, unpredictable boy. He would be *the* sought-after exotic type in today's gay scene—Hispanic, athletic, with a meaty butt, full lips, and dark eyes. He was fun, too, energetic and loud, always looking for ways to break rules. His room was three or four doors down the hall from mine in the dorm where our windows framed a view of cornfields and the faculty ranch-style houses downhill in the distance.

Macky was a tempter, repeatedly asking me to sneak down to his room after lights out, but I was too unsure of myself to act on this, afraid to be myself, and to some degree afraid even of him. What I was was suppressed—that's what I know now. Walking back to the dorm after dinner, he would catch up to me and startle me, "Hey, there you are, come down to my room after lights out and we can fool around." I didn't even know what he meant.

I had seen what happened to boys whose sexuality was conspicuous in high school—shipped off to live with relatives in distant places, or forced into pastoral counselling sessions. Frankly, I didn't want the attention. I had already had enough of the ridicule for which judgmental people are famous, so that the possibility of heightened scrutiny and analysis was just too much to bear. I had also heard whispered rumors about conversion, and it sounded like torture, evil acts done against youths by parents who refused to be embarrassed by their children's honest expressions of their immutable selves. In 1978, I just wanted to do my time in this prison-school and then get out with as little pain as possible. When I

## What's Love Got to Do with It?

didn't accept Macky's invitations, he started to accost me verbally with comments like, "What's wrong, fag?"—half joking, half serious, so I didn't quite know what to make of him in those instances. I didn't have the vocabulary or experiences to respond easily to his advances, and I didn't understand my own sexuality, suppressed or ignored at 17.

Our friendship soared at the beginning—long walks, lunches in the cafeteria, and tickling attacks or wrestling matches in his room that left me feeling violated. In the music department, we sprang into action on the piano, playing cocktail lounge-styled improvisations on famous hymns—made even more daring with his added Latin beat and my glissandos at the end of each phrase. *It was all just in good humor!* One of our music teachers caught us in the midst of a rollicking, irreverent hymn medley, and with a frown, told us to "play the music as it's written!" *Well, that's no fun.* Our piano duos in the music studios beneath the chapel were a highlight of high school. Looking back, I think we were basically dating. Our relationship exploded one evening when, after yet another invitation to his room after lights out, followed by my refusal, he couldn't take it any longer and screamed at me in front of bystanders, accused me of not caring for him, adamant that we weren't friends any longer. I had never seen such drama, and was embarrassed to have been the cause of it. I quietly walked to my room and shut the door. We drifted apart, not friends, but not enemies either.

My next crush happened at Southern Missionary College in Tennessee. During my sophomore year, a neighbor on my hall introduced me to a good friend of his, Kurt, an upperclassman, the son of an Adventist pastor, so I knew he came from a good home. He had the magnetism of a televangelist. With an eager smile and ready laugh, his gaze penetrated into mine as we chatted. I guess this was the first time everything clicked, and I felt vibrations of what, I don't know, lust, anticipation, intrigue—*ooh, what's gonna happen now?* We exchanged numbers, and, well, he knew where I lived, so it was only natural that he stopped by to hang out. He wasted no time, either. He was back for a visit that evening. And I had thought of nothing but him all day, his brown, naturally curly hair, his steady gaze. I had never been with a guy before this, and I was unable to block the feelings and thoughts that were pulsing through me. Between my brain, my stomach, and my heart, I was like a pinball machine, energy bouncing. Intuitively, I understood that as gay men we were not going to wait until the second date. Fundamentalist dogma and fear were cast aside, and I reached out with bold confidence toward my destiny.

Kurt was the hot young man who opened my heart to understanding what it means to be gay and shared with me my first gay experience. I suppose I should call it my coming out. That evening, on the day we met, we were sitting there in my dorm room talking about our upbringings, what each of us was currently studying, that sort of thing. I abruptly switched gears and explained to him that I had some conflicting thoughts and didn't have anyone I could talk to about them. He must have known where I was going with this, because he basically said, "Well, we should find out what that's about," or something similar that put me at ease. He pulled me close, put his arm around me, and made me feel comfortable as we talked. Comfortable, and a bit warm—dizzy even. I got up to open the window for some air, but he pulled me back. Within seconds, we took off each other's shirts and started to explore each other's torso. After a few minutes, we were completely tangled in

## What's Love Got to Do with It?

each other's arms, our jeans and underwear ripped off in a hurry. It felt as if we had eight hands between us. One thing led to another, and then another. We knew exactly what to do and it was entirely joyful, natural, authentic and affirming—we fit together. I find it interesting that often the most apparently conservative people are the ones to watch out for—they seem to have no inhibitions, no guilt whatsoever. Kurt did not recruit or groom me. At last I knew for sure what direction my life was taking, and I had no more fear. I was thrilled and uplifted because I knew with confidence whom I was meant to be and that there were other normal guys just like me to be found. To quote Madeline Kahn in *Young Frankenstein*, "Ah, sweet mystery of life, at last I've found you."[2]

This was in the early years of college, my teen years just barely behind me. During my freshman and sophomore years I witnessed 19- and 20-year-old guys and girls getting married, with an oft-repeated excuse usually laughed out, "It's better to marry than to burn." They were encouraged by faculty and staff, certainly by the pastoral staff, to get married. One friend, who had been dating a girl for only a month or so, told me, "Why wait?" *For a lot of reasons,* I wanted to reply. His attitude appalled me because these young people were throwing away their youth as far as I was concerned. And besides, I wondered, how can a 19-year-old guy know exactly which girl is right for him? Even then, I knew it was not possible to be mature enough to enter into marriage at that age. I was mortified for them, and I thought, there they go, quick to marry, then surely to divorce when they grow up. For those of us with no marriage plans, or the worst sin—not being half of a couple—a sort of anxious attention was directed at us because we were not progressing down the traditional path proving you belong, which was: meet a girl, get married, immediately reproduce—the primary goal in life for some.

Because of the constant watchful eyes in Collegedale, even in my small group of friends we were very careful how we acted and spoke; we remained guarded and dropped quiet hints or spoke of sex with understated innuendo. Under cloak of night, we'd slip out of the dorm, careful to place an undetectable object in a secluded side security door to prevent it from locking—a folded piece of cardboard or a pebble. This ensured a discreet reentry point. We slid into a friend's black Camaro and glided slowly out of the dorm parking lot, headlights off. About a quarter mile down the road, passing the Little Debbie's factory/bakery, we turned the headlights on and sped toward Chattanooga.

Alan Gold's Disco, which opened its doors in 1977, awaited us—it was our own Studio 54. You could feel the thumping bass all the way from the parking lot. Trembling with anticipation and excitement, we alighted from the car and walked in like we owned the place. No one checked IDs there, so I easily slipped past the bouncer. None of us ever hooked up at Alan Gold's, at least I didn't, but instead we just enjoyed the dance music and a few cocktails. At about 2:00 we would head back to the dorm, ears ringing from Donna Summer's "Last Dance" or Diana Ross's latest hit, "I'm Coming Out," which left us sweating, hearts pounding, floating with joy in the song's clear meaning. On the drive back to the dorm, we'd gradually calm down and return to a more reverent mood, bracing ourselves for another Saturday-morning sermon delivered by a man gripping a Bible and wearing a wool-polyester blend suit.

In my college years, finding a boyfriend was difficult. The bar scene was uninspiring, to be frank. We had no apps by which to

## What's Love Got to Do with It?

market our body parts or to give us the actual distance to another available guy. For me, it was just a waiting game—somewhere, sometime in my average day I knew I'd eventually run into the guy for me. Later, after I moved to Normal, Illinois, I learned that a small bar on the edge of campus "turned gay" one night a week. I'd go there on the appointed night, and sure enough it was full of men—other college students, a few older guys, townies, many of them with bitchy attitudes who just sat there quietly judging everyone as they walked in, like comparing steaks at the butcher counter. It was here that I met Jim. We hit it off instantly, shared a drink, and he offered to drive me home. I had my bike, so I didn't really need a ride, but Jim was insistent, and in the end we fit my 10-speed road bike in the trunk of his car. We drove for miles and ended up at his house on Lake Bloomington for a night of sex. In the gay scene of the 70s, 80s, and 90s, there were always labels, categories based on body types, and in those days I was what we call a Twink. Our affair only lasted a month or so, but it was a refreshing change of pace from the lack of interest I felt from guys my age in those college years.

By the time I finished undergrad and started graduate school, I occupied myself mainly with academic endeavors, yet I spent a lot of quiet time trying to figure out the clandestine gay scene. At the time, I tried everything I knew to put myself out there—dressing the part, or so I thought, wearing the right cologne, that sort of thing. I had a pair of Guess jeans in a trendy blue-gray hue with a leather codpiece that I wore regularly, confident they'd catch the eye of the right guy. Dressed just so, and with a western-style shirt one day or a rolled-neck linen shirt the next, I'd take my cigarette breaks standing in the hall (you could do that in the 80s) outside the Writing Center, waiting for my next tutorial session with undergrads who needed one-on-one coaching to meet their honors credits. I was invisible to every cute guy who walked by.

In 1980s Normal, Illinois, the gay scene was on the down-low, very insulated and discreet. Gays were difficult to find, at least for me. If I had been more of a gadfly, I'd probably have dated more men then. There were no books, no self-help guides, none that I could find anyway, to teach the budding gay man all the What, Where, and How to find romance in a busy world—in fact in a busy country where politicians are pleased when we remain hidden, invisible. The Gay and Lesbian Pride movement began on the night of the first Stonewall riots in New York on June 28, 1969, and more than fifteen years later I was still wondering why my people were so hard to find. I am impatient for a time when people can look past immutable details of our lives—to stop reducing us to our separate components of attractions, dimensions, abilities, colors. All this categorizing dehumanizes us to a degree and reduces us to data points.

After completing graduate school, I moved back to Chicago to start my adult life. I felt strongly that I had to make up for lost time, so I immediately began exploring the local gay-bar scene. I don't know why it is, but bars with themes touching on prison, hard manual labor, or old westerns seemed to be popular. They had such good, masculine names, too. It was code language so that anyone with any awareness would know they were gay. I didn't frequent all of them, but the names bring back memories. If you were into westerns, or at least western-style clothing and boots, there was the Manhandler Saloon on Halsted, and the Mine Shaft with its dimly lit bar area and unlit corners, and the Manhole—a place where you could dance until dawn, shirts off,

## What's Love Got to Do with It?

hot sweaty bodies pressed against each other. These were manly places, so poorly lit you had to grope your way through the shadows—and that was probably the point, made for interesting possibilities. The dress code was always denim and white T-shirt, so everyone looked a bit the same, like clones. There was the ever-popular Roscoe's, for a young, preppy crowd, and Sidetrack, the video bar, where every weekend a showtunes afternoon drew huge crowds. That party continues today, except when an old Madonna video comes on there's the inevitable question from a Gen Z-er, "Who's that?" And there was also the Eagle, with its original murals by Tom of Finland, and Cell Block, bars leaning more heavily on leather and uniforms, with their backrooms and basements where, frankly, anything could happen. And we have the Lucky Horseshoe Lounge, an old-fashioned tavern-like bar with its friendly bartenders and playful—even devilish—dancers who may pop onto your lap if you're in the mood. Whatever your pleasure, Chicago has something to offer.

On Friday evenings after work, the retail and business gays, myself included, from the Loop and North Michigan Avenue descended upon Gentry—the name itself tells you the clientele are a notch above (above what, I'm not sure)—a piano bar complete with chandeliers, decorated mainly in a subdued Art Deco style of black, silver, and mirrors. This was one of my favorite haunts, and I met friends there nearly every Friday. As I was an editor at the time with an office on Chicago Avenue, the two blocks to Gentry was an easy walk. Its most memorable headliner was Rudy de la Mor, who performed there for at least twenty years. Rudy was a slightly rotund man in his late 60s who always wore the most outlandish women's hats—hats with feathers, Easter bonnets, or Yves Saint

Laurent couture that could stop traffic—as his fingers effortlessly hammered out jazzy tunes to accompany his comedic, manly voice, his jowls jiggling along. Every performance included a tap routine in which Rudy led a rousing rendition of "42$^{nd}$ Street." All the patrons, quarters in hand, became the Rockettes for a few minutes, tapping our troubles away on table-tops or the bar—if you closed your eyes, you'd swear you were at Radio City Music Hall. When Rudy modulated into "Bringing in the Sheaves," everyone threw change into his tip bowl, and he'd thank each of us individually with a friendly leer, lips puckered into a kiss, or a campy wisecrack about one or other of our asses. All in good fun. His routine would be impossible today, because no one seems to carry change. When Gentry closed its doors, it signaled the end of an era.

But the late nights and casual sex—exciting for a while, I'll admit—became a bore. Something was missing. I joined the Windy City Gay Chorus to find camaraderie with like-minded fellows, and to sing—I had studied music, after all. Even though I was having a great time, it was still empty nonetheless. My entourage from the chorus, about five of us who became a tight-knit group, took to spending Friday and Saturday evenings together at one or another's apartment. We were a madcap bunch, really. We got together for every Chicago Pride parade from 1990 to perhaps 1995. During that period, most Pride days started with pre-parade cocktails at my apartment which was practically on the parade route. By the time we had our second round of drinks we could hear the parade approaching and would dash outside to find good viewing positions. Few things seem to last. We moved on to new interests, new friends in our lives, and drifted apart as each of us found boyfriends, or work took us away.

## What's Love Got to Do with It?

On one winter night, early 1990s, I was bored, beside myself with an energy that needed to be spent, so I dressed up and took myself out on the town. Arriving at a particular members-only club, I showed my ID to the bouncer and paid the cover charge. It's a club for men only—and today, I'm sure half the customers are gay-curious or "not into labels"—so at the time the clientele was predictable to a degree. The entertainment at the piano was no one of any particular merit, just some tenor mumbling through a jazzy number. Cigarette smoke formed a blueish cloud in the lounge, and I wandered to another area of the club. I ordered a drink and sat down at a small table, taking in the scene as it unfolded before me. After the jazz singer finished his set, a DJ in some remote outpost in the club turned on music to change the mood, an early-80s dance hit that began with a catchy rhythm on synthesizer, expanded with drums and violins, layered with bongos, which finally ascended to high disco with a bold saxophone riff. As Carol Jiani sang "Hit 'N Run Lover," with its hypnotic bongo rhythm, someone dimmed the lights and turned up the volume. It was difficult to see faces among the shadows, yet I felt oddly at ease in the dimness, anonymous even. Wandering further through the club's caverns, up one stairway then down another, I stumbled into an entirely new place it seemed, and a stand-up comic was on stage making cutting jokes about himself and the audience, the warm-up act for the main event—an acrobatic dancer who promised to take it all off. The room began to fill with men, clad in nothing but white towels, towels sometimes rakishly draped over a shoulder. A guy came here for one thing, so why not show it off? It is amazing how equalizing it is to strip away the outer layers of identity—suits, loafers, jeans, sneakers, and suddenly we all seem alike, on the same level playing field. That was Man's Country.

Bored with all this—or maybe because it was so intense—I left and went to another club. Not wanting to sit or stand in one place, I circulated among the crowd, restless, and that's when I saw him—a handsome, blond hunk of man who looked very relaxed that evening, just leaning against the wall with his drink. He noticed me, too. I circled in, passed him, and then circled back. I made the first move and introduced myself. He introduced himself, David, and we enjoyed a nice conversation. Later in the year, I was at a friend's apartment for a pre-Christmas holiday drinks thing, and I was nonplused by the crowd and conversation when I stepped into the bathroom for a break. There, mounted on the wall next to the toilet was a phone, a princess model in fact—*It better be, because I was dialing from the throne*. Without giving it a thought, I picked up the phone, dialed the Information operator on 411, and requested the listing I was looking for. When David answered, I said, "I don't know if you'll remember me, but this is James," and immediately as I started to say my own name, he interjected, his voice rising with enthusiasm: "Yes, I remember you." Our conversation went on for some minutes before I realized someone was knocking at the bathroom door, the party was spilling out into the night. We agreed to meet the following evening at a Halsted Street club.

I arrived early and, after checking my hair in the men's room, positioned myself at the bar so that I could see the door. David walked into Roscoe's Tavern right on time and greeted me with a smile and a hug. "I'm so glad I called," I began, and off we went on a courtship of sorts, seeing each other every weekend and some evenings during the week. He swept me off my feet. I felt imme-

## What's Love Got to Do with It?

diately comfortable and as if we had known each other for years. We could talk about anything. As weeks progressed, turning into months, I kept asking myself, "Could he be the one I've been waiting for?" I moved to a new apartment, closer to his place, because I was tired of my old neighborhood and I wanted to open a new chapter in my life by moving, and starting this new life with a clean slate. There's really nothing like a new apartment or house to give you that sense of newness. Even though I've moved my books and china, my clothes and furniture twenty times I'm sure by now, every time is a refreshing adventure. Unpacking the boxes is like Christmas, a new chapter begun.

Our courtship was like a staycation in a way. We were born planners and thought up interesting creative outings for every weekend, like going to the Art Institute and then dinner, having Thai food and taking in a classic film at the iconic Music Box, or roaming around different Chicago neighborhoods to discover antique shops, book stores, restaurants. We went out even when the weather was terrible, -30 degrees, we didn't care. We were enjoying ourselves no matter what nature threw in our face. There were times, deep in winter, when we were among the only patrons at the Music Box, or among only twenty or so customers at a small bar.

We both enjoyed film to such an extent that we often saw two movies a week, and when the Chicago International Film Festival was on we made sure we had tickets well in advance of the screenings, most of which were shown at the Music Box. We were there so often we had our own seats. Whether it's film noire, old horror classics, or comedies, we found that our favorite movies were often the same. *Some Like It Hot, Young Frankenstein, The Pink*

## James Philip Baran

*Panther Strikes Again*, *Christmas Vacation*, *Sunset Boulevard*, all rank in our top-ten lists, and when we watch a movie together we often will have the same reactions. But we don't always agree. For example, David couldn't tolerate the film version of *Who's Afraid of Virginia Woolf?*, while I argued that it's the best film ever made. Outside of that disagreement, we rarely have any.

Over time, we started talking about houses—what style we each liked, the architecture itself, what cities or parts of the world in which we'd like to live. Endless conversations circled around London, New York, Chicago, San Francisco. Since we are both culture people, we are attracted to cities, and more specifically cities with well-known symphony orchestras, opera and theatre companies. It's not that we're culture vultures, out every night for every performance, poetry reading, play, or opera. It's the fact that cities with symphonies and opera companies have highly developed cultural scenes, a large, well-educated audience, and, therefore, more opportunities for us to find a community of like-minded people. Our favorite city, our top choice of course, was and is London, not so much because of the cultural events, the museums, the theatres, but more because it seems that people there are respectful toward each other. Life there seems to have an elegant pace, and we always feel a sense of place, like it's the center of the known universe.

After a year or so of dating, I moved in with David in the one-bedroom condo he owned on Lakeview Avenue. Our first real home bought together, however, was a small cottage in southwest Wisconsin, which, as with all important purchases, was a spur-of-the-moment decision—"I've always wanted a house in the country," was one thing I recall saying at the time. The house itself, upon first seeing it from a distance, gave the impression of quiet

## What's Love Got to Do with It?

neglect, almost like Grey Gardens, slightly derelict. Once inside, the smell was overwhelming, bugs everywhere, and what's worse, there were five different kinds of floor coverings and about as many varieties of wood paneling. This is where we dove into a domestic life together with enthusiasm, remodeling, painting, buying appliances, even building bird houses for the garden. This small cottage was our spirit house—the place to which we decamped after an overly busy week dealing with all sorts of work-related demands in our jobs, David heading a well-known university museum, and me managing a magazine production department. Each weekend, our wrens, chickadees, cardinals, and sparrows awaited our arrival in the country. The first thing we did after unloading the car was to refill the bird feeders.

While we both love the outdoors, in fact prefer the outdoors when the weather is good, we also are very interested in maximizing our interior experience, so we put a lot of energy and resources into the places we live. In fact, we have owned eight homes together, so far. When we travel to interesting new places, Santa Fe, for example, where the light and landscape are inspiring, I inevitably pull out the laptop and fire it up, ready to search through Redfin listings to see what kind of houses are available here or there, what they cost, what amenities are included in the homeowners' association. Unlike decades past, now I also do a Google search to determine what, if any, LGBTQ+ community there is in the area. David just rolls his eyes when he sees Redfin on my screen—because he knows where this is leading. And he also knows that I know he's just as into it as am I.

In each of our homes, we both have spaces we declare personal, or at least focused more or less on one of us, his study or mine, but one of the most important aspects is the view. Many people enjoy television, and I am among them, but I'm also content to enjoy a glass of wine while gazing through the window at our view. In Wisconsin we had a secluded seven acres, and our living room view was of countless pine trees which, in winter, were covered with heaps of heavy snow, just like a typical Christmas card. That view remained ours for nearly seventeen years until, one day, we decided the house was simply not big enough for us for the long term into retirement. We found that we missed the city, and decided to move back to Chicago to immerse ourselves in its cultural offerings. Our new view sets Belmont Harbor right at our feet, past the traffic of Lake Shore Drive, an endless spectrum of blue water, white sails, and occasional clouds that drift across the scene like in a Turner seascape. We live behind those windows I so often passed as a child.

It was a cold winter evening when David and I decided to take a week's vacation somewhere different, somewhere decidedly warmer than Chicago, and we settled on Palm Springs because we had never been there. One week was all it took. We returned a year later and bought a Mediterranean-style house with expansive views of the San Jacinto and Santa Rosa Mountains, a view I have gazed upon countless evenings as the sun burnishes the landscape, cutting deep shadows as it sets over the mountains. As with other properties we've owned, we not only have the view and our rooms, we also have our favorite birds, too. There's the western bluebird, the black phoebe, the white-crowned sparrow, and the oft-misunderstood crow. Then there's my nemesis, the mourning dove, with its constant cooing. By far our favorite bird, though, is the northern mockingbird, which has an endlessly entertaining,

## What's Love Got to Do with It?

and at times hysterically funny, varied song, one that I can't help but chirp along to.

I am trying to find words to describe the indescribable. Day-to-day experiences hold meaning: cooking dinner of pork tenderloin with herbed new potatoes and broccoli, or assembling a lasagna Bolognese—the enticing aromas drift through the house and express contentment. Love is so much more than words, so far beyond. It is like time and space, endless, incalculable, and like the universe, infinite in possibility. It encompasses my whole being, so words really are inadequate. Time flows ever-onward, and I realize that in David I have seen a glimpse of heaven, had a peek at God, because David's patience and kindness, his joy and acceptance are a blessing sent from beyond.

David and I were raised in different parts of the country, grew up separately, lived entire lifespans before we met. And yet the universe set us before one another, and I said yes, this is enough for me, he is the one for me. David, I know, experienced the same realization. Dating, finding common ground, enjoying the things our culture offers—movies, theater, music, books, art, and travel, we continually build upon our love and our shared interests.

Significant experiences or events punctuate our lives. There's the time we spent in Munich and, upon entering a low-ceilinged bar, I unknowingly sat in a seat reserved for Werner Fassbinder. David's friends pointed out that apparently that's *just not done*, but being good-natured they let me sit there anyway. On another occasion, we were anxious the night of the presidential election of November 4, 2008, and lay awake in our friends' loft guestroom in their 500-year-old house in King's Lynn, England, awaiting the news. In another time and place, while remodeling our Wisconsin cottage, we had reclined awake, dozing slightly, atop army cots close to the Franklin stove, and listened to Hearts of Space, a radio program popular in the 1980s, tired from a day of work. David was there for me at my father's death, and again at the time of my mother's passing. I, too, gave him comfort with my presence and support after his mother's death and also after his father died. Our parents were from different worlds, but they each accepted us, individually and as a couple. They gladly wove us into their lives, and each treated us like family.

David and I met over thirty years ago, and today he's my husband. Like any couple, we have occasional disagreements, but they don't escalate into shouting matches—we're not at war. While big fights may be dramatic—think Liz and Dick in the 70s—the result being a salacious cover story in *Vanity Fair* or some other gossipy outlet like *Us* or *People*, we just don't let that happen. No issue for us can be earth-shattering, hair-pulling, glass-smashing. Even if I get annoyed with David on a rare occasion, the way he loads a dishwasher comes to mind, this passes in minutes because I know it's not worth arguing over—it is nothing compared to what we have built in our relationship. I have the same thought process for bigger issues when they arise. Nothing is so profound that it supersedes our love and commitment.

When same-sex marriage was approved in California, we looked at each other and agreed, "Let's do it while we can." We made our appointment at the Placer County Courthouse, asked my sister Bernie, who lived nearby, to be our witness, and on a sunny July day in 2013, became husband and husband, forever linked through our love and one state's legal approval. Two years later, June 28, 2015, the Supreme Court would find in our favor—in our

## What's Love Got to Do with It?

people's favor—in the case of *Obergefell v. Hodges*, where Justice Kennedy wrote so eloquently for the majority the following words: "Far from seeking to devalue marriage, the petitioners seek it for themselves because of their respect—and need—for its privileges and responsibilities. And their immutable nature dictates that same-sex marriage is their only real path to this profound commitment."[3]

Thank you, Justice Kennedy. While the Court's clear and wise decision, on the side of equality and justice, chokes me up even now, today we—and I mean all our people—must continue to be diligent by electing Democrats, because the current Supreme Court appears willing to revisit this decision; "the foundational underpinning of LGBTQ rights is up there on conservatives' list of targets …."[4] I must sound like a broken record when I ask, why can't people live and let live? Why do so many apparently want to relitigate cases that were already decided by a legitimate Court? Is it because they can't accept—or they refuse to accept—progress and reality?

\* \* \*

Back in September 1985, my English professor and mentor, Judith Roof, took me to see Tina Turner, who was in the middle of her historic Private Dancer Tour. As she danced across the stage, singing all her hits, I was like a child again, fantasizing about being her backup singer. Judith and I sang along to the songs, and my favorite—a perfect vehicle for Tina's sultry voice—was "What's Love Got to Do with It?" with its unanswered question hanging in the air, palpable like the rhythm and the beat pulsating from the ceiling-height speakers on stage. The poet in Tina sang it with feeling, with urgency.

The song held meaning for me because it pointed out the glaring fact that some people avoid love and only pursue sex, a physical transaction, and are closed to the emotional or intellectual facets. The emotional side includes a bit of romance, a lot of respect, loyalty, kindness, an overflowing generosity of spirit that, frankly, powers loving relationships in which both partners equally participate. It's two-sided, not one-sided. I had a few one-sided relationships, and fortunately they didn't last long—they shouldn't really be called relationships—they were just liaisons, each its own thing. Empty and disappointing, they left me hungry for something with substance. And I waited for it. And at last it happened for me on a night when I least expected it.

To me, love seems old fashioned for those who claim they don't have time for it, or think, perhaps, that modern relationships are best when kept simple, without deep attachments. The reasons are probably innumerable. Yet I think we all crave, long for, something deep and lasting. When someone first says those words—often dreaded in gay culture—"I love you," many guys shut it down, deny it, because it complicates matters, or they just aren't ready to take that step. *Update that Grindr account!* That's okay for some; I am not one to judge. We're all individuals, and we have the freedom to make our own choices.

Social media has idealized transitory relationships and brought us "content creators" with their workout and travel selfies. By contrast, I did all my chandelier-swinging before the era of social media, so there's no photographic record of my antics. (I don't know whether to be disappointed by that or relieved.) I have to admit, though, those content creators' almost unreal *joie de vivre* shows another, quite tempting life, even if it is temporary. With

## What's Love Got to Do with It?

such carefree, indomitable, all-consuming sexuality, they're almost toys, really! It's a big enough world with room for all of us. But if you're looking for lasting substance, you do have to consider that old fashioned idea of love. It will hit you when you least expect it, and a day comes when you find someone who aligns with your outlook, matches your spirit, and you realize you are content. You'll also hear yourself saying, "Yes, this is enough."

My heart's been broken a few times, but no longer. This love I live is built on mutual attraction, admiration, respect, tolerance, loyalty, shared goals and commitments, and a joy in seeing each moment together, whether that's dancing shirtless until 3:00 a.m., watching *Young Frankenstein* for the thirtieth time, sharing a smile over spaghetti Bolognese, or gazing out our window in silence. I have spoken these words and made the promise, "In sickness and in health, until death us do part," and I understand their meaning. The words are not owned by any one group of people; these words are universal and an honor to be spoken, heard, and understood. I know that one of us will be here for the other when that comes. Until then, we live every moment to its fullest, whether that's in some mundane task like cooking a stew or folding laundry, or in other activities that inspire us and bring us joy like cycling, hiking in the woods, looking at art, jetting to London, perusing Redfin listings, or reading our separate books, together, in peace, and in love. In the end, you see, love has everything to do with it.

# In Memoriam: Mater Doloresa

The early morning light on May 27, 2008, was heavily shaded by thick clouds. I sat, exhausted and inconsolable, observing the sky—a roiling black and grey mass blocking the morning light—as if it too mourned. A chilly wind off Lake Michigan blew across our high-rise balcony, as I began the long series of phone calls to inform friends and relatives who were by now awake. She died at 2:00 a.m. I last saw her in the early evening two days earlier, Sunday, May 25, the day before Memorial Day, when we shared a mid-day meal of chicken, peas, potatoes, and blueberry pie. I brought a small bouquet of flowers—white daisies, yellow and white roses. She was so delicate that day. I was afraid I might have a cold and feared I could pass it to her easily, so I kept at a distance, was careful how I breathed, did not hug or embrace her before I left. *My own most grievous fault.* I promised to come again "day after tomorrow" because I had much to do on the holiday, a day off from a stressful magazine job, the day off a chance to catch up on personal business, errands, housework. Her last words to me were a benediction, "God bless you. I love you," and I replied "I love you, Ma." And then I walked away. *Holy Mary, mother of God, pray for us sinners now and at the hour of our death.* The words of the Hail Mary still automatically roll off the tongue, repeated at every visitation before the coffin is closed. And I remember these words, taught to me when I was a child.

\* \* \*

Picture Carole Bouquet in the film *For Your Eyes Only* and you have an idea of my mother at age 24—agile, adventurous, lively, strikingly beautiful. If she had had the appropriate connections, circulated in the right New York circles, or was acquainted with Alexander Liberman at Condé Nast, she would easily have been a cover girl in the 1940s or 50s. There was even a rumor she had turned down an offer from Pablo Picasso when he was searching for a new muse. Her beauty surpassed many models of today. She could have been the Chanel spokesmodel for its eponymous No. 5 perfume, or at least a Bond girl. In her fifties and sixties, she was compared to Queen Elizabeth II in her style of dress—complete with diamond brooch—and the way she wore her hair. But in her twenties, she was a sought-after dance partner at the monthly St. Josephat Church socials in Lincoln Park. Along with two of her other sisters, the three eldest were nicknamed, in a gossipy tone, "Those Samp Girls" by neighbors, an almost notorious designation but intended as admiration.

My sister and I chose the flowers ourselves. Pink and white peonies, mother's favorite, with hosta leaves for a green backdrop—these would grace her coffin for the final journey to the Committal. She was proud of her peonies. Every year they sprouted forth from the east lawn of our suburban Brookfield yard, where I grew

## In Memoriam: Mater Doloresa

up. I imagine that the peonies are now untended, left wild, even weed-infested or leaning toward the grass, their luxurious, lavish blooms wet with a spring rain.

Looking back in time, usually with clearer vision—admittedly layered with a romanticized and wishful memory—I realize how easy it is to idealize and consider my mother in near-divine terms. But the facts are these: she had patience like a saint, and I was a challenge as a child, a challenge that surely caused her to curse and rail against me—the out-of-control, mischievous, free spirit in the house. I was the difficult child who tested her patience, and that is my grievous fault. My attempt to summarize the history of that girl, woman, and mother falls short because of my own limited knowledge of her history. I lean heavily on memories of my times with her, and the impressions, photographs, and family tales about her. Memories guided me as I created a posthumous portrait of her, a diptych entitled, "Mater Doloresa," a large-format photograph of her as a young woman (the original taken when she would have been about 20) layered over her favorite flower, the peony, with the second panel being a collage of old photographs, her eighth-grade diploma, a fragment of the 1940 U.S. Census page showing her family's names, pages from her mother's prayer book, and other scraps of memorabilia.

Doloresa Mary Samp Baran, a woman noble and dignified, was born in Chicago's Lincoln Park neighborhood on August 18, 1919, during the Spanish Flu outbreak. In her youth her family had very little in material goods (the children shared one toy, a firetruck), and yet she was blessed to enjoy growing up with seven siblings and a gregarious, loving mother. On June 12, 1947, the day of her wedding to my father, Frederick Jacob Baran, she was luminous, wearing a cream-white satin gown with an eight-foot veil crowned by a tiara woven of freshwater pearls and silk flowers. In photos from the day, her skin is like Carrara marble, her hair dark silk, her smile warm and genuine.

Except for stories told by my sister, aunts and uncles, I generally know little about her life in the years before my birth. She was her own person and had a life completely unto herself, then a life with her husband, before we children came along.

In every life there are things done and things left undone. I catch my breath on the words said in the Confession of Sin during the mass,[1] as the phrase is a reminder of our humanity, our fallibility, that we often fail. And yet we move forward, with any luck learning from those things done and undone, becoming aware enough of ourselves to grow into more perfect people. I'd like to think that my mother became that better person. And, by that example, I hope to emulate that in my own life.

I was born during the great blizzard of January 1961. Mother was taken to the hospital by one of the undertakers from Ewald Funeral Home on Southport, because no one could reach my father immediately at work. It's not hard to imagine the spectacle of a hearse pulling up to the emergency entrance at Columbus Hospital on Lakeview Avenue. After about twenty-four hours of labor, I finally arrived, at 1:10 p.m. on January 28. The nurses and doctor immediately took me to a kind of neo-natal intensive care unit, saying I needed oxygen. A hand-written note survives, certifying that I was baptized by a nurse because the medical staff thought I might die. This event would haunt my family for over a year, because they were told I might not develop normally due to oxygen deprivation during the birthing process. The hospital

## In Memoriam: Mater Doloresa

overbilled my parents for my days-long hospital stay. They billed for a circumcision which was not performed; my father did not believe in disfiguring a male child. And so, it was left to me, and I decided to get it done when I was 24. My father never forgave the hospital staff and, when asked, proclaimed his everlasting distrust of Roman Catholic institutions. Fortunately, and with some joy, over the course of my first year, it was noted that I developed as normally as any child, with laughter, recognition of other family members, and playfulness with the family dog, Duchess (she was apparently just as delighted with me as I was with her).

My curious, rambunctious behavior started early as I learned to walk, or at least roll about the house in a four-wheeled baby walker with bumpers padding the perimeter, not so different from the walkers used by elderly residents in nursing homes today. We had no Playschool toys, no heaps of plastic puzzles, tiny play houses, no Big Wheel in those days. What toys I had included genuine wood blocks, painted in many colors, with letters and numbers carved and painted on them. I had a sort of pyramid of donut-like multi-colored disks that had to be fit perfectly—large to small—so that they would form a complete cone shape in rainbow colors. With a clever sense of irony, I would sometimes purposely stack these donuts in reverse, carefully balancing them so that the fattest one was on top, completing the upside-down cone. When told this was incorrect, I'd just laugh, happy that I had broken some rule and did things my way. When I was about two or three years old I was given a full set of Lincoln Logs, with which I assembled small houses. I am not jealous of today's toys—video games, interactive lessons for preschoolers, and the generous families who heap iPads and smartphones on young children before they can even speak.

The 1960s were simply different from today; it was, quite honestly, a different world.

Mother raised me to be a gentleman. While we were not rich, she told me that nonetheless we came from people with dignity, people of good behavior—Kashubians. Good manners and respect for others are noble no matter one's background. At times, though, my instinct was to retaliate, because being a little gentleman was hard work—it required patience, kindness, respect, and something in my childish personality rebelled against these concepts. My mother set an example, and when I failed to live up to it she would correct me by explaining that it is better to be a gentleman than to be a bully, or to be rude, or to take more than other people—lessons a lot of people I've encountered seem never to have learned. She firmly told me to listen to my teachers, never hit a girl, and to never throw rocks or other objects. I was taught to sit still, pay attention, to be calm and quiet—things some members of Congress, clearly, never learned. When playing games with cousins, we were told to share the ball, to give everyone a chance to play. In my rearing, I in fact did not leave the confines of the house until I was at least four years old. I was not taken on an airplane as entitled parents do today, allowing their infants to terrorize other passengers by kicking seatbacks and screaming, all the while shrugging, "What do you expect me to do? He's a child." During my early years, children were simply not on airplanes. Similarly, as a small child I never went to funerals, weddings, or restaurants. People could learn a few good lessons by reviewing how things were done in the 60s.

When I was a child, my mother played perhaps the most important role in my life. She was ever-present, ever-guiding, ever-caring. My first memory of her is reaching out my hand to her while lying on

## In Memoriam: Mater Doloresa

my side in my crib or bed, and saying to her, *"Hold my hand."* But at my very young age I couldn't properly pronounce my Ds, so the words were uttered, "Ho my han." And I can still recall her grasping my small hand in hers, a larger, elegant hand, as I fell asleep. She hung our laundry outside on a line to dry. She loved this because the fresh air made everything smell like the outdoors, like new linen rinsed in spring water with a faint scent of lilac from the shrubs that surrounded our backyard. She often walked me to school, until I decided I was old enough to go on my own—at which point, for the first few days she would stand on the sidewalk and watch until I crossed the street at the end of our block. If weather was bad, she would meet me at Eight Corners, next to the Palucek Funeral Home, and take me to lunch at the little diner across the street on Grand Avenue. She often defended me when others did not; she would talk to teachers and the school principal when those individuals ignored the bullying. Those people in charge did not do their jobs. She taught me to stand up for myself at a time when she herself had no one to defend her. There were no toll-free women's help lines in the 1960s.

She made Christmas season magical for me in my early years, and I believed in St. Nicholas and Santa Claus. Sometime around the 5th of December I'd wake up to find a red mesh Christmas stocking near my bed with an orange, a Matchbox car, and some chocolates. Thinking it was all magic, that St. Nick had really been there, I looked for signs, footprints in the snow outside. On a December day when I was six years old, I came home in tears, despondent after my classmates confirmed the non-existence of Santa. She gently offered comfort then, and I began to grow up.

She lived through the Great Depression, which began when she was just ten, and it influenced her life thereafter. She worked hard at building a family. She nurtured us as children just as she helped raise her younger siblings after her father's death. She helped support her family when her father became too ill to work between 1935 and his death in 1939. After completing the eighth grade, she went to work at Wallace Press and later at Greenview Manufacturing, both in Chicago. She often fondly remembered her aunt Stella, who with her husband, uncle Frank, took my mother and her older sister on walks down Belden Avenue and through Lincoln Park and to the zoo, giving the girls new experiences on a day out. Neighbors in later years recalled "those Samp girls" with a smile, and wistfully noted how they were the talk of the neighborhood, classic sought-after beauties.

In a moment of reflection, my mother told me she had often hoped to become a school teacher or librarian. She was interested in making more of herself and guiding young minds. She was affected by tragedies, like the fire at Our Lady of the Angels School, December 1, 1958. It was a cold day, and in mid-afternoon she was outside walking casually, on her way to meet my sister at Sacred Heart School, when a woman ran by screaming that the school was on fire. Since the stranger was running in the general direction of my sister's school, our mother assumed the worst and ran all the way there, relieved to learn that it was not my sister's school after all. Still, she remembered that day all her life. After the fire, reports remained in the news for quite some time, that many children had died. That tragedy weighed heavily in her memory. But she remained young at heart, and I remember not thinking anything of her age, even as she entered her 80s. In her 60s, when I was in my 20s, she was ageless. In her 70s, as I was in my 30s, she was elegant and dignified, like Queen Elizabeth. In her 80s, my 40s, she began

## In Memoriam: Mater Doloresa

to slow down, but her complexion was still radiant, she still kept her hair styled. She finally accepted help with her grass cutting and yard work at about this time. I only noticed that she was in decline starting in her 87$^{th}$ year.

Mother was not a great cook, no gourmet. Her pork chops were on the dry side, and meat loaf was notoriously simple with no seasoning. Her potato salad, though, was second to none. Her recipes were simple and straightforward. She told me of the time she wrote to Campbell's Soup Company to discuss her vegetable soup recipe, which she happened to include with the letter. She always made this soup with large chunks of potato, green beans, corn, chopped tomatoes, turnips, onion, carrots, celery, generally any vegetable was an option. She told me that she never heard from Campbell's Soup regarding her letter, but that a year or two afterward they came out with their "chunky"-style line. It's pretty clear to me that the company simply used her recipe as a starting point, but never bothered to thank her or, more importantly, compensate her. She made a lovely sponge cake, slightly lemony, with powdered sugar topping that was simply divine, only it was such a production that I only recall her making this once or twice. Her chocolate-chip flat cake, kind of like a sheet of brownies, was rich with cinnamon and brown sugar. She would surprise me with this on the day I came home for a break from academy or from university. After baking this cake, the house smelled particularly welcoming; the fragrance of cinnamon and warm chocolate wafting through the house made it smell more like home on a chilly fall afternoon.

Conversations with mom were like sun dappled on waves, each sparkled refraction a lilting comment or laugh. Being fun-loving, she enjoyed the comedy of Carol Burnett, Tim Conway and Harvey

Korman, Bob Hope, Lucille Ball, Vicki Lawrence, and Don Rickles, all of whom appeared on the *Carol Burnett Show*. She loved it when they couldn't finish a skit because they were laughing so hard—Korman doubled over or Burnett facing the wall shaking with laughter. Then there were the more realistic antics and prejudices of Archie and Edith Bunker—who resembled my parents almost like they were relatives, precisely why I think she found them so funny. And there's the bold Bea Arthur of *Maude* along with Betty White of *The Golden Girls*, Judy Dench in *As Time Goes By*, and the incomparable Patricia Routledge of *Keeping Up Appearances*. She loved their comedy and planned evenings around their shows. It was all of a period—the 1970s and 1980s.

Not only did she enjoy funny TV shows, but my mother loved music, too. Country music singer Lynn Anderson with her song, "I Never Promised You a Rose Garden," the boy singer Heinji of Germany, and she regularly tuned in for the Chicago-area German radio program that was broadcast only on Sundays as she prepared the day's big meal. I recall her singing along to "Chanson d'amour," while the beef stew simmered on the stove. Then there was "Una Paloma Blanca." On the chorus, we'd all sing along from different rooms in the house—I can still hear the rapturous melody. This song was always played at mom's favorite restaurant, Chicago Brauhaus, on Lincoln Avenue, where we'd stop on weekends for a German lunch of Nuremburger brats, red cabbage, and German-style fried potatoes—throwing caution to the wind regarding cholesterol. The Brauhaus was decorated to replicate a typical German restaurant and bar, so that as you ate lunch you'd almost imagine yourself in Munich. She loved the music I played as well—Bach, Beethoven, Chopin, Brahms. She visited me when I was in college, and heard

## In Memoriam: Mater Doloresa

the Chicago Symphony Orchestra perform Dvořák's New World Symphony. She came to at least one department recital I participated in when I played a Brahms Rhapsody. Years later, David and I took her to see the *Nutcracker* ballet at Christmastime.

Over the course of her life, it doesn't seem like my mom got to go to many places, but she did enjoy travel and seeing different sights. She and Fred visited my sister and her husband in California at least once, touring vineyards. Photos from one trip tell me she had a nice time there, that she was at home in the California scenery and relished the visit with her daughter and son-in-law. My parents visited Europe twice; the first time, travelling to Switzerland and several other European countries for their 25th anniversary, and then we visited Poland in 1978. Our shared family experience, complete with dreams, broken or achieved, goals, hopes, plans made, successes, limitations (some surpassed and some accepted), disappointments and joys, laughter and tears, experiences and memories bonded and molded us more deeply than we realize. She came to terms with all this, overcoming some odds, was content, and found her place in this world. In fact, given her resources and upbringing, she was quite successful and happy being a homemaker and mother.

At our family home in Brookfield, she kept the house and yard clean and nicely trimmed for the forty years she lived there. She took care of the lawn and garden, partly out of love for the outdoors and the green space, but also because my father refused to touch it. He worked all day at Western Electric, so he was not lifting a finger when he came home. She liked to sit outside after the dinner dishes were washed, dried, and put away. Listening to the birds, and feeling the breeze took her back to an earlier time when all her family were together. She loved her peonies and morning glories, and would anticipate with joy their blooms every year.

Above and beyond the day-to-day errands, cooking, cleaning and yard work, my mother spent time reminding my father and me of the importance of being honest, reliable people. She valued integrity. She taught me that honesty is more important than always being right. She gave me many gifts, too many to name, both material and spiritual. I was often the self-centered child, in my adolescence and even in early adulthood, too caught up in my momentary needs to be concerned with hers. *My own fault, my own most grievous fault.* I was quick to accept all her many gifts, and so quick to be off and about my own business. Mother lived to see me become a success, and I am thankful to her for all she did to help me, from the example she provided, to defending me from the offenses of bullies at the terrible primary school in Brookfield, to helping me pay off student loans. It took her generation to launch the next generation into success in the U.S. I cannot adequately express my gratitude.

I think my mother knew I was thankful, without words, but whenever I visited or called she might have known. For we are family and nothing can really separate us. We know each other, even though we may have moments of surprise or questions, disagreements, or celebrations. We know each other deeply. I am hopeful and confident that she knew my thankfulness, just as I know she was thankful for me. Before she died, she said, "God bless you," with tenderness and depth of meaning like a benediction, knowing that it was probably the last time she could say this to me. She spoke this as she sat peacefully on her sofa, poised in dignity, noble and quiet.

## In Memoriam: Mater Doloresa

How is it possible to summarize a relationship with a parent, or with anyone really, whom you've known your entire life? Nothing is adequate, no words, and even memory fails somehow. But over the course of time, it's the being there, being present that seems to count most. I recall clearly that I sat with her on Sunday, May 25, 2008, and after lunch I took her for a stroll—she in a wheelchair and I walking, pushing her along in the garden at the Methodist Home, an overcrowded nursing home where she was recovering from pneumonia. We sat under a small tree, a Japanese maple, its branches outstretched. As we settled into conversation, a bird began chirping unusually melodically and beautifully—a bird I could swear was not native to the Midwest. The bird landed on a branch nearby and remained for quite some time, perhaps ten minutes, entertaining us, as dappled sunlight cast gentle pools of pink and golden light upon us through the branches of the red-leafed tree. I began to imitate the bird, as is my silly habit, chirping and clucking back at it above our heads, no more than a few feet away. Mother sat there, humored, as I chirped along. She laughed like she did so often before, a lilting, soft laugh that faded slightly at the end, and said to me, "Even when you were a child, you always were chirping to the animals, talking to them." She was there when I rescued five baby rabbits from a lawn mower, but sadly they could not thrive without their own mother and one by one died.

Back in her room, I gave her a manicure, washed her hands, soaked them, trimmed her nails and moisturized her skin. To my memory, she always had hard-working hands, worn, wrinkled, aged well beyond her own age, two knuckles quite pronounced in their position, molded where the thumb and forefinger form to the shape of a lawn-mower handle, rake or broomstick. I wanted to ease those hands, but time moves beyond our control, and I didn't get the chance. That was something outside my ability. I'm proud to be this woman's son—glad that she is my mother.

\* \* \*

And then there was another visit.

The place was in mist. There was no sense of location, I was not in a room and I was not outdoors. Although the surroundings were vague and out of focus, this did not disturb me. There was no sense of weather, no wind, no cold, and no heat. There was a feeling that it wasn't night, and yet it wasn't day. Light emanated from some central place, undefined, like a physical presence. I was in the light, and in the mist at the same moment. But there was no sense of time. It was not night and it was not day. The place was quiet, peaceful, a place to rest, and it was serenely quiet.

Then I saw her—my mother. She was wearing one of her favorite dresses, pink, pale pink speckled with white, and light emanated from the space and from us. We were unified in the light. Her hair was beautiful, like she usually had it set at the beauty parlor, dignified, light, gentle curls—her hair was always fine, like mine. I inherited my baby-fine hair from her. She stood there next to me and was speechless, that is to say that she did not say a word. I did not greet her, and I was not surprised to see her. She did not speak to me at first. I was not surprised, and did not speak as if surprised. It was as if this was entirely natural, a thing of nature, expected even, not to be confounded with reason, cause and effect, what, where, why. We just were. She was present, with me, and I was present, with her.

## In Memoriam: Mater Doloresa

The light I observed came from nowhere, yet it was everywhere, the light filled the space, even with the mist, and the space was radiant. Mother's dress was luminous, as if light came from within the fabric, and her face was fine, opalescent. She was about the age when I was in high school, perhaps 55 to 60, younger than I am today, and I understood this, and it was not a surprise—it simply was.

At last, we greeted one another, not with words but as if we knew each other's presence and nodded acknowledgment. We did not face each other straight on, but seemed to be side by side, as if observing some scene, as yet unrevealed. Then I spoke and said something, the words not really coming from my mouth, but more like projected thoughts, "Mother, how are you here? You really can't be here, can you?" And this was in complete peace and calm and spoken with entire quietness. She slowly turned to me and said, "I needed to see you, to check on you." This was spoken, or I heard it, not directly from her mouth but simply there, sensed. Like she was there, seen, present but perhaps not present in some way. Aware of myself, I questioned again, quietly, in peace, "Why are you here? How can you be here? You are gone, and yet here you are."

She repeated, "I needed to check on you."

Without a breath, confused yet calm, I stated quietly, "It must have been difficult for you to come here."

She nodded slowly and said, "Yes, it was difficult. But I wanted to check on you. I wanted to see you." She continued, "I love you," the words whispered, present.

And I replied in quiet, in peace, placing my arms over her shoulders to embrace, "I have always loved you."

Her visit was not long, and the scene evaporated into dream, then I awoke, warm, peaceful, calm, facing a new day, aware that this dream was unusual in that I was so aware of my place and my interaction with my mother, a brief conversation from beyond, real but unreal, not surprising but welcome and simply there. The day was August 5, 2021, thirteen years, two months and nine days after her death.

I believe that this vision was not a dream. It did not have the fantastic, illogical, inexplicable, stream of consciousness, jumping from one bizarre scene to another, skipping from place to place or time to time inexplicability that dreams have. This was a visit, a conversation, and it was set in a place, albeit undefinable or unknown to me, yet it was a real place. And she was there, present. And I was there, present. And there was peace.

\* \* \*

In the year after mother's death, my sister and I gradually disposed of her dresses, scarves, coats, furniture, and other possessions. The *National Geographic* collection filled my car three times, as we shuttled various items to the local Goodwill donation center. She no longer needed the clothes, books, glassware. Life had become a burden, and she set that burden down and took up another journey on May 27, 2008. A difficult thing for us was to realize that it's okay to give away, discard, even forget the physical possessions, because they no longer mattered to her, and they should not matter to us, except we cling to some objects as reminders of her presence in our shared past. I have the old washboard my mother used before she got her first washing machine, also the old ceramic "God bless our home" plaque, the Seth Thomas mantle clock, and some old photos to remind me of my ancestors

## In Memoriam: Mater Doloresa

and my mother, kept securely, discreetly, archived. My sister has mother's bureau and double dresser, mother's (and grandmother's before her) wooden plant table, a few lace table cloths made by ancestors in Poland or just after their arrival in Chicago in the late 1800s, whom our own mother would have known in their old age, even touched, the finger prints faded but still there, passing their presence on to us—reaching out to us as if to speak, to say things that had not been said before.

Like a religious relic, I have guarded the last birthday card my mother sent me. She signed it and added a personal note, "May you have a long and fulfilled life. God bless you always." Thanks for this, I told her, it shows unconditional acceptance and joy for me.

I pray that God grants the peace and light promised to us all in the heavenly kingdom which is beyond our limited human understanding. I take comfort in these thoughts: For whoever believes in Him shall not perish but shall have everlasting life.[2] God, she believes in you. Look not on her shortcomings, forgive her sins, known and unknown, and look on her kindness, her deeper being, the fact that she was a humble person, a servant of yours and ours who helped us when we were sick and in any need. Lord, reward her in your kingdom with every blessing of eternity, rest, refreshment, joy and peace.

Every time I see a peony, I think of my mother.

*Rest eternal grant unto her, O Lord; and let light perpetual shine upon her. May her soul, + and the souls of all the departed, through the mercy of God, rest in peace. Amen.*[3]

# My Father and Mr. Hyde

Even as an infant, I had a highly developed sense of danger. Sudden, loud noises practically made me levitate out of my crib. Doctors said I was highly strung, nervous, but could not explain the cause of this to my parents. By the age of one, I had developed an aversion to my father. I reacted violently to his smell when he tried to pick me up. I am told I even slapped him once as an infant, and I would often become stiff as a board—a wooden plank—when I resisted his touch or his efforts to hold onto me.

It isn't that I disliked my father. I wanted to be with him, wanted to sit on his lap, wanted him to take me along wherever it was he went every day. But his smell was off-putting, even to an infant. It was the combined odors of skin oil, Fels Naptha soap, Lucky Strikes, and whiskey.

We never were able to get close, to bond, my father and me. Seems like we were orbs revolving in some planetary system, forever passing on our separate rotations and always moving away from one another. He was part of another time and place, separate from me, and as the years added up one after another our distance grew more pronounced. This comes as no surprise when our secrets are revealed—secrets exorcised by the telling.

My parents met at Greenview Manufacturing Company, where my mother had already been working for a few years and was at that time in charge of the tool shed, a secured room where portable, expensive work gadgets were kept. When employees needed a specific tool, they had to check it out, sign for it, and my mother supervised this operation. She had also worked as a packer, a sort-of general laborer, when she first started at Greenview in the late-1930s, and had been promoted once already to punch press operator, a relatively dangerous job requiring steady hands and alert attention.

During World War II, my father was a sergeant in the U.S. Army Air Force (today's Air Force became a separate branch of the military after WW II), and was stationed in Agra, India. He joined the force on February 10, 1942, and was discharged October 9, 1945, after serving in Squadron R, in the 3502$^{nd}$ AAF Base Unit. His Army Enlisted Record indicates he was an Instrument Repair Man and attended army school to be an Airplane Instrument Mechanic. He also received a Good Conduct medal. He died on January 3, 2003, in hospice care in La Grange, Illinois. In the end, his war service entitled him to a two-gun honor guard at his burial.

Fred and Doloresa were married on June 12, 1947, and St. Josephat's church was decked out with garlands and bouquets of white and pink roses, chrysanthemums, and lilies. The few photos show a crowd on the bride's side of the aisle, but only a handful of people on the groom's. Family legend tells the story of the priest inquiring about where the bride was, perhaps ten minutes after the wedding was scheduled to begin, as the organist played the preludes a second time. After a quick search, someone realized that the bride

## My Father and Mr. Hyde

was left at home. And so, one of the undertaker's men from Ewald's Funeral Home drove the hearse over to grandma's house on Janssen Avenue and found Doloresa waiting there patiently for her ride to church. What a scene it must have been, a hearse pulling up to St. Josephat's and a bride getting out from the passenger side. After the nuptials, the reception was held at grandma's house, and people enjoyed the wedding dinner in shifts, eight at a time, because there was only room for eight to sit at the dining table. There is a photo of mother with her veil off and her face radiant. She was a natural beauty in her day. Aunts and cousins have told me that my parents were very much in love.

In the immediate years after their marriage, my parents lived at 1746 W. Diversey Parkway in Chicago, in a ground floor apartment immediately below Fred's father, John. My sister was the first-born, and she arrived on July 9, 1949. By the time I was born, my sister was 11 and in fifth grade at St. Bonaventure School. I came along in 1961, during the great blizzard on January 28. Sometime between our two births trouble began. In 1967, my father filed for divorce, but, after witnesses were called and testimony reviewed, the court denied his request and issued a Cease and Desist order. It's been helpful to remind myself that our parents were people, independent individuals, before we became part of their lives.

Father was 46 when I was born, and he had undiagnosed smoking-related health issues, so when it came time for me to play baseball he was already well into middle age and barely able to keep up with me, let alone teach me how to play ball. We played catch once, and he was sweating and out of breath in no time. But he did manage to teach me to ride a bike. I was about seven when we were in Sears one day, at Oak Brook Center, a sprawling outdoor mega mall—in fact one of the first of its kind—and we were possibly shopping for shoes when I saw an electric-blue boy's bike with high handlebars and a matching blue banana seat with a big red reflector at the back. I lit up. I had to have it, and dad knew it, and he bought it then and there. We took it home in the trunk of the Chevy Biscayne, and he promised he'd teach me how to ride.

As he was a hands-off father, my dad thought I might easily learn to ride all on my own. From a work pal, he acquired an old rusty set of training wheels that didn't quite fit so the bike leaned about ten degrees left or right, but if I was riding it down the sidewalk I managed to keep it upright. In about a week I was dissatisfied with the training wheels, found them more burden than help, and asked my father to remove them. But I kept falling down without the trainers. Then my dad tried to push me from behind and run with me to keep me upright. This took about three or four tries. He was winded from smoking all those Lucky Strikes and couldn't keep up, so he had to let go of me after only a few running strides. I'd gradually lose control and fall. But around the fourth or fifth attempt something clicked. Suddenly, I grasped how to control the pedals to keep my speed, and coordinated my arms to steer properly. I was off. I flew down the sidewalk and stopped at the end of the block. This time I didn't fall. I was on top of the world. This new skill made me feel powerful, and a sense of independence took hold of me. I could go places on a bike.

Except I was not allowed to go off my block. Well, what good is that? I would wait, perhaps weeks, or even months, before I decided to go off our block and explore further. The rules were established, and I broke those rules whenever I decided that my own judgment was more relevant.

## My Father and Mr. Hyde

*Bless me father, for I have sinned.* In my mind, the confession is between me and God, no one else is necessary. But then the story won't be known if it's kept a secret. And the confession will remain silent.

Telling the story of a difficult, even painful period in my life, exposing it to fresh air and light of day helps make sense of it so that someone new might learn that secrets can be hidden by a kind face, honest eyes, a quick smile. Looking back, I never quite knew if conversations with my father would be jovial—a bit of fun and games, or foreboding—like Walpurgisnacht, with a bonfire of accusations. Like the tale of George and Martha in Albee's *Who's Afraid of Virginia Woolf?*, the telling is the exorcism.[1]

\* \* \*

My first memory of my father is of me sitting on his lap at the kitchen table. He is behind me, holding me, reluctantly as usual. He just came home from working at his father's house on Diversey Parkway, a short bus ride away from our home on Winchester. He is still smoking Lucky Strikes, and the ashtray sits to our left on the neat, cloth-covered table, a trail of smoke grazes my ear, wafts around to my nose with a sharp burning that makes it difficult to breathe, closes my sinuses, and stings my eyes. Still I sit there, content for some attention at the kitchen table. Then I am lifted, I assume by my mother, but there may be another in the room, my sister perhaps, and I am placed on the floor to play. Crawling about the room, I look up in fear at a great big brown-colored steel box—the central oil heater which glows yellow, amber, and red. I see the bold gold starburst pattern in the linoleum as I crawl about, feel its coolness to the touch. Then I am lifted again, taken to the bed with high bars on it that sits between my parents' larger bed and the wall. I close my eyes.

Wakened. Loud voices in a distant room. The bedroom door is closed, but I see light from the kitchen sending streaks of light under the door, shadows of motion, someone walking back and forth, pacing, on the other side. Does not feel right. "You're hurting me," someone says. Mother comes to bed alone, holds my hand briefly after I ask her to, "Hol my han." I am two or three at this time and unaware of the disagreements on the other side of that door.

Years later, when I am allowed to watch television past dark, I am fascinated and drawn to films about houses with secret rooms, priest holes, and hidden passages between the walls. In our cape cod in Brookfield, there are four such secret places for me to hide as a child. I am glad they are there. I am able to hide from the one who calls himself my father. To the outside world—neighbors, school teachers, priests, aunts and uncles—he appears to care, looks concerned, asks pertinent questions about my development, my interests, my classes. In private, he is someone else, his face changes, reddens, bloats, he smells of whiskey.

In warm weather, I feel free. I am allowed to be outside of the house until almost sunset. I feel safe among the bushes, and the shrubbery still hides me when my mother calls my name from the back door of the house. I know it must be dinner time, and so I return to the house, tentatively sit at the kitchen table where I eat in silence. My father's food turns cold while he has yet another Seagram's in his basement lair, a place I do not like to go. It smells of whiskey and damp. I think I've seen a gun there. There are oil cans, odd tools strewn about, and a ramshackle desk with no draw-

## My Father and Mr. Hyde

ers and a lamp bolted to its side. Mother calls to him and there is no answer. As we eat, my mother asks me where I've been, what did I do today, what friends did I play with, and if I learned anything interesting in school. We grow silent as we hear the father's footsteps climb from the basement heavily, slowly. A leaden cloud settles over us. The evening at home has begun.

Conversations with my father were usually like thunderstorms. Things that I sense I should not hear are said. Things that I am certain cannot be right are said—*barked*—at my mother, even at me. Accusations. Bad words. In school I am learning new words every day. The words have meaning. The words I hear in the evening are often hurtful, purposely used to degrade, and as a young child even I know they are used as weapons. *Not good enough! Dumb! Stupid! Never amount to anything!* At five years old, I am smart enough to know these words are bad, and also that they are untrue. At five years old, I know I have to do something to save myself, to save my mother, yet I understand that I am powerless, and so I calculate how long I must wait before I can leave. Secretly at night I write numbers on a note pad I have hidden under my mattress—an exercise to plan an escape. I am aware of the number eighteen, that I must wait until I am that old before I can do anything. Lying still, I count the years on my fingers until I fall asleep.

*I wish you were never born. I should have never married you. You're hurting me, stop that.* Terrible words strung together in haste, in anger, or in despair.

*I wish I had a different father. You are not my father.*

As I continue to grow, I begin to cultivate my imagination. At first, it's just magazines, copies of *Architectural Digest*—I have no idea how I got a copy of this—and as I turn the pages and look at the lovely decorated rooms on the page, I escape there, so organized, planned, with every beautiful thing in its place. I somehow live there, in the magazine. I am increasingly quiet and stay in my room where I arrange my books and a few objects, everything in its place. I paint my room sky blue. My space occupies a corner of the house, and it looks just like a room in that magazine. My windows frame secluded, suburban views of pine trees and wild flowers. I also read *National Geographic* magazines cover to cover, transporting myself to far-off places, and have my small but growing collection of books which offer escape, stored neatly in my mid-century modern white bookcase.

On a Saturday when I am about 15 or 16, I have practiced the piano for much of the day, and later in the evening Svengoolie is to host Creature Features on TV. No doubt it will be an entertaining black and white horror film. I anticipate it eagerly, imagining that it may be a mummy, a werewolf, or a vampire that will take my imagination to flight on this evening. The father has been distant, quiet all day, in his basement hideout. After the movie has started, its eerie music and clever cinematography setting the scene, I hear heavy steps coming up the basement stairs, a stumble for a moment, a bang, then suddenly he is beside me, listing a bit, almost unrecognizable—the face swollen, his expression one of sweating anger, and a fetid odor rises from his skin. There is a slight aura of danger in the room as he sits down on the piano bench and, for a moment, seems to watch the film on TV. I restrain my nerves, relax a bit and think for once he will be calm, will sit for a few minutes and enjoy this with me. The fragile peace is broken when he leans toward me, breath like a distillery, and Mr. Hyde tells me to turn off the TV, growls lowly that I am under *his* roof and therefore will do

## My Father and Mr. Hyde

as *he* tells me. I hesitate, so Mr. Hyde raises his voice like an angry general, "If you don't do as I say right now, I will chop up this piano and burn it in the yard, piece by piece." Heart pounding, I keep looking at the TV; I try to remain calm, steady, disconnected from this assault, and when at last I turn to reply, I calmly and with decisiveness tell him, "Fine, do what you want. But if you lay a hand on my mother again, I swear I will kill you with my bare hands."

Now he turns quiet, taken aback surely, perhaps calculating a next step. And Mr. Hyde is gone. I believe he finally understands what verbal abuse is now that it is directed at him, at last. Like the aftermath of an exorcism, he seems calm, aware of himself again. After years of receiving threats and verbal violence, I could take it no longer. I knew that if I let it continue, it would likely only get worse. Looking back, I momentarily feel the shame, regret, for conscience tells me I shouldn't have spoken to my father in such a manner. But then he never should have said the things he said, acted in the ways he acted. What goes around comes around. I feel no real regret—he never hit my mother again.

*"Fear no more the frown o' th' great, Thou art past the tyrant's stroke ...." (Cymbeline, Act IV, Scene ii)*[2]

I could end his story here, but it would be incomplete. I'll share another side to the story to peel back the hard crust and reveal other facets about the man, my father. There were many times when he showed genuine concern, helped me even. He took time off from work to find a new school for me when I was in fifth grade. He drove with me to Collegedale, Tennessee, to collect my property so I could move back to Illinois and attend a new university. He encouraged me to study, explained that travel was a great educator and even enthusiastically wrote out the check for my first trip to England in high school, at that time an affordable $400.00—airfare and lodging included. He was enthusiastic when I told him of a skydiving trip I took. We talked about other journeys to faraway places, and he told me with excitement that he always wanted to visit Australia. My mother, listening to our conversation, only added, "You should go. As for me, I'm not taking a nineteen-hour flight. That's just too far." There are good memories, albeit only a handful. He was changeable, could go from jovial to belligerent over the span of a single breath, and so I was always careful around him, watchful.

Years after his death, as I sorted through a small box of his belongings, among the military medals and memorabilia I found his wallet. Tucked inside, behind his pilot's license and his National Geographic Society membership card, along with his Social Security card and his Masons Life Member card, was a small photograph—my high school senior portrait. This discovery startled me—took my breath for a moment. Was he proud of me, that he kept this photo? I assume so, though in day-to-day life he certainly didn't show it. But why else would one keep such a photo? I keep that wallet as I would a religious relic.

After I left university, indeed after I was established in my career, my father acted more calmly, more congenially, and actually seemed to be interested in my life. He no longer used his old dismissive judgment, "You'll never amount to anything." He asked about my work and seemed dumbfounded when I explained the writing and editing process, or discussed magazine production workflow. Shaking his head, he said, "Wow, I can't imagine it. You do *all that*

## My Father and Mr. Hyde

on a computer?"—eyes focusing on some far-off point, staring into space, as if trying to picture the world I occupied. He accepted my boyfriend, my partner, David, with acquiescence and treated him kindly, as if he knew he had been beaten, or at least that history had taken its course and this could not be changed.

On a special visit to my parents' home—my sister visiting from the west coast where she had been living for thirty years—we prepared a family dinner. We were all together again, the family of four. As my sister Bernie and I put dinner on the table, my mother smiled with joy. This was something she had done for us countless times, an infinite litany of meals. Through her smile and light conversation, I could see echoes of pain in her eyes as we sat at the same table we'd sat at so many times over the decades. And my father talked of his life, as if knowing he was nearing the end of his time. This dinner was around his 87$^{th}$ birthday, and he told us, "I've lived, had a good job, a wife, my children are educated. When I die, I'll be gone, I won't exist. So, just burn me. I don't want a funeral, no visitation. What's that for anyway?" In the end, we followed his wishes and had no visitation. The Illinois Cremation Society handled all the details.

My father's long-lost brother, Leo, joined us at the *après*-cremation luncheon we held at one of the finer restaurants in La Grange. His visit came as a surprise, as I'd never met this uncle and had only heard father's stories about the "good-for-nothing" siblings. *Honestly, I thought he was dead.* As we dined on salmon filet and crisp steamed vegetables, uncle Leo asked my mother an odd question: "So, wasn't the house in my father John's name? Did he leave any money?" My mother seemed ready for this, and didn't miss a beat. Without even stopping to put down her flatware, she quietly said,

"Leo, no, the house is not in John's name, and frankly, there's nothing left for you," and with that returned her attention to her salmon and vegetable medley. We never heard from uncle Leo again.

Several weeks after my dad's inurnment at Graceland Cemetery, our cousin John, the man who gave me my first tour of the family funeral home all those years ago, called me at work and asked if I was free for lunch. We had often met for lunch when John needed to submit death certificates to City Hall, apply for an exhumation permit, or run other errands downtown, so it was no surprise that he asked if I was free that particular day. It was a bright, unseasonably warm February day, and we lunched in Greek Town at the always-popular Athena Restaurant. We talked—a pleasant conversation, really—chatting about nothing in particular, my work and his, this and that, how the funeral business isn't what it once was, how the Polish neighborhood where the Baran Funeral Home stood was now changing, mostly Hispanic families moving in and the business declining.

I was savoring my Mediterranean Shrimp entrée when the question came, asked in an almost breezy, casual manner: "Wasn't your parents' house in your grandfather's name? Did he leave money for the family?" *Had I heard correctly?* Wasn't this the same question that old uncle Leo asked my mom? *She's going to laugh when I tell her about this!* Putting down my fork, I set the record straight—hoping it was for the last time. "No, John, my parents' house is *not* in grandfather's name. He's dead, you know! And so there's nothing for you or anyone else; whatever is left belongs to my mother." He was visibly taken aback—I was perfectly clear in my answer. I nearly laughed, though, at the time recalling how I hadn't believed my father, how I had thought he was imagining

## My Father and Mr. Hyde

things, perhaps making up dramatic stories—decorating the family lore—when he had spoken many years before of relatives crawling out of the woodwork looking for money. The unapologetic nerve! The audacity! These relatives had no shame. And whenever I recall that conversation, I think of my father, and I smile.

# The Three-Ring Circus

Blazing a trail into the business world with a liberal arts degree was a challenge at first—even my parents thought I was clowning around at the time. Seriously, I didn't know if I'd ever stop needing to prove myself. Representatives at placement firms and headhunters had no idea what to do with a guy with degrees in Music and English. *Wasn't it their job to cleverly find appropriate career opportunities for their clients?* So, I tried my most authoritative voice and explained that having an English degree meant that I had verbal analytical skills—I could read and write, sort fact from fiction, and that these skills were necessary for success in business. Yet, all they were interested in at first was my typing speed. What a slap in the face! I soldiered on, though, trying the juggling act as a writer for a public relations firm, then moving to a high-wire act in marketing. Eventually, I found my way. The fact is, though, in more than one job I felt underpaid, manipulated, or exploited—if it wasn't one thing, it was another. One boss even said, "This is a competitive business. You're paying your dues"—something unheard of today. Yet I was hopeful, always looking to succeed at what was in front of me, and then imagining where that experience might lead. With each job disappointment, I'd only chalk it up to experience, and use that awareness as I searched, like an archaeologist, for that hidden, rare opportunity. Diligence and determination were key to my success. I kept in touch with headhunters and people like myself at other companies, always seeking information that might lead to a better position. Unlike my father, who had one job for thirty years, I worked for seven employers. When I'd cheerfully announce that I'd found a new, better job, my mother would shake her head and say, "Why can't you keep your job? Stay there; they'll promote you." And I'd explain that, apparently, at that time—in the 1980s and 90s—people usually had to move to another company to find that promotion, that step up the ladder.

With a degree in English, and interests in magazine publishing, photography, books and other creative endeavors, I envisioned myself one day at *Architectural Digest*, except Paige Rense wasn't going anywhere anytime soon. She had a firm chokehold on her position as Editor since the 1970s and was still at the helm of that publication. I periodically talked with representatives at placement firms in Chicago and New York, and every conversation seemed to point, almost predictably, to dead ends—either this publisher only hired after an internship (nonpaying), or that publisher didn't hire entry-level people, or—the worst humiliation of all—the salary range was so low a person would need multiple roommates just to cover rent. One east coast placement specialist breezily intoned, "I've got a few internship possibilities here that might interest you." I was skeptical, though; "Do any of them come with a paycheck?" I boldly asked. "Hmm, I see your concern," was the only response she could muster, which answered my question. My

## The Three-Ring Circus

next head hunter wheezed in a three-pack-a-day New Jersey accent about another nonpaying internship—croaking, *"It's a really good one!"* I could hear her exhaling smoke. I replied, "I'm sure it is, but I'm only interested in full-time paid positions." During my early job searches, I learned that it was not uncommon for a magazine to get over three hundred résumés for a single entry-level editorial position. Of course, if you can imagine the sheer height of that stack, you begin to realize how daunting the task was for the person doing the hiring, and so how much easier it is to just ask around and get word-of-mouth applicants. But I remained diligent and kept looking. One of these days, I thought, it'll be me who's in the right place at the right time. I bolstered myself by keeping a good perspective; someday! Someday, I'll find the job of my dreams.

I started my work life, or career such as it is, at a Public Relations firm. After of couple of years' busy work that bordered on boring, managing multiple projects like a juggling act, I finally got to write press releases, but by now I was no longer interested, felt constrained, undervalued, and decided to look for a new job. After months of writing cover letters bragging about my meager achievements with decorous prose bordering on fiction, I visited yet another placement firm, this one specializing in publishing, and shortly thereafter landed on my feet in an editorial position for a periodical. With my foot in the door, I felt that I was finally on the right track.

My new supervisor and I had a congenial relationship at first, and he would often take me to lunch at a local place we liked—Gino's East, where deep dish pizza is king. At one such lunch meeting, after taking a long sip of his Coke, he told me he thought gay or bi people make the best editors and designers—just dropped that comment like Barack Obama's mic at a White House Press Dinner.

## James Philip Baran

Taken by surprise, I didn't know what to say, so I just smiled and agreed, "I suppose that could be a valid point"—a deflection, hoping he didn't already know that I'm gay. At that time, I was firmly in the camp of keeping work and personal life separate; I had many conversations with gay friends who were harassed at work—some who had even been fired when their sexuality was discovered.

Over the years, I worked in public relations, editorial, and marketing, then in a series of engaging freelance design and writing assignments, and I even owned my own publishing consulting studio—an energizing and enjoyable Barnum and Bailey's of daily sales pitches, estimated-tax payments, contortionist production schedules, and editing projects. In other words, I was Chief Flunky and Managing Director, all in one. As time passed with weekly client lunches at white-tablecloth eateries and 16-hour workdays, spring rains turned to summer warmth, then fall leaves skittered past my office window. On one such afternoon, gazing from my window at the burnt umber and crisp gold outside, I wistfully recalled the joys of employer-provided benefits and paid vacation time. When a former work associate called me, we chatted and laughed, regaling each other with our various projects, clients, and successes. Then she mentioned she was going on a cruise, and I was jealous of those paid vacation days. We concluded our talk after she told me she wanted to pass my name along to a friend who was looking for a design "maven." Noting her interesting word choice, I let my imagination conjure the offices of *Architectural Digest* and *Vogue* as I said, "Please do, I'm always happy to explore new opportunities." I hung up, and then threw a load of towels into the washing machine. Such is the glamor of owning your own company.

## The Three-Ring Circus

A year or so later, it was again one of those deliciously warm fall days when my phone rang. I had been wistfully eyeing a boat on the river from the window at my new freelance gig, thinking about what the weekend might hold. Out of the blue, a publications executive called to introduce herself. Katherine was her name, and as we talked she inquired if I'd consider going back to full-time, working for one magazine, heading up my own department. Ignoring the warning signs and reasons why I went freelance in the first place—and since I'm gullible to a fault—I agreed to meet for a conversation, my palate whetted, my interest piqued. I visited their plush association offices on LaSalle Boulevard near the Chicago River a few days later. I could almost smell the paid vacation time.

At first, this was only a get-acquainted meeting. "I just had to meet this guy everyone's so enthusiastic about," was how she cheerfully welcomed me as we strolled down the hall from reception to her corner office. *"Everyone?" Did I have a fan club? Who was she talking to?* I perused a copy of their association magazine and indicated it was comparable to the work I was currently doing. After an hour or so of congenial conversation, I thanked her for her time, still not quite sure of the landscape. I had nearly forgotten about her when about two months later she called back, desperation barely disguised in her voice, saying her magazine design "maven" was leaving, and would I be interested in seriously discussing the position. Katherine—she'd later insist that I call her Kate—took the time to ask more detailed questions about my background, leading up to how much notice I'd need to give. I in turn asked about how things worked there, polite and careful not to be too bold, not to offend. With years of experience at this

233

point, I felt I knew what to look for—surely there was a viper under a rock somewhere, and I just had to find it. I wanted to be direct, so I asked why the maven was leaving, that sort of thing, were there issues with staff or workload? What I really wanted to ask was, "Is the status quo defended at all costs?" or, "Are there systemic problems here?" To put it in simpler terms, in today's lexicon that translates to, "How messed up is this place?" But I couldn't dare be that bold.

Kate was a good talker, though, and I liked her—maybe it's because she reminded me vaguely of my mother. She only had an indefinite idea that perhaps the maven was burnt out, or so she said, though she admitted, with a wave toward the doorway, "Well, we do have *a few* personalities around here." *Aha! A clue!* She held her cards close, though.

Kate seemed reasonable, straightforward, a shoot-from-the-hip kind of leader, and that's what reeled me in. She was interested in me, enjoyed leafing through my portfolio, employing the irresistible flattery that gets me every time, and then asked me to return the next day to meet the team—four or five editors. They were ready for me when I arrived promptly the following afternoon, all sitting at an oval conference table, an empty seat for me in their midst, while Kate paced the room. They were all smiles—sometimes nervous smiles, I'll admit—peppering the meeting with non-challenging questions here and there, such as, "Could you outline a basic editorial-to-production workflow?" I obliged. Then, "How many projects do you usually juggle at any given time?" Hmm, I tried to lighten the mood with, "Well, isn't one magazine a whole bunch of projects?" After a pause, I continued, "I just do everything I can until I find a good finishing point, then move on to another piece,

## The Three-Ring Circus

keeping them all updated on a master checklist." After the editors left, Kate enthusiastically threw up her hands and said that my experience was *exactly* what she was looking for. I asked again about "challenges," but was assured things ran smoothly in this circus.

After a couple of days, she phoned with an offer. I thought I had played hard to get, and after some negotiation on workload, salary and vacation time, I accepted the position. I felt powerful, that I had pulled a coup in securing her agreement to offload a set of responsibilities unrelated to the core job. "Don't worry about those things, the advertising materials, I've got someone here who can handle that," was all she said. *Easy peasy!* I arrived on a Monday morning, and after signing some HR paperwork, I was paraded around to meet the staff. After a long first-day luncheon, I got down to work, the ring-master of magazine production. I sorted through emails, then answered dozens of voicemails, and finally pushed several editors' submissions through the workflow. I was confident that all I had to do was whip this three-ring circus down to one ring and everything would fall into place. But balancing acts can be tricky.

This job was both the most challenging and the most rewarding during my career. Challenging, like training elephants to stand on one leg—everyone seemed to have their own work style, and their own workflow. And it was rewarding, as in being well-compensated. At last, those benefits I wanted. Four weeks of vacation. Retirement contributions every year. Health and dental! I had almost forgotten about such things. I went about each day cheerfully, keeping in mind the salary and benefits, glad that I didn't have to drum up business any longer. I was staying on top of things, and then juggling the mini projects from contributors who needed some extra help—a custom photograph or illustration for one article, extended deadlines for another. To quote Gilda Radner's character Roseanne Roseannadanna, "Well it just goes to show you, it's always something ...."[1] I had matured in this job, and crises were par for the course. Tired of being persona non grata over my hated task of establishing those pesky production deadlines—always a lose-lose gamble, I stopped asking for items, just to see what might happen. To look at it with humor, and to balance my perspective, I'd just repeat the old mantra: "It could be worse." I was eager to keep a professional and cordial attitude, though, so I usually kept my mouth shut. Over time it all became second nature, predictable even. I was smiling through the tears.

During the last years of my tenure, one of our new hires—a gregarious woman with whom I got along swimmingly—needed extensive one-on-one time with various staff to learn quickly about our association's work, how all the pieces fit together. My half day with her was spent covering magazine production workflow and relationships between our departments for materials or information handoffs—identifying the key point-persons. In today's lexicon, we spoke about our "teams," "ramping up," and "deliverables." I found this detached management rhetoric amusing, like a deflection from understanding the actual work. I was sad to see her leave; she was talented but resigned in about a year, which, in turn, resulted in a jittery atmosphere in her department until a replacement came aboard and was "brought up to speed."

Over the years, there were new hires, including a complete transition from one management team to another, new human resources staff, new departmental directors, people retired or left for other opportunities, and, as anyone might expect, there were

## The Three-Ring Circus

occasional terminations. All these human transitions inevitably contributed to workplace evolution, new ways of doing things—a new work culture. Our new executive brought with her a new vision, one that encouraged input and perspectives from all of us. We had monthly staff meetings, regular opportunities to get to know each other, learn about the latest organization challenges and goals, and to acknowledge each other's contributions. Lunch was often brought in—now that's progress! Instead of a "Do-as-I-say-or-I'll-replace-you!" attitude, the new management approach was to thank us for work well done and to ask if there's anything we might need to make our jobs easier. *Imagine!*

Annual performance reviews rolled around every year in the fall. It was during one such review period that I noticed that everyone else in my department had already had their meetings, and I wondered what the holdup could be with mine. I recalled that only a few weeks past someone from another department had been terminated, their departure sudden, late one afternoon, and they were not seen again. Just as this idea took hold and festered in my thoughts—connecting some imaginary dots—my phone rang late in the afternoon shortly before the end of the business day. Modern technology being what it is, my office phone's LCD screen identified the caller—Charlotte, our chief executive. I caught my breath. My heart skipped a beat. *What does she want with me, and at 4:00 in the afternoon?* I answered my phone tentatively and heard a cheery voice pipe in with, "Hey, got a minute? Pop on down to my office—I want to have a word." I staggered down the hall, hands sweating, heart pounding. *Is this what it feels like to have a heart attack, I wondered?* I "popped" my head in at a friend's office, bracing myself against her doorjamb, "Have you

237

seen our department head lately? His office door's been closed all day." Distractedly, she looked up from her laptop, "No, what's wrong?" My throat dry, I croaked, "Nothing, I just wondered." Somewhat relieved, I continued down the hall. As I approached the executive suite, I felt a tightness in my chest and heard my blood pulsing through my brain—*ba-thump, ba-thump*. Charlotte was on the phone but waved me in and pointed to a chair while she completed her call. As I settled into the plush leather cushions opposite the Big Boss, I scanned the shelves on one wall, sagging under the weight of crystal awards and other honors.

She began to speak. "I'll get to the point. We're both busy, and I know you deal with a lot here—," and as her voice trailed off, there was a ringing in my ears. *That damn tinnitus!* I was confused and hadn't quite heard. *What was that?* She handed me an envelope across her expansive desk, and, with my hand shaking, the first thought that came to mind was that it might be a severance letter. *So, this is how it's done!* She could see I was trembling, and with a diamond-encrusted wave urged me, "Go on, open it," as if to mock me. Inside was a check—and a personal Thank You note. To say I was surprised is an understatement. With sweat running down my temples, I choked out, "I thought I was being terminated." She threw her head back and laughed loudly, deep burnished blonde curls tossed over her shoulder, clearly finding this funny, and asked with a chuckle, "Why on earth would you have such an idea?" I explained that it's not every day I got a call to come down to the executive suite, and she assured me with a smile, "That's because I don't *need* to talk with you every day." In her opinion, bonuses were an appropriate acknowledgment of the team's successful work during a challenging year. After a pleasant

## The Three-Ring Circus

conversation, both of us laughing over my momentary misunderstanding, I thanked her and glided back to my office, lightheaded, dizzy.

As time went on, I was promoted, there were salary increases and occasional bonuses, which added to my overall satisfaction. I realized I was held in some esteem. But still, after ten years I also realized that, really, the challenges were the same every month, twelve times a year—it was a monthly magazine, after all. We'd get together for a content meeting to discuss the next issue's articles, and the team would go their separate ways and not be seen for two weeks as they worked diligently on their content. It's anyone's guess how—or if—this works now, in the post-pandemic time of unsupervised remote work and possibly a four-day work week.

After years of this now-predictable fun house, I decided I needed to learn some new tricks and embark on a new adventure, achieve a new level of empowerment. So, I met with a financial advisor and, together, we strategized and designed a plan. This plan involved numbers, in fact a number of days and a number of dollars. Then I created a custom countdown calendar and posted it above my credenza. As the days, weeks, and months wore on, daily office dramas became white noise. It was a pleasure to look at the calendar periodically, pondering the future. Each date on it was coded with a small number in an upper corner, and the numbers went in descending order over time. It started with 890, and before I knew it I was marking off key milestones of 500 days, then 300, then 200, until one day the number was 30. It was quite by coincidence that on that day our annual 401(k) deposit was made, so I carefully logged into my retirement account and checked the balance. Numbers confirmed, I reached for my phone and called my supervisor.

I still remember the conversation we had. "Hi, are you busy? Is it okay if I pop in for a minute?" And I walked down to his office, somehow light on my feet, head high, back erect, possibly a little light-headed. I closed the door and took a seat. He hadn't finished his morning coffee and had a curious, distracted look about himself. I began slowly, "My husband David and I've been talking and have decided that we need more time for ourselves. We need more time to do the things that give us the most satisfaction." He looked confused for a moment, as I recall, dumbfounded even, so I elaborated. "You see," I paused and smiled, "I'm giving you my notice." Thirty days later, I said cheerful goodbyes, shook a few hands, got a couple slaps on my back, and with that I jumped off the merry-go-round.

# Wanderlust

By now you know I have a thing for travel. The trip doesn't begin for me at the destination, but at the actual point of departure. That feeling of power as I'm pushed more deeply into my seat on the upper deck of an A380, Rolls Royce engines whirring quietly as we rotate off the runway, wings flexing. It's a feeling like no other, the whole act of becoming airborne a miracle, really. Taking flight is also where my imagination soars—a fantasy of a white dove flying, mockingbirds swooping, purple martins with operatic chirps and their dance in the air—as we leave the ground far below.

Then there's the slow onward progression of a train as we depart Union Station with a gentle rocking, the clatter of steel wheels navigating the rail junctions as we shift from one track to another and make our way slowly at first, through the Chicago suburbs, then faster, *Westward Ho!*, through the uninspiring landscapes of Iowa and Nebraska, finally into the snow-brushed Rocky Mountains past Denver where the scenery takes our breath away and mountain deer dodge the train as it glides past.

David and I mapped out a cross-country road trip for one of our journeys from our home in Palm Springs to our Chicago place. We left the lush landscape of our planned community and set out driving through the Sonoran Desert, a hot and desolate landscape of grayish-brown, rocky, low mountains and gray-green scrub brush with burnt, sandy soil. Within a few hours the landscape changes, delighting our eyes with reddish soil, sage-green flora, more scrubby bushes. We bypass Sedona this time, not for any particular reason, though it looks and feels a bit overweight. There are groups of day-trippers jamming the parking lots and in lines for T-shirts and cotton candy. Been there, done that. We were the only gay couple visible for miles when we visited for Cinco de Mayo, and our aesthetic tastes—probably our gay instinct—led us to the real art galleries of Tlaquepaque.

By the time we reach our first-night's destination—Winslow, Arizona—we are ready for a break, butts tired from sitting for eight hours. Our oasis is a fine one, La Posada, where the restaurant—The Turquoise Room—attracts visitors from far and wide, but mainly those driving the historic Route 66, who also want a gourmet dinner and a comfortable night's rest. The landscape here is a sort of plateau, flat but you know there are mountains nearby; you can see them in the distance. The air is thinner, and the light is starting to get that otherworldly radiant quality only found in this part of the American southwest, a light that makes everything more vivid. Each room at La Posada is named after a famous film star from the 1920s, 30s, or 40s, possibly because in those days Hollywood starlets would spend the night here on their cross-country rail journey from New York to Los Angeles in the years before jet travel became the time-saving, more glamorous way to go. We are in the Greta Garbo room on this particular stay.

On our way to dinner, we stop in one of the hotel's galleries where the owner's provocative art is on permanent exhibit.

## Wanderlust

From a distance of twenty feet I cast my eyes upon a painting of Nancy Reagan. I can't help but guffaw when I get close and see tiny portraits of Ronnie in her eyes, where the pupils should be. The painting has a strange buzz, like it's vibrating, as if the paint itself has a nervous condition. Then there's Jackie Kennedy, and you guessed right, she's in a pink Chanel two-piece suit complete with pill-box hat designed by Halston, the sacrilegious detail here being a bullet shooting through the King of Hearts from a deck of cards. It's shocking to my sensibility, and I wonder if the artist felt any shame about this subject, but I can't avert my gaze, there's something arresting in it. And finally, we come to Hillary Clinton staring from the bottom of a fish bowl, two sharks circling above. *Aha!* I realize there's a theme, these paintings form a series—the First Lady as entranced co-conspirator, helpless witness, or anxious quarry.

Out of the gallery and past the bar, we arrive at the dining room. David requests a quiet table near a window toward the back of the restaurant. As the Covid-19 pandemic is still quite present, we veer away from the braying, over-served retirees at one table and lead the host as far away from the bar as possible, to a small table at the back. The menu is uniquely southwestern, with deep-fried squash blossoms filled with a Mexican cheese, beet and walnut salad with a raspberry vinaigrette, and such entrées as Bison Short Ribs—really, they should rename it a singular Short Rib, because one is all you get, and honestly one is all you need. I order this, and David settles on the Elk Filet Medallions, a tender, succulent treat that almost makes me jealous. It's a repast that leaves us sated, even a bit stuffed, and we need a walk about the property before retiring to the Garbo room to be left alone.

The next day, after our breakfast of strong coffee and a southwestern omelet (naturally), we pack and head for the car. Day two takes us across New Mexico and to another artsy destination: Santa Fe. Along the road, the landscape becomes a living southwest painting—sage bushes in a soothing powder green, the soil a dusty burnt pink, so palpable to the eye that I have to stop the car and scoop up a handful of the stuff to take home in a zip-seal plastic bag so I never forget how it really looks. By now the light has that radiant quality, clear and blueish, so colors become startlingly vibrant—as if everything is lit from within, the blue of the sky almost too blue, unreal really, the reds, dusty eggplant, ochre and burnt umber of the rocks and soil like rich velvet, their textures visible from a distance. Like so many places I visit, whenever I'm in Santa Fe I immediately want to move here. David gets nervous as I fire up the laptop, a glint in my eye, to start reviewing Redfin listings. *I can't help it!* It's one of the few places where I truly feel at home, accepted, like this was meant to be, as if my Circadian rhythm is in tune with the surrounding landscape. There's no better way to explain it. Friends and acquaintances think I'm crazy, a bit off, but it's true, there are places where the energy of the geography and landscape truly feel like they match my aura, help me breathe more freely, or even give me more energy.

We've been to Santa Fe often enough that I feel right at home the moment we exit the freeway from Albuquerque—right into bumper-to-bumper city traffic, everyone here for the same reason: to get their piece of the southwest. We've stayed at hotels near the cathedral, generally clean and passable for a night's stay, but usually a bit worn around the edges, no ice in the freezer, a dripping tap, that sort of thing. Of chief importance when booking a room is to ask about parking. Believe me, you need parking, because this town gets crowded—it is *the* place to be in northeast New Mexico. We pass on the overbuilt Eldorado Hotel; it just looks too big for our idea of a laid-back stay, so we now choose Inn of the Governors, an intimate two-story hotel where each room has its own kiva for those chilly winter nights, and in the summer it just makes me happy to look at it. After unpacking, we have time to walk around the square and admire the many shops offering crystals and geodes, kachina dolls, sheepskins, shearling coats, hand-made Lucchese western boots, and even a shop selling hand-embroidered southwest-themed women's overcoats in brilliant southwest colors of turquoise, orange, purple, red, green—the very thing every woman from Chicago's North Shore needs.

The galleries beckon, as if calling my name—*James, come hither, we have lovely paintings!* In a trance, I'm slightly breathless—*could it be the elevation or the aromatherapy candles burning near the door?* I glide in, my attention caught by a large oil by a local artist depicting a southwest mountain scene with a river and a few cacti casually punctuating the canvas, painted in the ravishing, earthy colors we saw on our drive into town, striking shapes barely outlined but oozing an authentic, studied style.

After a glass of cool white wine at the Hotel St. Francis' bar, we slowly walk back toward the square and pause at an antique shop with ancient polychromed figures carved in wood carefully displayed in the window and on shelves further inside the gallery. Like Oscar Wilde, "I can resist everything except temptation,"[1] and so I grab David's arm and we head in. It's a small space, rather cluttered and dusty overall, but the objects are a delight to the eyes, each ancient figure unique, carved of wood, bits of polychrome worn away. They each tell a story, have a history. We learn that these are religious Santos figures, hand-carved figurines representing saints that were set up in small roadside altars in Slavic countries in remembrance of the dead or to celebrate a saint's day in the Catholic liturgical calendar. We agree on a large blue-polychromed St. Joseph, partly as a remembrance of our trip, partly because it will add a certain vibe to our eclectic art collection, but also because of our Anglo-Catholic religious interests. And Joseph is, after all, the patron saint of real estate transactions. Nothing in the jumble of rarities has a price tag, so it takes some negotiation to settle on a mutually agreeable price. We pay and are on our way, with St. Joseph under one arm, encased securely in bubble wrap. Once we are home, I research Santos figures in order to learn more about their history, and of course I can't find any information about them. No matter what words I choose, every Google search for a Santos figure results in an unending array of bobble-heads in the likeness of a disgraced member of Congress. And just then it occurs to me that I once predicted that a day would come when the internet would become useless.

After Santa Fe, it's downhill from there—at least for a while. Mid-morning on our third day's journey we cross into the Texas panhandle, and I subconsciously lock the car doors and try to look as Republican as possible. The drive across the panhandle is uneventful, the landscape a perfectly level, treeless pancake. It's a wise idea to check the weather often while driving through here, because tornadoes can pop up almost any time. U.S. Route 40 takes us directly to Amarillo, where I feel a bit safer than I did on the open road. We relax into an overnight at one of the finer motels with free parking just off the freeway.

## Wanderlust

Since we are now in beef country, David suggests a steak dinner, so we choose The Big Texan. This is not just any steak house—it's a "steak ranch." Call them up, and they send a Cadillac limo to your motel, complete with three-foot wide steer horns mounted where the hood ornament normally is. They don't take reservations at The Big Texan, but while you wait for your table you can entertain yourself in the lobby Shootin' Gallery. After your dinner, there's a candy shoppe, ice cream stand, and brewery bar to keep you entertained and where you can buy more goodies to take on your continuing journey. If you haven't heard of The Big Texan, let me explain its claim to fame: the "72-oz. steak challenge." This is not for the faint of heart, or the tender of stomach. In the movie version of this cardiac nightmare, *The Great Outdoors,* John Candy orders the "Old 96-er" and miraculously finishes it, gristle and all.[2] But here in Texas you get a shrimp cocktail, baked potato, salad, roll with butter, and the 72-oz steak. Just like the movie version, if you finish the entire meal within one hour, you eat for free. If you are brave—and hungry—you should know that just like John Candy, you'll be seated on a sort-of dais in the center of the restaurant with a countdown clock ticking down the minutes above your head. People will loudly cheer you on, even take bets for or against you, all in good fun, of course. The courteous staff have thought of everything. If you should become ill while masticating, there is a convenient plastic-lined waste receptacle next to the table. Perusing the menu, I opted for the smallest steak they offered, an 8-oz. sirloin that I couldn't finish.

Day four of our journey east took us into Oklahoma. When driving across Oklahoma, you'll want to make sure you've got plenty of CDs to choose from. I can hear your inquiring minds now. *Why, you ask?* Because no matter how many times you scan your car radio, it seems to only stop on riled-up preacher stations; and if you pause long enough, you'll hear the fear of God in their voices. After listening for a minute, I realize that these radio evangelists need to get out more, travel, meet some new people. As my father told me many years ago, "Go see the world and you'll learn something"—that's my advice. From the way they sound on the radio, the whole country—democracy itself—seems to be a threat. We drove as fast as we could, stopping only for gas.

While the road trip excites us, and we get to see interesting and varied landscape, interact with different people along our way, the trip is nearly over before we want it to end. It seems we quickly make it to the relative safety of Chicago's city limits—with its traffic, democrats, and unions.

\* \* \*

New York is always an exciting destination, even for work. In 2007 I was honored to be a speaker at Folio:Show in New York City. This is *the* magazine industry conference, with keynote addresses and seminars for editors, art directors, production teams, and publishers. My organization had won the top redesign award the year before, so my presentation was on "The Elements of the Redesign." Earlier in the day, I agreed to meet up with my good friend, Bruce, from our college years. Bruce and I had gotten to know each other our junior year, and we even rented a house together for a time. Before my presentation that afternoon, we decided to meet in front of the Met at 6:00. He mentioned something about the opera, that he was going to try to get tickets. This sounded like a great idea, although I was preoccupied at the time with my presentation.

That evening, I arrived a bit early and stood near the plaza in front of Lincoln Center's impressive marble and glass modernist buildings. As I stood there, I noticed the red carpet and the phalanx of professional photographers lined up off to one side. I was confused for a moment, and then concerned as I realized this was opening night, as in THE gala *Opening Night* evening at the Met, the place to be, at the center of the known universe for music and celebrity. I recalled my earlier conversation with Bruce and decided there's no way he could pull this off. Surely, it's sold out. There were rows upon rows of seats set up in the plaza in front of the opera house itself, which had a giant screen mounted above the outdoor balcony. We'll never get in, I thought, as I waited, feeling out of place in my gray Brooks Brothers business suit.

When you stand in front of Lincoln Center on opening night, you can bet you're going to see some famous faces, and it was quite a parade. As I observed the scene unfold before me, a bearded man in black evening wear hurriedly walked past, a bit distracted, decidedly Italian, dark hair, slightly portly but in a dignified, life-well-lived sort of way. *No, can it be ...?* I couldn't recall his name at that exact moment, or I would have called out like an old chum to say how much I enjoyed his work. Then three visions in Italian couture walked toward me, like Roman goddesses in ethereal fluttering-flowing silk gowns like clouds, a brunette and two blondes. Gorgeous. I could smell their enticing perfume from twenty feet away, when one called out with a bejeweled wave, "Placido! Wait for us." As they glided past me, stilettos clacking slightly on the pavement, long hair flowing in the breeze, I was enveloped in a cloud of Acqua di Parma. *So, this is what wealth and fame look like up close—and smell like.* Yes! It was him, I realized too late, as he was gone, already on the red carpet. I could hear a flutter of shutters—*ka-chuuh ka-chuuh ka-chuuh*—getting those publicity shots in frantic fast motion, the very sound of fame. If I were straight, I would have dashed to catch up to Placido, and with a masculine boys-will-be-boys attitude, nudged him, "If you need any help with the girls, I'm your man! You take the brunette, and I'll take the tall blonde"—a salute to Marty Feldman's Igor in *Young Frankenstein.* But just then, I spied a lonely man alighting from a black sedan. Now he's on the red carpet and a photographer begins to shoot, that familiar paparazzi sound perking my ears—*Who could it be now?* But a tall woman in sleek Jimmy Choos with a clipboard in her hand intercepted him, gently guided him off the red carpet, and barked toward the cameras, "Don't bother—he's not on the list." How humiliating.

That evening was memorable for seeing Bianca Jagger and Willem Dafoe. I nearly bumped into Barbara Walters, but she was not stopping and got away quickly as I raised my hand in a wave, *"Barbara! ... Love you, darling."* At last, dusk was falling, and traffic had built up to a tizzy, frantic people pushing past, scarves flowing in the cooling breeze, perfumes wafting, and it was nearly curtain time. At last, there's Bruce, with his girlfriend, Kathi, wrapped in a pashmina, and we hug and share quick hellos. I waited with Kathi as Bruce bolted toward the box office: "I don't know how he's going to get tickets. It's opening night—this has to be sold out." Kathi only smiled, "Somehow he always manages." And he did. Within ten minutes he strolled back to us, smiling broadly, "Okay, let's go," three tickets in his hand. *Some people have a gift.*

## Wanderlust

We sat under the stars and watched on the big screen, enthralled in the magic of the evening. With a big moon high above us, I felt like we were extras in the opera house scene from *Moonstruck*. The music began, and Natalie Dessay delivered an electrifying performance as Lucia in Gaetano Donizetti's *Lucia di Lammermoor*, what was then and still is my favorite opera. The thunderous applause at the end of the performance went on and on, curtain call after curtain call, roses thrown, a bouquet brought on stage, and then we watched, curious for a moment as a camera-operator followed Natalie and the rest of the cast as they ran backstage, then down some fluorescent-lit cinder-block hall, making a sharp turn, the camera nearly hitting a pole or some other object. "Where on earth are they going," I wondered aloud, and then there they were, on the balcony to greet us, outside, their adoring and grateful audience. A historic night! A historic performance! Unique, memorable, once-in-a-lifetime experiences like these are what make travel rewarding and meaningful. Evenings under the stars, with good friends and like-minded strangers, privileged accomplices sharing secret moments in time and place.

\* \* \*

When you feel the call of wanderlust, there's really no place like Rome. A year before the Met opening night, my sister Bernie wanted to visit Italy, and I thought that was a fine idea. Always one for a trip abroad, I put on my tour director hat and we made reservations for a two-week visit. I had been to Rome before and knew all the great sites, even some secret ones. David even advised me, "As long as you're going all that way, you may want to take a side trip to Pompeii and Capri." We took his advice, and the excursion out to Pompeii was a highlight of our visit. We saw ancient mosaics depicting such gods as Priapus and frescoes depicting citizens of Pompeii. There was also an active archeological site where scientists had just unearthed the pumice- and ash-encased remains of some poor soul who had perished in the 79 A.D. Vesuvius eruption. The next day we took a boat to Capri, and I walked about the island, hiking all the way up to the ruins of Villa Jovis which was built by Emperor Tiberius. After my hike, I met up with my sister and we hired a small boat to take us to the Blue Grotto. It was crowded with tourists, all waiting their turn in small boats holding no more than four people each, and we eventually went inside. The water refracted and filtered the light as it enveloped and washed over us in blue, green and aquamarine, the effect almost spiritual, otherworldly. We capped off our day with a meal on the edge of the bay in Marina Grande. When travelling, one must always savor the food.

The best part of the eternal city awaited us on our return from Capri: the Sistine Chapel and the Vatican Museum. For this excursion, you must be patient, with a good breakfast in you to keep up your strength, because this is probably the most over-run place on earth, possibly 20,000 or more visitors a day. To get into the museum, everyone must stand in an impossibly long line leading to the entrance. On the day my sister and I went, I dashed over early to save our place in line. At six o'clock in the morning you'd think there'd be no one there, but I was wrong. Still, I was one of the lucky ones to be among the first 2,000 in line, a line that wrapped around most of the Vatican City wall. Once inside, though, the crush of the crowd and its constant push forward makes it very difficult to stop anywhere to enjoy any individual work of art. And the art itself is unparalleled. A large, one-of-a-kind lavish basin (think of it as a large tea-cup saucer, perhaps ten feet across) is made of Imperial Porphyry, a stone only found in Egypt. That fantasy in purple stone is big enough to bathe in, and probably was, because it is referred to as Nero's Bathtub. Then there are innumerable marble busts of emperors and popes. Every painting, every sculpture is a masterpiece worthy of its own art history seminar. Even the floors and light fixtures in this ornate building are works of art. I thought, if the Roman Catholic Church wanted to do something about worldwide hunger or homelessness, they could just sell off a few masterpieces and take care of the situation. I am hopeful that the current pope will eventually act on this—live the Christian mission. After all, he does have the power and authority.

St. Peter's Basilica is an awe-inspiring building and probably what comes to mind when one thinks of Rome or the Vatican. People recall it from the televised funeral of Pope John Paul II, on April 8, 2005. It's featured on television in the moment when white smoke wafts from the chimney above the Sistine Chapel signifying that a new pope has been selected. The building's sheer size inspires awe as the cameras scan the scene in the moment the new pontiff greets the people for the first time from the balcony high above St. Peter's Square, cheers echoing off the travertine walls. It's a sound whose echoes transport the imagination across centuries past. The basilica is built, quite literally, on top of an ancient cemetery—a necropolis—or city of the dead. The current building was completed in 1626. Roman Catholic traditions indicate that Saint Peter was crucified—martyred—on the site of Emperor Nero's Circus, and that the saint was then buried nearby. Today, a reconstructed map shows the proximate locations of the necropolis, the circus, and the basilica. And I recall my father's advice from long ago: "see the world and get an education."

Peter's execution, burial, the necropolis—all called to me, captured my imagination. So, I did some research. That work paid off with a rare treat during our visit to Rome—the Vatican Scavi tour, a half-day guided walk through the necropolis beneath St. Peter's Basilica where only a dozen people are allowed at a time. This tour isn't open to just anyone—there's no signage with hours posted. One must complete a sort of application form online, then wait for a response from the Vatican Scavi office. I was one of the lucky few, fortunate to obtain reservations about a month before our visit. A highlight of this extraordinary small space was when our guide pointed to the bones of Saint Peter himself, or more accurately, bones *possibly* of Saint Peter. After the tour, we were pleasantly surprised to be escorted up a small spiral stair and allowed to exit into the crypt—the level where John Paul II and other famous—and infamous—popes are buried in lavish tombs, encased first in a cypress casket, then sealed—in fact welded-in—in an airtight zinc layer, and finally fitted inside a plain outer casket of elm.

To travel is to eat, and when in Rome you'll eat, eat, and eat! Visiting new places, walking around all day, builds up an appetite. Every meal we had was a delight to the senses. One of my policies when I travel is that when I find a really good restaurant, I go there often. Every day for a week we had lunch at the same place on Piazza Navona, with its inviting outdoor tables, pigeons landing on the pavement nearby. Also when I travel, my ulterior motive is to expand my cooking ability or my wardrobe. In Rome, I was on a mission to refine my basic Bolognese sauce, so I ordered spaghetti à la Bolognese one day, and then alternated with their Lasagna à la Ragu to see if I could decipher the ingredients by sight, taste and texture. Having an interest in cooking, I tried over the years many different Bolognese recipes, and none of them quite satisfied me—something always seemed to be missing. Finally, one day I broke the ice and asked our waiter, a rather jovial man, if he would humor me and write down the ingredients for the sauce. I thought he'd just ignore me, guarding the secret family formula, but to my surprise he sauntered over with our check, and beneath it was a list of ingredients, though I was left to figure out the proportions myself, and translate the list from Italian. Back at home, I started with an old Bolognese recipe, plus my notes from Rome, then compared and adapted it with the ingredients available at my local grocery store. After a half-dozen attempts, I found the proportions I preferred, and the resulting sauce is hearty, thick, making it perfect for spaghetti, pappardelle, tagliatelle, or for lasagna, too. Now, every time I make this, I think of those carefree days in Roma.

* * *

**Bolognese à la Roma** (adapted by James Baran)
Preparation time: 30 mins
Cooking time: 2 hours
Equipment: 8- or 10-Qt stock pot, 12-inch skillet, Cuisinart or other food processor

**Ingredients:**
2.0 oz (approx.) uncured/uncooked Pancetta (4-5 thin slices)
1-1/2 cups minced carrots
1-1/2 cups minced celery

1-1/2 cups minced sweet onion such as Vidalia
4 Tbsps. unsalted butter
4 Tbsps. good Italian olive oil
1 lb. – 1-1/4 lb. ground beef, 85/15 or 80/20
1/3-lb ground veal (optional)
14-20 fresh Basil leaves, minced (adjust number to your flavor preference) OR 1 4-oz tube Fresh Basil Paste, usually near the lettuces and fresh herbs at the grocery store
1 4.5-oz tube Cento or Napoleon brand Double-Concentrated Tomato Paste
2 28-oz cans Cento brand San Marzano Tomatoes, with juice
1 14.5-oz can tomato sauce
1/2 cup dry white wine (Italian pinot grigio works well)
salt and pepper to taste
Choose a pasta: Spaghetti, Tagliatelle, Pappardelle are best pastas for this sauce; pick your favorite grated (or shaved) Parmesan or Parmigiano Reggiano for serving

**Directions:**

1. Freeze the uncooked/uncured Pancetta (once frozen it will easily slice); when frozen, cut into 1/4-inch slices, then cut again crosswise so that you have little square bits approx. 1/4-inch in size (slightly larger is okay, too), and set aside.
2. Using a food processor, pulse into a near-pulp (in separate batches) the carrots, onion, and celery, keep separate and set aside. This is your *Mire Poix*.
3. Open canned tomatoes and dump them into a large, 8- or 10-quart stock pot. Using a dinner knife, roughly chop the tomatoes.

4. Put olive oil in a large skillet (12-inch is best), add the butter, and heat.
5. Once butter and olive oil are bubbling, add diced Pancetta and stir until fat renders, or slightly longer, but do not brown. You want the Pancetta to stay pink.
6. Then add the minced carrot. Add this first because the carrot takes longer to soften. Cook for three or four minutes, stirring constantly.
7. Add celery and onion, and continue to stir until fully combined.
8. Cook the *Mire Poix* over a medium heat until it achieves a slight golden sheen, 8 to 10 minutes.
9. Pour cooked *Mire Poix* into the stock pot.
10. Using the same skillet, add a little olive oil and brown the ground meat, breaking it up into small bits as it cooks. Add a few twists of fresh-ground black pepper and a few pinches of salt, to your taste.
11. Once meat is browned, about five to eight minutes, drain grease from the meat as much as possible and add meat to the stock pot.
12. Add tomato sauce and stir until blended.
13. Add entire contents of tube of basil paste (or the basil leaves) and entire tube of concentrated tomato paste, and stir well until blended.
14. Add the white wine, and stir.
15. Bring to a bubble over medium heat, then reduce to low heat and simmer.
16. Simmer, stirring every fifteen minutes (you don't want any ingredients at bottom of pot to burn), for 2 hours. When done,

turn off heat and cover until pasta is ready to serve.
17. Prepare your favorite pasta, and use one soup ladle of sauce per serving. Top with grated Parmesan or Parmigiano Reggiano, and serve with a hearty crusted Italian bread if you like, such as Turano brand. Leftover sauce may be divided, using the ladle to estimate serving sizes. Once cool, you may freeze.

(Notes: Do not use: red wine, garlic, milk or cream. For freezing: when cool and in freezer containers, put down a layer of plastic wrap directly on the sauce surface so that no air touches the sauce. When this is frozen, the plastic wrap prevents freezer burn to protect the sauce flavor. Keep in mind that you can customize this recipe to your own liking. If, for example, you love onions, then go for it, add more. Make it your own, and you should enjoy it your way.)

As they say in Italy, *Buon appetito!*

\* \* \*

My wanderlust was sparked during my family's first European trip in 1972, when I was 11. That trip coincided with my parents' twenty-fifth anniversary. We flew Swiss Air to Zurich, a ten-hour flight on the new McDonnell-Douglass DC-10, which became my favorite airplane. It was sleek, quiet, modern, with a galley below deck accessed by a narrow elevator. The plane featured large windows, and doors that opened by sliding into the ceiling. I was impressed by the technological advances that made the DC-10 the most advanced aircraft to-date. Always interested in trying new dishes, I recall the delicious food we were served on that flight. The first course was baby shrimp served on a bed of lettuce with a side of herbed butter and cream along with French bread—a First-Class treat and a very European dish. The main course was steak with mixed vegetables—and we were in economy! My father and sister enjoyed a glass or two of red wine. When the cabin lights were dimmed so that people could sleep or enjoy the movie that was projected onto the bulkhead at the front of our cabin, I could see the Aurora Borealis outside the north-facing airplane windows, an otherworldly and magical experience for me. My father brought along a copy of *Europe on $5 a Day*, by Arthur Frommer, in order to plan for reasonably priced accommodations that allowed us to spend more money on meals. We usually stayed in family suites in various hotels, but in one or two cities our parents shared one room, while my sister and I shared another. There was seldom a bathroom in the room itself, so we had to adapt to the European-style hotel's design where toilets and showers were shared facilities. Altogether, we spent about six weeks that summer in Europe, visiting Switzerland, Lichtenstein, Germany, Austria, Belgium, Denmark, Norway, and Sweden, with a week-long second visit to Lichtenstein, my mother's favorite place.

My father had bought EurRail passes for us so that we could travel across Europe via train for one flat fare. In retrospect, this was a most ingenious and economical way to travel. Today, there really is no all-inclusive travel pass, and you have to buy individual tickets for every train trip. On one of our overnight train journeys, two Italian girls joined us in our 6-person First Class compartment. Their conversation sounded romantic and interesting, lyrical and poetic. I did not speak or understand Italian, except for the few phrases I'd heard many times, such as *Mi scusi* (or scoozi!), *molto bene, ciao*, or *arrivederci*. These girls' attire was so different from what we knew in the U.S. that my mother declared it indecent. I recall one of the girls wearing what appeared to be just a large tank top-style dress, very thin, very revealing. And their gold jewelry and perfume were alluring. I quietly suggested to my father that we take a train to Italy in order to see Rome and maybe Venice, but my mother intervened, saying, "No, I don't think that's such a good idea." She had heard rumors about Italian men's behavior—bold comments or lurid leers at women as a display of machismo—which probably worked better on their own egos than on the women to whom they directed their attention. At that time, crime was also a concern. And at one of our train-station stops, we had met another American family who told us their luggage had been stolen in Rome.

Toward the end of our trip, on a sunny day in Lichtenstein, mom prepared a European-style lunch of fresh-baked rolls, ham, cheese, fruit and pastries that she had purchased in the shops on the main street in Vaduz. My father rented a red Volkswagen, and we drove above the capital city to a park-like setting behind the castle. Once there, we found a smooth area where we could sit on the gentle slope looking down toward the castle and at the city and countryside far below. When we were finished with lunch and cleaning up, a distinguished couple walked past us. My mother, ever the smiling extrovert on this trip, greeted the couple and said hello. The woman asked, "Are you enjoying our country?" It seemed an oddly possessive question, but nonetheless we all nodded and my mother said, "Yes, we are, very much." Departing nods exchanged, the couple went off down a narrow path. Eventually, I could see them disappear through a tall gate at the side of the castle. A day or two later, in a Vaduz gift shop and still remembering the simple lunch we had that sunny day, my mother found a copy of the royal household's cookbook. There on the cover was a photograph of the two people we saw on that hillside, the Crown Prince and Princess of Lichtenstein. My mother delighted in telling her own stories of the trip to relatives and friends upon our return home. It was a vacation that changed her life.

As our Swiss Air DC-10 landed in Chicago signaling the end of our holiday, I asked my father if we could go back the following summer. He only laughed and said, "You've got the travel bug now."

*  *  *

I don't have a travel bucket list. That's something I've never quite understood, as if destinations were merely game pieces to be collected, or boxes to check on some list. But I have always been drawn to centers of culture—cities that are vast storehouses of history where art, poetry, food, and people thrive, remembering their past while building a future. My first trip to London was during my senior year in high school. A brainchild of our history teacher, the trip was planned as an educational tour of London and Paris for two weeks over the Christmas break. When I told my father about the trip, he immediately asked, "Who should I write the check to," and added that, "Travel is a better education than books will ever give you." His response, and indeed his enthusiastic support, were a surprise, and I had to suppress my excitement in case he reneged on his offer to pay for this trip. This was, after all, an unusual expression of largesse on his part, and I was dubious about his intentions.

In the end, he wrote that check—$400 for airfare and accommodation, and then he even gave me some spending money for the trip.

Our tour group left Chicago's O'Hare International Airport a few days before Christmas, 1978, aboard a TWA 747, plush seats upholstered in thick red, white, and blue fabrics. At the check-in counter, we were allowed to select our seats from a large 747 floorplan displayed on the wall behind the counter. Whatever seat numbers were up there meant those seats were available. I wanted to take charge on our trip and show off the fact that I was a seasoned world traveler accustomed to flying, so I convinced a few of my classmates to join me in selecting seats in the far-forward economy cabin, rows 7 and 8. I said to my friends, "Oh, sit up front with me. We'll be in front of the wing where we'll see the leading-edge flaps and look into the engines as we take off." To convince them further, I also noted, "When we land, we'll be among the first to disembark the aircraft." I gave a wave to the check-in agent and requested seat 7A. My three friends followed along and got adjacent seats.

With only two weeks to explore and learn about the history of our destination cities, we spent every day in a variety of activities at historic sites and other interesting locations. We toured Westminster Abbey, a rarefied place—a major repository of British history—with the tomb of Edward the Confessor hidden behind the high altar in a separate chapel, along with more royal burials such as Elizabeth I. I was fascinated by the carved effigies, and engrossed in the inscriptions. This is like being inside a time capsule of British history, and it captivates my imagination to this day. We learned about Perpendicular Gothic architecture, with the most notable examples in the Houses of Parliament and Westminster Abbey's interior. We visited the British Museum and saw Egyptian treasures taken by British explorers in the 1800s—huge granite statues so large and heavy it was impossible to imagine how they were transported such a distance. The Rosetta Stone and the Elgin Marbles were highlights of our visit to the museum. Those British explorers and archaeologists did it the old-fashioned way—they just took things. Well, they did have permits to dig and explore, but still, it seemed to me they didn't know when to stop. On a more pedestrian excursion, we went to Madame Tussaud's Wax Museum, founded in 1835 by the French wax sculptor Marie Tussaud. This didn't impress me at all. Wax reproductions in various people's likenesses? Preposterous and silly, I thought. Yet when you pass it today, there is a line of tourists that wraps around the block.

 The London weather was typical for winter, cold and damp, rainy and windy. It was hard to stay warm. Our accommodation was in our sleeping bags in the social hall of a church. I was in high school; I wasn't concerned with the quality of our arrangements. I was thrilled to be there, learning more about history and seeing sights far from home.

 On our journey to France, we took first a ship across the English Channel and then a train to Paris to discover that the weather was no better there. Here, once again, our accommodation was in a church social hall. There was no heat, and it was cold, but we were glad to have the place to rest at night. We visited the Louvre and saw the Mona Lisa and other masterpieces. We went to the top of the Eifel Tower and then walked along the River Seine. I was enthralled with the architecture and interior space of Cathedral Notre Dame, and we were lucky that an organist was practicing while we were there. I enjoyed the reverberation when an organ piece ended, its final chord released but the sound echoing from back to front and then back again like a wave washing over us. I could practically see the sound waves dancing. Magical! I wanted to go to Père Lachaise Cemetery to visit the graves of Oscar Wilde, Frederic Chopin, Georges Bizet, and the niche of Edith Piaf, but my friends thought that was creepy and voted against the idea.

On our way back home, we encountered a significant travel disruption, something that is common nowadays but was a surprise then. After boarding our British Airways 747 for the return flight, we simply sat there—for about three hours, cooped up in the plane, and I could see baggage sitting on the ground. Heathrow Airport ground crews had gone on strike just as we boarded, so there was no one to load our baggage onto the plane, in fact, no one to load any plane. Once the flight was cancelled, we were told to keep our boarding passes, that they'd be used the following day, and we deplaned and were herded onto busses headed for hotels. None of us knew where the others were. We didn't even know where our chaperones were. At least I had a roommate, Norbert, who stuck with me, and we ended up in a group at the London Penta Hotel. In our room, Norbert went into the bar cabinet and pulled out small bottles of Scotch and shook them gently, jokingly giving me a thumbs up signal. I declined, and in the end he didn't open those bottles. We watched TV for a while and then took ourselves out to dinner, adolescents free in London, free from supervision. We could have disappeared, never to be heard from again—something I'd fantasized about many times as a child.

The following day our flight departed on time. We had had an adventure, saw great inspiring sites, buildings, art, enjoyed the food, smelled the air, and saw how people live in these different places. My life as an American would never be the same, because

## Wanderlust

I'd tasted a few rare delights of European culture and seen British life and the way people presented themselves, more elegantly than those in the U.S.

My wanderlust is always sated in London. Since that first visit in 1978, I have been back at least thirty times over the years. I've travelled to many countries, and my love for travel only increases. Today, Business Class is the new Coach, and in domestic travel the only perk in First Class is being the first to deplane. But I won't be deterred. I'm living my life, and travel is just as important as the air I breathe, the water I drink. Why? Because travel teaches me about the world.

\* \* \*

I was hard at work at my magazine job on the morning of September 11, 2001, when I overheard a commotion coming from the main conference room. I could hear staff members shouting and even crying. People started running down the hall outside my office. I stopped what I was doing to see what was the matter, and I walked down to the conference room. There, on the television, I saw one of the World Trade Center towers in New York with a cloud of smoke billowing from it. A news announcer was narrating the scene like it was some Orson Welles-style "War of the Worlds" broadcast, updated for modern America, telling viewers that a plane had flown into one of the twin towers. The reporter rhetorically asked how such an accident could happen in broad daylight, and I thought it no accident, that clearly it had been done on purpose, like a military attack. The images were so terrible, I initially refused to believe it was real—it was like a movie. As

## James Philip Baran

I watched the news commentator discuss the situation, another plane flew across the TV screen and burst into the second tower. I was stunned, and then I knew this was real. I stumbled and fell into a chair and watched as the scene grew momentously worse, and then the inevitable happened, the towers collapsed in a cloud of unearthly dust—plaster, steel, concrete, asbestos, glass, paper, office records, machines, building components, and in the midst of the cloud, people. All lost.

The horrors of that day affected us all. In the office, we soberly went about our work. Some people left to go home. The streets were crowded with people rushing to Union Station to board trains back to the suburbs, worried that an attack could happen in Chicago. Suddenly, every high-rise office building seemed like a dangerous place to be. The national response was to shut down American air space. No planes flew for at least a week after that date, our national defenses on high alert.

I had scheduled a visit to England beginning the following week. I was anticipating my trip with relish, a chance to get away from the day-to-day of my job and to see some of my favorite sites in London. David had introduced me to his good friend Julian and his partner Anthony, and I was to visit and stay with them for a week. I was looking forward to this new adventure, but now became worried. During the days that immediately followed the attack in New York, I tentatively watched the news, read the papers, and emailed my hosts in London. While I was full of shock and sorrow for New Yorkers, the families who lost their loved ones, and for the victims of the attack, I was also angry. Livid is more like it. How is it that some people seem to have a mission to kill others? This existential question has bothered me ever since that day. But moreover, I vowed to myself that I would not shrink in terror; I would not be bullied and terrorized into hiding. I was determined to go on with my life, pack my bag and go on my trip.

That next week, my United Airlines 747 departed on time. Security at O'Hare was unusually smooth. The reason? There were almost no people there. Most travelers had cancelled their trips and were at home watching the news. I soldiered on. The 747 carries up to about 400 passengers in a typical American-style three-class layout, and I was seated in Business Class, on the quiet upper deck. After takeoff, we seemed to glide effortlessly at about 1,500 feet over the city, and the pilots waited until we were over Lake Michigan to accelerate and climb to cruise altitude. I was among four passengers on the upper deck, along with two flight attendants. After the seatbelt sign was turned off, I wandered through the plane; I counted at most thirty passengers on board—one man in First Class, a handful in main-deck Business, and the rest scattered throughout Economy. It was an eerie feeling, the plane being nearly empty. I asked a flight attendant why the flight hadn't been cancelled, and she informed me that the plane was needed in London for a reposition and another flight the next day. No wonder we were aloft with only about fifty people, crew included, our group hardly covering the cost of fuel. Nevertheless, I settled in for a comfortable flight.

During my stay in London, I went to all my favorite places: the Victoria & Albert Museum, Tate Modern. I enjoyed pleasant walks on Kensington High Street and the King's Road. I explored Chelsea and took note of the famous residents who once called Cheyne Walk their home, including actors Elizabeth Taylor and Laurence Olivier, writers Henry James and Bram Stoker, and rock musician Keith Richards who, apparently, still lives there. The lives lived, the books written, the film scripts studied here enrich the history of this short but storied stretch of road. I observed the shoppers on Sloane Street avidly pursuing fashion like a nun might commit herself to religious devotion. London seemed perfectly normal, if quieter than usual. My friends Julian and Anthony were most welcoming. They lived in an Edwardian Arts & Crafts vicarage next to the church where Anthony was vicar, Saint Barnabas and Saint James the Greater, Walthamstow, a rambling eight-bedroom house with drawing room, dining room, ground floor and first floor studies, a separate kitchen and larder, a coal fireplace for every room, and with a walled garden of shrubbery, roses, and vines. At night I could hear the eerie cries of foxes as they roamed in search of food and companionship.

Julian had received an invitation to the rededication of a famous historic house, and he invited me to accompany him. It promised to be a splendid event with the former Prime Minister, now Dame Margaret Thatcher, reopening the house for the public.

She stood in the warm fall sunlight, statue-like in a heavy royal blue, floor-length gown lavishly embroidered with vine-like patterns, with a brooch near her left shoulder in diamonds, emeralds, and rubies—she had the look of an HRH. Standing there conspicuously, the center of attention, stoic, as if she were like a stake driven in, with satin gloves encasing her hands and hair sprayed into a helmet, she was a vision in advancing age, and incidentally, she was also blocking the front door. The occasion was the much-anticipated reopening of Doctor Samuel Johnson's 18th-century Gough Square home; it now stands as a museum memorializing his many contributions to the art of the English language. I stood nearby with Julian, casual yet attentive, practically leaning on the bronze statue of Hodge, Johnson's beloved cat, now mounted on a small pedestal, perpetually ignoring the little oyster set before him.

At last Margaret Thatcher spoke, repeating from memory a prepared statement thanking donors and curators, thanking us for coming to Doctor Johnson's home museum after such a long closure due to remodeling. Her short speech finished, she turned to walk inside and invited us to accompany her to view the newly remodeled interior. In minutes we were inside as well, all thirty or so attendees who had been summoned by engraved invitation, where waiters in white tie offered us champagne off silver salvers, and where we could mingle and view the rooms.

Julian cleverly, instinctively, knew just where to stand upon entering the drawing room. My bold, subversive instinct tempted me to call out, "Mags!" with a wave, as if hailing an old friend, but I held back. Instead, I stood with the calm restraint and dignity of a member of Parliament. Julian and David go back forty-five years, to the time when David worked at the Victoria & Albert Museum while he was living and studying in London. He met Julian there, who was at the time a curator in one of the departments.

The former PM was the first to be served champagne, but in a moment we held our own glasses of Bollinger, *the* champagne of the British upper class. After a moment of taking in the pale gray of the walls, the sparse decor, we found ourselves bumping into her, *Herself*, and she initiated the conversation. "And how *kind* of you to come out this afternoon," were her first words, a heavy emphasis on *kind*, and off we went, coasting along a chatty romp that included pointed comments on the excellent restoration of the house, how the plaster workers toiled all those months rebuilding entire walls, how the security system surely was upgraded, what with all the crime in the city nowadays. "And are you from London?" Dame Thatcher inquired of me, to which I replied, "Actually, I'm an American," sharing that I reside in Chicago, explaining that I had just flown over only a week after the September 11 terrorist attacks. *I wondered to myself, if I tell her I'm gay will she recoil? Will she walk away?* But I'm not an instigator of trouble—I tend to let sleeping dogs lie. I was a guest here. This larger-than-life woman had kept gays at a distance during her life at 10 Downing. It wasn't my place to point out her shortcomings, failures, and where she might have done better if she hadn't been so iron-willed and unable to accept diversity at a certain time in history.

"How terrible, how ghastly those attacks were," Mrs. Thatcher continued, leaning in closer like an old chum to inquire quietly whether I had any friends or relatives affected personally by the tragedy, anyone at all in the towers that day. No, I was relieved to report, no relations, but my friend Bruce was evacuated from his office within a few minutes after the first plane penetrated one of the towers in a huge conflagration of fire, black billowing smoke, and falling debris. Margaret went on to say that it was shocking that the Imams made no statements condemning the attack, and that it was a real shame what the world is coming to. As I had travelled so soon afterward, she was curious to learn if I had any trouble with my journey, and I had to admit that it had been the easiest trans-Atlantic flight I'd ever taken. I explained that it seemed to me that immediately following the terror attacks Americans cancelled travel plans, fearing that more hijackings, more terror attacks, were going to take place. Little did we know that Al Qaeda had really shot its wad on its one big day, having taken years to plan and implement it, to recruit certifiable lunatics, to train them to steer planes, to coach them in tactics to take over jumbo jets, all well-coordinated and in sync on the day. I, however, was not one to panic. I would not have unknown terrorists, or anyone for that matter, bully me into cowering and hiding. I was going to live my life, travel, and fly whenever I damn-well pleased.

While talking with Mrs. Thatcher, I was impressed by her personal style, her ability to engage with me, someone she did not have to impress or bother with. It showed me she had that clever knack shared by conversationalists (and good politicians) who can talk with and hear perspectives from all sorts of people. She seemed to respect me, my story. Julian and I said our good-byes and retired to the nearby Ye Olde Cheshire Cheese pub for a hearty hot lunch.

The next day, I purchased a copy of *The Times*, and there she was, Dame Margaret—"Mags"—photographed standing in front of Johnson's house, a photo larger than the headline on the front page which read, "Thatcher speaks out on terror."[3] I read the story with interest—I was there, after all. I'm no celebrity, no influencer, but I thought the least they could have done was include a quote or two from the dashing American visitor—something, anything. But nothing! No mention of me in conversation with the former PM. How humiliating. It just goes to show you the media will always rely on familiar names—people with some degree of celebrity—to sell papers.

Thatcher died in 2013, after years of retirement when she went out less and less, performed fewer and fewer official duties. After an unusually large funeral at St Paul's Cathedral, she was cremated and inurned under a simple stone marker along with her late husband, Denis, in the sidewalk leading to Royal Hospital Chelsea, behind a wrought iron fence and locked gate. It occurred to me that the family could have just as easily bought a nice crypt at Brompton Cemetery or Kensal Green, but a public figure should be in a place of prominence.

And today, as I recall meeting her, I can see the cold bronze of Hodge's statue, the gray-black cobblestone pavement, the rustling leaves filtering the sun. Margaret Thatcher ended up with the same affliction as her pal Ronnie Reagan had so many years ago—dementia—and faded into old age. She lived out most of her final days in her white rowhouse on Chester Square in Belgravia, where I easily found it, the only house with no address plaque, a stark memorial to the once-powerful Iron Lady. And in the fall sunshine these many years later, I can still see the elaborate embroidery of that dress fit for royalty.

\* \* \*

David and I enjoy travel and can't help but return to our favorite places—cities where we feel at home. Outside of Chicago, London is the city where we feel most comfortable. When I first started visiting that city, I needed a guidebook and map every day, and I was momentarily lost when deciding on what train to use on the Underground, or what bus to take. Now, though, after perhaps thirty visits, I just walk out our door and head toward my destination, bus and Underground are like second nature to me. It's no wonder I feel at home there. We have our favorite restaurants: Wagamama for modern Asian noodle dishes, Côte for classic French-style fare, and Sheekey's for special-occasion dining, where the *Maître d'* always recognizes us and welcomes us back.

## Wanderlust

We visit our old haunts every year. The Victoria & Albert where there is usually a special exhibit, the Tate Modern, or Tate Britain if we want to bask in the light of "Norham Castle, Sunrise," an ethereal painting by J.W.M. Turner, one of Britain's most celebrated artists. Then there's the National Portrait Gallery. And we always seek out recitals and concerts at venues such as St. Martin-in-the-Fields, although concert-going there is difficult and less and less enjoyable due to nightly protests and other bombastically loud activities in nearby Trafalgar Square.

It seems we're drawn to London for other reasons, too. Usually, our secondary, ulterior motive is to update our wardrobes, and Jermyn Street in Piccadilly with its men's haberdashery shops is a perennial destination. Boutiques catering to men's fashion needs such as Charles Tyrwhitt for shirts, Jeremy Hackett for well-made Italian wool or fine cotton trousers, or Russell and Bromley for Italian leather shoes and belts. I used to buy my clothes at Marshall Field in Chicago, but then Macy's took over, and over time it seems everything has slid downward in quality, with limited choices as well. For example, where are cotton socks? Today, too many items are made in China, or Italian-made fashion is limited in choice while outrageously priced. I'm not a clothing snob, but I do look for quality, and the choice is better in London while the prices are similar to those in the U.S.

And it's not always about eating out, seeing art that's only here, and shopping. As Episcopalians, we are part of the worldwide Anglican Communion, and therefore we have a church home anywhere we go, with many excellent churches in London. We've been to mass at All Saints Margaret Street, which was designed in 1850 in a high Victorian gothic architectural style with intricate inlaid stone floors and hand-painted tile friezes along an entire wall—the building itself is a three-dimensional work of art. We fit right in here because their mass is so similar to that of our home parish. But we always make sure to get to Chelsea Old Church for matins. The building sits on the north side of Chelsea Embankment at Old Church Street—you can't miss it because there's a large statue of Sir Thomas More in front, facing the river. The church has been there for more than 700 years. It was partly destroyed during World War II in 1941, and was rebuilt and restored by 1950. We have a number of friends at Old Church, and every time we visit there's another chance for lunch or coffee, with lively conversations about the state of politics in the UK or in the States, because, really, there's always something interesting going on in one place or the other.

For a recent visit to London, David and I wanted to do something different—we wanted to mix things up bit—so we booked our transportation on planes, trains, and a big ship. We flew British Airways, on their Airbus 380, carefully selecting our seats on the upper deck in Club World for seclusion and quiet. For our return journey we booked the Queen Mary 2, currently the world's only true ocean liner, a ship designed for speed and smooth sailing, even in rough weather. Once back in the states, and after a few days' visit with my old friend Bruce at his home in the Adirondacks, we booked a train trip on Amtrak from Albany to Chicago, an overnight ride on the Lake Shore Limited. The plans were set, reservations made.

It was September 8, 2022, one week before our scheduled departure, and I was having a relaxing afternoon in the sun. Early September in Chicago is often the last time you can enjoy summer-like weather, and the evenings turn chilly quickly. I recalled the news from London earlier in the week, that the Queen had met with

## Wanderlust

Liz Truss to invite her to form a government and become Prime Minister. The photo published with that article gave me a chill. Her Majesty looked frail and weak, with unusual dark patches on her hands, as she stood for the photograph in a cashmere sweater in front of a roaring fire at Balmoral Castle, a cane supporting her. The image struck me; I had seen that look before on the hands of aunts, felt that look in my mother the last day I sat with her, such weakness, such tiredness. And I said to myself, "It won't be long, now." So, as I sat on my lounge chair in the afternoon on the 8th of September, I was already on edge when my phone rang. I hadn't had a chance to look at the *Washington Post* or *New York Times* apps that were buzzing when my sister called to say, "She's died." And I didn't even have to ask, "Who? Who died?"

Why was I so shaken by the death of Queen Elizabeth II? I was witnessing the passage of history. I'm an American. I never met the woman, the queen, and yet she impressed me. This is why I was so affected, moved, by her death. I'll admit, there is some romance about royalty, but honestly, I'm not obsessed with the Royal Family Inc.—it is a business, after all. As world leaders go, though, Queen Elizabeth II was England's head of state the entire length of my life, since before my birth, so she was the only living monarch I knew of and saw in the news. She gave a continuity to England that set it apart from other countries. And here's why she impressed me: as a world leader, Queen Elizabeth never made a wrong move, at least not that I knew of. She was beyond reproach—an example most world leaders could emulate. Apart from Barack and Michelle, Jimmy and Rosalynn, or George and Barbara, Elizabeth was the only world leader in my lifetime that wasn't followed by some scandal (nefarious arms sales), misdeed (appointing family members to

Cabinet posts), or embarrassment (an affair conducted in the Oval office). She was someone to admire and look up to as an example. And her resemblance to my mother was uncanny. From her hair style, her simple dresses—complete with diamond brooch—her shoes and handbag, to her smile, she looked like a sister to my mother. Maybe I'm setting my own mother on a pedestal with the comparison, but to me they looked a lot alike, and my mother always had a sense of nobility about her.

When we arrived in London that September, it was a solemn city. Plays we had booked were cancelled, concerts and shows cancelled, too. City workers were busy setting up steel barricades. Traffic signals were being taken down along the procession route so that the solemnity of the funeral would not be disrupted by blinking traffic lights. On the day, I stood near the Albert Memorial in Hyde Park. It was quiet, somber, as I stood at the steel barrier, like a stake driven in. I stood there, in one place, unmoving until after the cortege of three motorcycles, the Queen's hearse, and a few accompanying Land Rovers passed slowly by. Leading up to that moment, the park, and the people in it, were sober and quiet. Even with a large crowd of people standing twelve deep on each side of the road, there was near silence. We could hear the distant cannon salutes over the Thames, ninety-six cannon blasts—one for each year of her life, along with the steady far-off toll of Big Ben. Such was the stillness in the crowd, all of whom came to this place out of respect and to say a final farewell to the woman they all felt they knew. Later that evening, at the completion of the Committal service which was broadcast "live" on television from St. George's Chapel in Windsor Castle, all London churches rang out peals of bells. The church one block from our flat rang its peal for three hours that evening. The passage of history was palpable in an elegant, respectful way. No one does a funeral like the British.

London returned to normal in a day or two. The feeling as I walked the streets on those days was as if a page had turned, a chapter had ended, and a book closed as the leaves turned gold, deep red, and fell to the ground. We'd still see large photographs of the Queen throughout London—in store windows, larger than life on banners hanging here and there, and on magazine covers. But as is necessary and realistic, Britons and their visitors as well as the entire world itself, carried on and cast our gaze forward.

Our departure in October, while a sad farewell to our second city, set us on an adventure aboard the Queen Mary 2. Seven nights at sea with no wi-fi, no internet, no emails—this is what I call joy! The voyage, or "crossing" as it is referred to, is a rare chance to step away from technology, unwind, forget about the world's innumerable problems. We enjoyed long walks around the ship, the planetarium show, and live entertainment with the Kingdom Choir—the singers who performed at Prince Harry and Megan Markle's wedding. We didn't just eat—*we dined*—on Beef Wellington, Sole Meunière, boeuf bourguignon, poached salmon. Our *Maître d'* not only took care of our seating arrangements and ensured everything was to our liking, but he made the desserts himself every evening. Bananas Foster one evening, Clafoutis (baked berries with a pancake-like batter on top) on another, chocolate mousse, crème brulée, and a traditional cheese course with fruit on yet another night. The desserts were a delicate and decadent finish to our dinners. We don't eat that way every day, that's for sure.

When at sea, it's a wonderful experience to sail through a good storm, not just a thunderstorm, but tumultuous seas with high winds and large swells. I love it when the on-board speaker system chimes three times, and the officer on the Bridge announces that all passengers are to stay indoors, avoid their balconies (in fact, ensure all balcony doors are bolted), and under no circumstances try to walk on the decks. To some, this is terror at sea—to me, it's like going to an amusement park, and I want it to go on and on. We had the joy of rolling through three days of Force 7, 8, and 9 winds. During this rough weather, it was still easy to eat in our dining room as it is located on deck 2 of the ship, low and close to the water, so there was very little rolling motion. But when we returned to our stateroom, we had to steady ourselves—"hip to the rail," as one seasoned passenger called out to me, signaling that we literally walk down the halls with one hip gliding along the rail—a good way to balance oneself, especially if carrying drinks or a tray of snacks.

We also read books we'd brought along, attended Church of England morning prayer on Sunday, which concluded with the sea-inspired hymn "Eternal Father, Strong to Save," which is in the Anglican and Episcopal hymnals. As the ship rose and fell on the waves, we sang a line made more meaningful in the drama of our moments on the ocean: "O hear us when we cry to thee for those in peril on the sea."[4]

Each evening we had a glass of wine or cocktail in one of the ship's bars. There's the Chart Room, a plush lounge with large windows and deep-cushioned sofas where a small jazz ensemble regularly offers a satisfying selection of jazz hits or other toe-tapping tunes to keep the patrons entertained and drinking. On one evening we tried the Laurent-Perrier Champagne Bar, for champagne of course. But when the sea is rough the best place for a drink is the Commodore Club. Just below the bridge, the club's angled win-

## Wanderlust

dows let you look out over the expansive bow of the ship, and if the waves are good they'll crash over the bow and spray the lounge windows. Whenever this happens, customers raise their glasses in a toast, "Whooo," and share a few laughs—like children on a rollercoaster.

And before we expected it, we were arriving in Brooklyn. Each trip we take has its beginning and its end, each moment an exciting opportunity to embark on new experiences, meeting new people, learning, savoring, and setting our sights on yet-to-be new horizons. In the vocabulary of every journey, there are certain words that grab my attention and echo with excitement and possibility: "Flight attendants—please take your seats for takeoff," and the inevitable, "Good morning, ladies and gentlemen, welcome to London. The local time is ...."

*And off we go!*

# The Old Apple Tree

Brookfield, Illinois, in the 1960s was nicknamed "Tree City USA." This was embossed on a metal sign mounted below the larger "Village of Brookfield" sign at the edge of town. At the time, I thought this meant we were unique, and that our town was special, the only place with this nickname, or subtitle, but now I am sure there are other towns with this same designation. My family lived in a red brick cape cod on a street with large elm trees whose branches spanned the road and covered many of the house roofs as well. It wasn't a bad street; it was pleasant looking, and yet ordinary. The neighborhood mainly had bungalows, some wood frame, others brick, then a few ranch-style houses, tiny really, and then a variety of two-story homes, with a few cape cods as well. The only exceptional thing about the place was that it was surrounded by trees. We had the largest tree on our block, enormous really, its branches reached upward eighty feet, and large forked branches at least forty feet long arced over the street and over our house, giving shade in the summer heat. In the fall, of course, this tree produced acres of crisp brown leaves, which I was expected to rake. The piles were so immense that I just left them here and there, in the front yard, in the back yard, ten or fifteen feet across and at least five feet high in the center. My mother would help divide these piles and move the mass in dribs and drabs to the front curb where, on a given week in November, the village would send a great big truck to suck up all the leaves, just like a vacuum cleaner.

We moved to Brookfield when I was five years old, and oddly enough I apparently had a say in the choice of this house. When my father took me along to see houses with a realtor, I ran around the back yard and announced that it was a "house in the park." It was a phrase that stuck. The setting was park-like, a large elm shaded the house in front, while a forest of eight or ten blue spruce, cedar and fir trees defined the property border to the west in the back yard, with a meandering border of peonies, phlox, hostas, morning glories and various wildflowers on the east edge of the yard, and a large, overgrown lilac bush hiding the alley from view. Yew bushes and cedar also dotted the property in the front and the back of the house. But the best part of the yard was a slightly crooked apple tree. It was old and tall and only bore scrawny, pock-marked fruit, but the spring blossoms were fantastic with their sweet fragrance and delicate beauty. All in all, it was picturesque, a setting for a Monet painting. My imagination was captivated by the outdoors, and I loved being outside.

The first time my mother saw the house was on moving day. (I never knew why she didn't accompany us on the day we first saw it.) I don't recall her initial reactions; she was busy directing movers to place the sofa here, the dining table there, and so on, and I was told to stay out of the way.

The house interior was typical of the time—a living room, dining room, kitchen, bath, and one bedroom on the ground floor,

## The Old Apple Tree

with a larger bedroom under the eaves on the second floor. This room felt a little strange to me with its dark, knotty pine walls, heavily varnished with an aged, yellow pine color, a cedar-lined walk-in closet for my mother, and built-in pine plywood bookcases and desk near the stairs. I spent hours each day exploring the secret passages under the eaves, hidden panels in the pine that popped open if you applied just the right amount of pressure. As a young child I was enthralled with movies about old houses haunted by ghosts, with secret rooms accessed only via secret passages. Inside our house, there was only storage space beneath the eaves, but to me it was a hideout. Sure, it was dark, but I could take father's flashlights up there and create my own little getaway place, my boy-cave. Days later I'd hear my father, a bit miffed, wondering aloud, "Now, where did that damn flashlight get to?"

In the summer and fall as I was growing up, whenever I came home from school or returned from a bike ride, I'd climb the old apple tree in the center of the garden. At first, I had to haul myself up very carefully, but eventually I became monkey-like and was able to climb a good fifteen or twenty feet up into the forked branches. There I would sit, legs dangling, rocking a bit, looking out past our roof and the neighbors' roofs, gazing across the entire neighborhood. Birds would alight on nearby branches, doing what they do best, twittering and chittering along, pecking here and there, scratching about, searching for grubs, ants, other small insects, or seeking tiny twigs for nest-building. I would chirp along with them, finding their hopping and bobbing amusing. I saw squirrels, too, and rabbits, and I made up names for all of them. Our dog, Duchess, would lounge on the expansive sun-drenched lawn below, not knowing where I was. I could see she was looking for me. She heard me come home, bang the door closed, toss my satchel down, then go out again. *But where is he? He's supposed to throw me a ball.* I was aloof, having escaped the cares of my day, and in my tree.

But this idyllic peace would not last. Our next-door neighbor Dorothy was on the lookout all day, for just what I have no idea even now, but she was definitely the nosey neighbor. She would peer out of her kitchen window, sometimes opening it wide so she could lean out, to see where I was and what I was doing. As soon as she felt she had the situation assessed, she disappeared from the window and, shortly thereafter, I could hear the phone ringing in our house. Sure enough, it was her, calling to tell my mother what a nuisance I was being, climbing a tree, running around the yard, and *shouldn't someone keep an eye on him?* My mother, ever the diplomat, tried to assuage Dorothy's fears that a seven-year-old would burn down her house or wreak havoc or generally run amuck, but that woman could only leave me alone for a few minutes. I felt there was no privacy at all. I was just a kid, but I knew I didn't need constant supervision. *The nerve!* I was forced to nickname her The Vulture, or Vultch for short, because she hovered menacingly, as if waiting for death. Mother thought the nickname funny and appropriate if, admittedly, a bit disrespectful. We laughed together about it, which lightened the atmosphere, assuring me that my mother trusted me more than the gossip next door.

When the weather was good, I spent most of my day on my bike. I would leave the house, having asked my mother for permission to ride my bike, and I would not return until dinner time. Mother would ask, "Where is it you go all day? Who are your friends?" I'd explain that, "Jack and I rode bikes, but then we met up with Linda, and Jack doesn't like Linda, so we said good-bye

## The Old Apple Tree

and I rode around with her." As I got older, we had to raise the seat inch by inch on the bike until I was clearly too big for it. When I got home, if I was early and it wasn't dinner time, I'd go directly to the backyard garden and climb my apple tree.

In summertime, the only thing that could get me down from that tree was the Good Humor ice cream truck. When I heard its bells, I'd climb down from my perch, run to the house and upstairs to my parents' bedroom. My mother left her cast-off purses behind the mahogany dresser, and she apparently had forgotten about the innumerable quarters, nickels, and dimes in some of them, money enough to fund at least two or three summers' ice cream bars. I would rush downstairs, mother would call out, "Jimmy, don't run in the house," but I'd be out the door before she could finish admonishing me. I'd wait by the curb for the ice cream truck along with other children up and down the street, and when it stopped all the kids from our block would run, forming not a line but a mob at the service window. For fifteen cents, or a quarter, I was able to get an Orange Dreamcicle, which was part orange sherbet and part vanilla ice cream, or a red, white, and blue berry-flavored, rocket-shaped popsicle. Then I'd nonchalantly walk back home, sometimes I'd run into mother, hands on her apron-covered hips, ready for me with a note of surprise, "You'll ruin your dinner, young man, and then what will I do?" I'm still not sure if she expected an answer to that. I'd head back to my tree to enjoy my ice cream.

As I grew into an eight- or nine-year-old, and school-yard harassment was on the rise, I learned to protect myself by sometimes hiding. The fragrant apple tree was a summer hideout, a jungle gym, a silent companion—it was a secret perch from which I could observe the world. I shared it with no one. None of my friends were permitted to climb it. It was special to me. This was the place where I could think, where my imagination could fly, where I'd imagine being grown and no longer need to hide myself, while a warm breeze gently swayed the tree high above the grassy lawn below. Oddly enough, that strange feeling of being in danger, of being wary of strangers, never quite left me. Even in adulthood, I watch for signs of prejudice, potential violence, and quickly assess situations or places in which I might be unwelcome or threatened. But no harm ever came to me in the apple tree. My only companions there were the birds, the robins, cardinals, and the sparrows, and an occasional blue jay. All of them twittering away in the branches nearby—none of them were threats. It was calming and exciting all at once—the scenery from my perch on a branch and the breeze rustling the leaves. Some days, up in that tree, I'd observe the clouds floating past, or I'd see the vapor trails of jets high above and wonder to what far-away places they were heading, whether those travelers were escaping something or happily going forward to find something new.

 When I was 17 and at boarding school, there was a bad wind storm, and trees throughout our town were damaged or downed. One victim was my old apple tree; it had broken nearly in half at the main trunk where a large, thick branch had grown into its own secondary trunk—a gash that left the whole tree weakened. My father called a tree expert who told him it was hopeless, and they cut down the tree. When I returned home for a scheduled break from classes, I took in the sad, empty scene. Where there should have been a glorious leafy tree there was nothing but a stump with an open space, a void with open sky above it.

 Over the decades, I have remembered that apple tree and the sense of tranquility I experienced in it. It's a peace and joy that

## The Old Apple Tree

cannot be bought or built but simply must be found. That apple tree bore silent witness to many years, time unfolded upon time, the annual family Fourth of July picnic, a conga line, mother's August birthday parties, seasons come and gone, leaves raked into piles, a dog running for a ball, the boy playing catch with a friend, laundry hung on lines to dry in the fresh air of lilac and peony. One day it offered gentle shade for a beloved guinea pig's funeral; on another it presided over rabbits nibbling grass before they dashed under great hosta leaves to hide from a pursuing dog. And it witnessed a child become a young man. Today that tree is gone. Its great branches that bore so much beauty and lived through innumerable seasons surely made fragrant fire wood after the tree was felled, all part of nature's perpetual cycle.

That old apple tree had been my special hiding place. I could climb into the branches and not be seen. Sitting up there, in my green cotton khakis and tan summer shirt—my little boy's archaeologist uniform—I'd daydream of future exploits and expeditions, imagine the friends I would find, camping trips to come, bicycle rides ahead, schools I'd attend. I didn't know then all the friends who would come to be like a litany of saints to alight with me on a branch here, a bench there, sharing experiences and ideas, each of us enriching our times together with the food of fellowship, kindness, understanding. I would daydream about fantastic scenes from a book I'd just read—a journey to the earth's center, or an underwater city. I dreamed in my childish way of the work I imagined I might do, places I'd visit—Italy, Egypt—gazing up as a jet flew overhead. *Where could they be going? Wasn't that just yesterday? Last year?*

In a flash, the past is past, and here I am in my home looking at the sparkling waves on Lake Michigan, then casting my gaze back, knowing that all these things have happened, not exactly as I had imagined in childhood, but achieved in my own way, with freedom of choice, freedom of thought, and determination.

There also are those things I'm not proud of, opportunities missed, goals lost or abandoned. There's the childhood ceramics class, and the feel of wet clay in my hands. I enjoyed pressing leaves and other objects into the clay to form patterns that reflected nature. Then there was my second-grade painting class. If only we had then had in our house a book on Abstract Expressionism, I might have developed an effortless, random style. Also, there was my fantasy of becoming an archaeologist and working in Egypt. As I grew into adolescence, several of my classmates discovered gymnastics, and I enthusiastically wanted to join in, too. The athletic movements, flying through the air, the clever balancing acts all inspired me. But that opportunity never got off the ground. The career in music I had envisioned in childhood and adolescence didn't materialize either, but I'll not complain or shed a tear. Were these experiences abandoned efforts or all part of a learning process, exploring the world and how I fit into it?

The experiences I had led me onward to other interests, other successes. It's not for me to regret or judge the fates, God's plan for me, whatever words I might use to give it a name or explain it. I never baked a cake with my mother—that's a regret; I could have learned her technique for mixing the chocolate batter just as she did. And I lament not offering to pray with her on that last day I saw her as we talked; I failed to provide some comfort at a time when it might have been needed. But maybe this is some ghost of guilt misplaced—I'm only human. *Mea culpa, mea máxima culpa.* At least we had that afternoon, that last talk, and sat together under

## The Old Apple Tree

the tree with low branches where a bird sang for us on a sun-dappled day in May.

Whether these memories are good or bad, I'm not sure I can sort them one way or another. But they are part of my tapestry. Is there closure? Are there blessings here? Do things come full circle? Some mysteries are beyond human capacity, and I have to accept that. I am just glad for the journey itself. There are many lessons along life's path, and many unanswered questions. I am fortunate that I was allowed to learn, to explore ideas, and to become myself without government interference. I'm grateful to my parents; in the long course of events, they did their best. My father, it seems to me, was trapped by toxic masculinity, which presented itself in anger, disappointment—perhaps even disappointment in himself. My mother lived in meekness, acquiescing to the vows she took in marriage, and was faithful until the end. No matter their limitations or circumstances, no matter what may have happened in our lives, they encouraged me to read and allowed me the freedom of thought that my soul needed to flourish.

Like alpha and omega—the beginning and the end—the old apple tree flashes again in my memory as a sentinel, a signpost, a marker. I have never forgotten my apple tree, now gone these many years. It was my companion, and it offered me compassionate shelter from the noise and violence of the world. It raised its strong branches toward the sun and supported me on a bough where I could sit, think, and feed my imagination, where I saw my future, a place where I soared above the house, out above the trees and among the birds as we flew in the clear blue light of the sky.

# Appendix: Sources and Further Reading

### Introduction
1. Pilkington, Ed. "Speaker Mike Johnson calls separation of church and state 'a misnomer.'" *Theguardian.com*, Guardian News & Media Limited, November 15, 2023, https://www.theguardian.com/us-news/2023/nov/15/mike-johnson-separation-church-state-misnomer. Accessed January 3, 2024.
2. Baran, James. "A Gay Man's Journey through the Adventist Church." *Adventist Today*, October 7, 2021, https://atoday.org/a-gay-mans-journey-through-the-adventist-church/. Accessed June 9, 2023.
3. "Save our children." *Wikipedia.org*, Wikimedia Foundation, Inc., https://en.wikipedia.org/wiki/Save_Our_Children. Accessed January 20, 2024.
4. Miller, Susan. "'War' on LGBTQ existence: 8 ways the record onslaught of 650 bills targets the community." *USA Today*, Gannett Satellite Information Network, LLC, March 31, 2023, https://www.usatoday.com/story/news/nation/2023/03/31/650-anti-lgbtq-bills-introduced-us/11552357002/. Accessed April 19, 2023.
5. "Judge rejects trans lawmaker Zooey Zephyr's effort to return to Montana House." *PBS.org*, Public Broadcasting Service, May 23, 2023, https://www.pbs.org/newshour/politics/judge-rejects-trans-lawmaker-zooey-zephyrs-effort-to-return-to-montana-house. Accessed June 9, 2023.
6. Breen, Kerry. "What to know about the 'Tennessee Three': Why were two of the Democratic lawmakers expelled, and what happens now?" *CBSnews.com*, CBS Interactive, Inc. April 12, 2023, https://www.cbsnews.com/news/tennessee-expulsion-house-democrats-expelled-what-happens-now/. Accessed May 1, 2023.
7. "Banned in the USA: State Laws Supercharge Book Suppression in Schools." *PEN.org*, PEN America, April 20, 2023, https://pen.org/report/banned-in-the-usa-state-laws-supercharge-book-suppression-in-schools/. Accessed June 1, 2023.

8. "Which states passed laws restricting school curriculum?" *USAfacts.org*, USAFacts, December 7, 2022, updated March 30, 2023, https://usafacts.org/articles/which-states-passed-laws-restricting-school-curriculum/. Accessed June 9, 2023.
9. Schroeder, Pete. "How Republican-led states are targeting Wall Street with 'anti-woke' laws." *Reuters.com*, Reuters, July 6, 2022, https://www.reuters.com/world/us/how-republican-led-states-are-targeting-wall-street-with-anti-woke-laws-2022-07-06/. Accessed January 5, 2023.
10. Burga, Solcyre. "Tennessee Passed the Nation's First Law Limiting Drag Shows. Here's the Status of Anti-Drag Bills Across the U.S." *Time.com*, Time USA, LLC, March 5, 2023, updated April 3, 2023, https://time.com/6260421/tennessee-limiting-drag-shows-status-of-anti-drag-bills-u-s/. Accessed May 13, 2023.
11. "2023 anti-trans legislation." *TransLegislation.com*, Trans Legislation Tracker, https://translegislation.com/bills/2023. Accessed January 22, 2024.
12. Natanson, Hannah; Tierney, Lauren; and Morse, Clara Ence. "America has Legislated Itself into Competing Red, Blue Versions of Education." *WashingtonPost.com*, The Washington Post, April 4, 2024, https://www.washingtonpost.com/education/2024/04/04/education-laws-red-blue-divide/. Accessed April 4, 2024.

### Finding My Vocabulary

1. Christian. *Merriam-Webster.com Dictionary*, Merriam-Webster, https://www.merriam-webster.com/dictionary/Christian. Accessed June 1, 2022.
2. Woke. *Merriam-Webster.com Dictionary*, Merriam-Webster, https://www.merriam-webster.com/dictionary/woke. Accessed June 1, 2022.
3. Value. *Merriam-Webster.com Dictionary*, Merriam-Webster, https://www.merriam-webster.com/dictionary/value. Accessed June 1, 2022.
4. Culture. *Merriam-Webster.com Dictionary*, Merriam-Webster, https://www.merriam-webster.com/dictionary/culture. Accessed June 1, 2022.
5. Gay. *Merriam-Webster.com Dictionary*, Merriam-Webster, https://www.merriam-webster.com/dictionary/gay. Accessed June 1, 2022.

Appendix

**Valley of the Guinea Pigs**
1. *Creature Features. Imdb.com*, Internet Movie Database, https://www.imdb.com/title/tt1178757/. Accessed January 12, 2024.
2. *The Abominable Dr. Phibes*, directed by Robert Fuest, (American International Pictures, 1971). *Wikipedia.org*, Wikimedia Foundation, Inc., https://en.wikipedia.org/wiki/The_Abominable_Dr._Phibes. Accessed January 12, 2024.
3. *The Mummy's Hand*, directed by Christy Cabanne, (Universal Pictures Company, 1940). *Wikipedia.org*, Wikimedia Foundation, Inc., https://en.wikipedia.org/wiki/The_Mummy%27s_Hand. Accessed January 12, 2024.
4. *The Mummy's Tomb*, directed by Harold Young, (Universal Pictures Company, 1942). *Wikipedia.org*, Wikimedia Foundation, Inc., https://en.wikipedia.org/wiki/The_Mummy%27s_Tomb. Accessed January 12, 2024.
5. *The Mummy*, directed by Karl Freund, (Universal Pictures, 1932). *Wikipedia.org*, Wikimedia Foundation, Inc., https://en.wikipedia.org/wiki/The_Mummy_(1932_film). Accessed January 12, 2024.
6. "Hill of the Seven Jackals" (plot detail). *The Mummy's Hand*, directed by Christy Cabanne, (Universal Pictures Company, 1940). *Wikipedia.org*, Wikimedia Foundation, Inc., https://en.wikipedia.org/wiki/The_Mummy%27s_Hand. Accessed January 12, 2024.

**Dead and Buried**
1. *The Pink Panther Strikes Again*, directed by Blake Edwards, (United Artists, 1976). *Wikipedia.org*, Wikimedia Foundation, Inc., https://en.wikipedia.org/wiki/The_Pink_Panther_Strikes_Again. Accessed January 12, 2024.
2. The Committal. *The (online) Book of Common Prayer*, bcponline.org, (Pastoral Offices. The Burial of the Dead: Rite Two). The Church Hymnal Corporation, New York, p. 501.
3. The Committal. *The (online) Book of Common Prayer*, bcponline.org, (Pastoral Offices. The Burial of the Dead: Rite Two). The Church Hymnal Corporation, New York, p. 502.

**My Family Tree**
1. Pomerania. *Wikipedia.org*, Wikimedia Foundation, Inc., https://en.wikipedia.org/wiki/Pomerania. Accessed October 11, 2023.

2. Kashubians. *Wikipedia.org*, Wikimedia Foundation, Inc., https://en.wikipedia.org/wiki/Kashubians. Accessed October 11, 2023.
3. Dudek, Mitch. "When a $2.2M home sale fell through on 'Windy City Rehab,' Alison Victoria found a buyer to bail her out: Her boyfriend." *Chicago.suntimes.com*, Chicago Sun Times, December 28, 2021 (print edition December 30, 2021), https://chicago.suntimes.com/windy-city-rehab/2021/12/28/22824525/windy-city-rehab-alison-victoria-janssen-lincoln-park-michael-marks-flipping-hgtv-discovery-channel. Accessed January 8, 2024.

## All in the Family

1. Timm, Jane C. "Fox News and Dominion reach $787.5 million settlement in defamation lawsuit." *NBCnews.com*, NBC Universal, April 18, 2023, https://www.nbcnews.com/media/fox-news-settles-dominion-defamation-lawsuit-rcna80285. Accessed May 1, 2023.

## Love for Sale

1. Zagórzany, Poland. *Wikipedia.org*, Wikimedia Foundation, Inc., https://en.wikipedia.org/wiki/Zag%C3%B3rzany,_Gorlice_County. Accessed January 18, 2024.
2. Kielce pogrom. *Wikipedia.org*, Wikimedia Foundation, Inc., https://en.wikipedia.org/wiki/Kielce_pogrom. Accessed October 14, 2023.
3. *Beyond the Forest*, directed by King Vidor, (Warner Bros., 1949), *Wikipedia.org*, Wikimedia Foundation, Inc., https://en.wikipedia.org/wiki/Beyond_the_Forest. Accessed January 18, 2024.
4. Sto lat. "Good luck, good cheer, may you live a hundred years." *Polishamericancenter.org*, Polish American Cultural Center, https://www.polishamericancenter.org/StoLat.htm. Accessed January 13, 2024.

## The Journey of Coming Out

1. "What does not kill me makes me stronger." *Wikipedia.org*, Wikimedia Foundation, Inc., https://en.wikipedia.org/wiki/What_does_not_kill_me_makes_me_stronger. Accessed January 20, 2024.
2. *A Return to Salem's Lot*, directed by Larry Cohen, (Warner Bros., 1987), *Wikipedia.org*, Wikimedia Foundation, Inc., https://en.wikipedia.org/wiki/A_Return_to_Salem%27s_Lot. Accessed on January 20, 2024.

Appendix

3. Establishment Clause. *Wikipedia.org*, Wikimedia Foundation, Inc., https://en.wikipedia.org/wiki/Establishment_Clause. Accessed January 18, 2024.
4. Fundamentalism. *Wikipedia.org*, Wikimedia Foundation, Inc., https://en.wikipedia.org/wiki/Fundamentalism#Christianity. Accessed January 20, 2023.
5. Conversion therapy. *Wikipedia.org*, Wikimedia Foundation, Inc., https://en.wikipedia.org/wiki/Conversion_therapy. Accessed January 18, 2024.
6. "Position Statement on Issues Related to Homosexuality." *Psychiatry.org*, American Psychiatric Association, psychiatry.org/Position-2013-Homosexuality (PDF). Accessed January 20, 2024.
7. "Resolution on Appropriate Affirmative Responses to Sexual Orientation Distress and Change Efforts." *apa.org*, American Psychological Association, https://www.apa.org/about/policy/sexual-orientation. Accessed January 20, 2024.
8. Heshmat, Shahram. "Why does music evoke memories?" *Psychology Today*, Sussex Publishers LLC, September 14, 2021, https://www.psychologytoday.com/us/blog/science-choice/202109/why-does-music-evoke-memories. Accessed January 15, 2024.
9. "Southern Adventist University Transgender Student: 'The Church is Dangerous in Situations Like Mine.'" *Adventist Today*, February 16, 2022, https://atoday.org/southern-adventist-university-transgender-student-the-church-is-dangerous-in-situations-like-mine/. Accessed October 12, 2023.
10. Rights of privacy. *Britannica.com*, Encyclopaedia Britannica, Inc., Britannica.com/topic/rights-of-privacy. Accessed January 16, 2024.
11. Integrity. *Merriam-Webster.com Dictionary*, Merriam-Webster, https://www.merriam-webster.com/dictionary/integrity. Accessed January 20, 2024.
12. Miller, Susan. "'War' on LGBTQ existence: 8 ways the record onslaught of 650 bills targets the community." *USA Today*, Gannett Satellite Information Network, LLC, March 31, 2023, https://www.usatoday.com/story/news/nation/2023/03/31/650-anti-lgbtq-bills-introduced-us/11552357002/. Accessed April 19, 2023.
13. Seibold, Loren. "My Church Supports the Killing of LGBTQ People in Uganda." *Adventist Today*, April 28, 2023, https://atoday.org/the-silence-is-deafening/. Accessed April 29, 2023.

14. Baran, James. "Connection to Draconian Uganda Bill Raises Questions About Adventist Leadership." *Spectrum*, May 27, 2023, https://spectrummagazine.org/views/connection-draconian-uganda-bill-raises-questions-about-adventist-leadership/. Accessed May 28, 2023.
15. Yoon, Sungjoo. "I'm a High School Junior. Let's Talk About 'Huckleberry Finn' and 'Mockingbird.'" *New York Times*, The New York Times Company, April 18, 2022, https://www.nytimes.com/2022/04/18/opinion/school-book-bans-students.html. Accessed January 22, 2024.
16. Diaz, Jaclyn. "Florida's governor signs controversial law opponents dubbed 'Don't Say Gay.'" *NPR.org*, NPR, updated March 28, 2022, https://www.npr.org/2022/03/28/1089221657/dont-say-gay-florida-desantis. Accessed April 5, 2022.
17. Thunderdome. "[A] gladiatorial arena," where "conflicts ... are resolved by a fight to the death." *Mad Max Beyond Thunderdome*, directed by George Miller and George Ogilvie, (Kennedy Miller Productions, 1985). *Wikipedia.org*, Wikimedia Foundation, Inc., https://en.wikipedia.org/wiki/Mad_Max_Beyond_Thunderdome. Accessed April 12, 2024.
18. Fascism. *Wikipedia.org*, Wikimedia Foundation, Inc., https://en.wikipedia.org/wiki/Fascism. Accessed January 20, 2023.
19. Kay, Jennifer. "Republican State AGs Sue Biden, Claiming Social Media Censorship." *Bloomberglaw.com*, Bloomberg Law, May 5, 2022, https://news.bloomberglaw.com/tech-and-telecom-law/republican-state-ags-sue-biden-claiming-social-media-censorship. Accessed October 12, 2022.
20. History of Homosexuality. Historiographic Considerations. *Wikipedia.org*, Wikimedia Foundation, Inc., https://en.wikipedia.org/wiki/History_of_homosexuality#Historiographic_considerations. Accessed March 1, 2024.
21. Christian. *Merriam-Webster.com Dictionary*, Merriam-Webster, https://www.merriam-webster.com/dictionary/Christian. Accessed January 20, 2024.
22. Warfield, Phillip. "Anna Knight and the Case for Reparations." *Spectrum*, April 8, 2022, https://spectrummagazine.org/news/anna-knight-and-case-reparations/. Accessed October 1, 2022.

Appendix

23. Aamodt, Alex. "Transgender Student Faces Uncertain Future at Southern Adventist University." *Spectrum*, February 17, 2022, https://spectrummagazine.org/news/transgender-student-faces-unclear-future-southern-adventist-university/. Accessed October 1, 2022.
24. Golden Rule. *Wikipedia.org*, Wikimedia Foundation, Inc., https://en.wikipedia.org/wiki/Golden_Rule. Accessed January 21, 2024.

### The Graduate Student

1. "Old sins cast long shadows." *AgathaChristie.fandom.com*, Fandom. https://agathachristie.fandom.com/wiki/Old_sins_cast_long_shadows. Accessed December 1, 2023.
2. "A rolling stone gathers no moss." *Wikipedia.org*, Wikimedia Foundation, Inc., https://en.wikipedia.org/wiki/A_rolling_stone_gathers_no_moss. Accessed January 21, 2024.

### What's Love Got to Do with It?

1. The Fates. *Greekmythology.com*, https://www.greekmythology.com/Other_Gods/The_Fates/the_fates.html. Accessed January 28, 2024.
2. *Young Frankenstein*, directed by Mel Brooks, (20$^{th}$ Century-Fox, 1974). *Wikipedia.org*, Wikimedia Foundation, Inc., https://en.wikipedia.org/wiki/Young_Frankenstein. Accessed February 12, 2023.
3. *Obergefell v. Hodges* (2015). *Constitutioncenter.org*, National Constitution Center, https://constitutioncenter.org/the-constitution/supreme-court-case-library/obergefell-v-hodges. Accessed January 20, 2024.
4. Elliott, Philip. "The Fight for Same-Sex Marriage Isn't Over. Far From It." *Time.com*, Time USA, LLC, March 14, 2024, https://time.com/6899864/same-sex-marriage-supreme-court-biden-trump/. Accessed April 1, 2024.

### In Memoriam: Mater Doloresa

1. The Confession of Sin. *The (online) Book of Common Prayer*, bcponline.org, (The Holy Eucharist. The Penitential Order: Rite Two). The Church Hymnal Corporation, New York, p. 352.
2. "That whosoever believeth in him should not perish, but have eternal life." St. John 3:15. *The Holy Bible* (KJV). The World Publishing Company.
3. The Committal. *The (online) Book of Common Prayer*, bcponline.org, (Pastoral Offices. The Burial of the Dead: Rite Two). The Church Hymnal Corporation, New York, p. 502.

James Philip Baran

**My Father and Mr. Hyde**
1. Albee, Edward. *Who's Afraid of Virginia Woolf?* 1962. Atheneum, New York, 1983.
2. *Cymbeline.* Act IV, Scene ii (lines 264-65). William Shakespeare. The Arden Shakespeare, Methuen, 1980, pg. 133.

**The Three-Ring Circus**
1. Roseanne Roseannadanna. *Wikipedia.org*, Wikimedia Foundation, Inc., https://en.wikipedia.org/wiki/Roseanne_Roseannadanna. Accessed January 12, 2024.

**Wanderlust**
1. *Lady Windermere's Fan* (1892). Oscar Wilde. *Wikiquote.org*. en.wikiquote.org/wiki/Oscar_Wilde. Accessed January 19, 2024.
2. *The Great Outdoors*, directed by Howard Deutch, (Universal Pictures, 1988). *Wikipedia.org*, Wikimedia Foundation, Inc., https://en.wikipedia.org/wiki/The_Great_Outdoors_(film). Accessed January 29, 2024.
3. McCue, Jim; Bale, Joanna; Webster, Philip. "Thatcher speaks out on terror," *The Times*, October 4, 2001, p. 1.
4. "Eternal Father, Strong to Save." Music by John Bacchus Dykes (1823-1876), words by William Whiting (1825-1876), no. 608, *The Hymnal 1982*, copyright © 1985, The Church Pension Fund.

# About the Author

James Philip Baran is a designer and fine-art photographer. During a 25-year journal and magazine publishing career, he spoke at conferences and served on the board of a publishing industry group. His photography has been exhibited in California and Illinois, and his work is in private collections in the U.S. and Canada. James holds a bachelor's degree in Music and a master's degree in English. He lives in Chicago.

www.ingramcontent.com/pod-product-compliance
Lightning Source LLC
Chambersburg PA
CBHW030326010526
44119CB00027B/388/J